Last One Down the Aisle Wins

Last One Down the Aisle Wins

10 KEYS
TO A FABULOUS SINGLE LIFE NOW AND AN EVEN BETTER MARRIAGE LATER

Shannon Fox and Celeste Liverside

Thomas Dunne Books/St. Martin's Griffin New York

THOMAS DUNNE BOOKS.
An imprint of St. Martin's Press.

www.thomasdunnebooks.com
www.stmartins.com

Book design by Patrice Sheridan

LIBRARY OF CONGRESS CATALOGING-IN-PUBLICATION DATA

Fox, Shannon.
Last one down the aisle wins : 10 keys to a fabulous single life now and an even better marriage later / Shannon Fox and Celeste Liversidge. — 1st ed.
p. cm.
ISBN 978-0-312-62805-5 (alk. paper)
1. Single women. 2. Man-woman relationships. 3. Marriage. I. Liversidge, Celeste. II. Title.
HQ800.2.F69 2010
306.81'53—dc22

2009047596

10 9 8 7 6 5 4 3 2

This book is dedicated
with much love to our fabulous daughters,
Lucy, Ava, Chloe, and Callia.
With great hope that
within its pages you'll
find a little direction and
even some inspiration as
you grow into the women
you were created to be.
How blessed we are to walk beside you
as your life journeys unfold.

Contents

Acknowledgments

Many thanks to Dan Lazar, agent-extraordinaire, for your rapid-fire enthusiasm for our message, your steady and wise guidance through not-so-smooth sailing times, and for always being gracious. To Toni Plummer, for your editorial expertise and for putting our passion into print. To Jill Schwartzman, for your warmth and encouragement from the outset of this important project.

To our courageous clients and all the women who have shared their stories, for your ability to look inside yourselves and move forward with great hope for the future.

To our amazing moms for the myriad ways you have lovingly poured into our lives to make us who we are today. For cherished friends and beloved family who cheered us on from the beginning, through the middle, to the end. And most of all to our incredible husbands, whose support and sacrifice allowed us all the late nights, early mornings, and the "you can do its" we needed. We love you.

To Shannon, the best coauthor and friend a girl could ever hope for. Your wit, wisdom, and disdain for emoticons is forever in my heart. Who knew that our many state-of-women-today discussions of the past two decades would eventually find their rightful home in these pages? I love you, my friend.

To Celeste, no one else in the world could have convinced me while I was very pregnant with my third child that we could pull off writing a book. No one else could have finished my sentences perfectly. No one else would have laughed hysterically at my late-night brilliance (most of which never made it to print as we realized that funny at 3 A.M. is decidedly *not* at 7 A.M.). No one else would have displayed your loyalty and grace. I am humbled and grateful to have worked alongside you. You are a true friend and I love you.

Last One Down the Aisle Wins

Chapter 1

The Keys to Happily Ever After

Are you tired of hearing about the skyrocketing divorce rates in our country? Does it scare you to think that your future marriage has a less-than-50 percent chance of survival? Do you feel helpless to improve your odds of having a successful marriage? What if we told you that we know the key to more than doubling your chances of staying married? And what if we told you that this key was something you can use right now, whether you're single without a prospect in sight, in a serious relationship, or engaged to the love of your life and knee-deep in *Brides* magazines? How much would it be worth to you? Would it be worth five easy payments of $29.99 plus shipping and handling? Or how about just the price of this book?

Here's the key: **Don't marry young.** In fact, don't get married until you're thirty. According to the National Center for Health Statistics, your chances of staying married more than double if you get married after the age of twenty-five. That's right, the old "50 percent of all marriages end in divorce" statistic is literally cut in half for those who marry for the first time after twenty-five. Marriage and family researchers, Marcia and Tom Lasswell, concluded that "divorce rates are lowest for men and women who marry for the first time at age twenty-eight or later. The chances for a stable marriage increase as both partners reach the age of thirty." And after many years of working with women on the verge of divorce, we wholeheartedly agree. But it's not that there's something magical about turning thirty. There's a lot more to it than sitting back, biding your time, and waiting for your thirtieth birthday to roll around. If you're serious about improving your chances of choosing a great husband and having a fabulous marriage, there's a lot you need to be doing *now,* before you walk down the rose-petaled aisle.

So what qualifies us to be the Keepers of the Key? For the past sixteen years, we have been working with women in crisis—Shannon, in her psychotherapy office, with women and couples who were trying to save their troubled marriages; and Celeste, in her divorce law office, with women whose marriages were already beyond saving. We've listened to women pour their hearts out and share their stories of disappointment, regret, disillusionment, and guilt over their failed marriages and unrealized hopes for the future.

How It All Started

As best friends in our twenties, and just starting out in our professional practices, we'd often commiserate about how frustrating it was to enter our clients' lives after the damage to their marriages had already been done. At that point there was nothing we could do to turn back time. We wondered if there was anything that could be done to better people's chances of having a successful marriage, or were we all just destined to be random victims of the depressing divorce statistics? As big fans of marriage and out of a desire to have great and lasting marriages ourselves someday, we decided to investigate. We were determined to figure out what leads to the demise of marriages and if there was anything to be done to prevent divorce before saying "I do."

After discovering consistent patterns in our clients' stories, we came to two important conclusions: First, the choices we make before we're married, even long before we ever lay eyes on our spouse, have the biggest impact on the success or failure of our future marriage. And second, happy marriages are born out of fulfilled single lives.

Armed with this knowledge, we were determined to find a way to encourage single women to live their lives to the fullest in their twenties so that they could make better choices, have some great experiences, and hopefully enter marriage with no regrets. Writing a book was the obvious choice if we were serious about reaching the single women of the world with our message of hope. We didn't get very far on the whole book idea back then because we were so busy traveling, pursuing our careers, and making the most of our own twenties.

Sixteen years, two marriages (just one each!), and six children (three each!) later, we have an even better vantage point. Our personal experiences of marrying at twenty-nine and thirty have reinforced our message that having a fabulous single life leads to an even better marriage later. Throughout the next twelve chapters, we'll share many stories from our clients, mentor relationships, focus groups, and interviews with women of all ages and stages of life. We are so appreciative of these women (whose names have been changed) for their willingness to honestly share their experiences, even the painful ones, in the hope that others will benefit.

VANESSA

Vanessa is a former therapy client who, at twenty-three, was sure she had found her soul mate. She and Greg met their junior year of college and had been inseparable ever since. If this wasn't love, she didn't know what was. By all accounts, Greg was a great guy—athletic, handsome, funny, and incredibly romantic—everything that Vanessa had always wanted in a husband. Vanessa had never experienced such intense passion with anyone, ever. "Our chemistry was intense, and I always felt safe when we were together. My parents loved Greg, too. They were always telling me how relieved they were that I had Greg to take care of me now that I was graduating and 'going out into the real world.'

"I was pretty nervous about walking down that aisle on my wedding day. I knew I wasn't ready to be anyone's wife and couldn't shake the nagging feeling that there was more I should have done with my life before getting married. But I knew that I loved Greg and he loved me. Besides, my parents had spent a small fortune on the wedding, and my friends and family were all there, expecting me to say 'I do.'" So she did.

A little less than five years into her marriage, it became painfully obvious to Vanessa that she had made the wrong decision. She had changed so much during those five years and felt a million miles away from Greg. Fighting was a constant in their relationship. Many of the fights were about money, of which there never seemed to be enough, even though Vanessa had a decent-paying job. The credit card debt was spiraling out of control, and Greg had been through three jobs since the wedding and as many periods of unemployment. "I didn't understand why he wasn't more motivated to try to find work but seemed content to just sit around and wait for the phone to ring. When Greg found out that I had called my parents to help out with our rent, it caused a huge fight. What else was I supposed to do? He hadn't worked in five months!" Despite her guilt, Vanessa quickly began losing respect for Greg.

Vanessa reconnected via Facebook with a girlfriend from college who had spent the past two years working with a nonprofit in Paraguay. Hearing about her friend's incredible experiences learning a new language and exploring a new culture made Vanessa long for the freedom to just pick up and go. She tried to talk to Greg about the possibility of working abroad, but he made it clear he had no interest in leaving the comforts of the good ol' U.S. of A. and couldn't understand why Vanessa would want to, either.

Religion also became a problem between them. "Greg and I always considered ourselves to be spiritual people, but decided back in college that organized religion wasn't for us. When a friend from work invited me to her church several months ago, though, I felt a very strong connection there. I started going to church every Sunday and invited Greg to go with me, but he had no interest. We just don't seem to have much in common anymore."

Why had Vanessa been so naïve to think that she could make a decision about whom she would spend the rest of her life with at age twenty-three? That "intoxicating" love she had felt so strongly toward Greg had slowly worn off and was instead replaced by feelings of resentment and distance. She was miserable, ashamed, and full of regret. Why hadn't love conquered all?

Vanessa wasn't just a silly little girl in love, nor was she reckless in her decision to marry. She was a college graduate, had known Greg for a few years before they got engaged, and had the support of her family and friends. Most important, Vanessa truly believed she was in love. And she probably was. But, that's just it. At twenty-three, Vanessa lacked the ability to really know herself or her future husband. It was the life she had *yet* to live that would bring about the growth and maturity she was just starting to experience now, at twenty-eight. From this new vantage point, Greg already looked a whole lot different than he had sitting across from her in their college cafeteria.

MARIN

Marin got married a week after she turned twenty-four. She graduated from college and then spent a year getting her teaching credential. She and Erik had been dating for five years and knew they were meant to be together. Marin's family loved Erik like a son, but still encouraged Marin to wait a few years to get a job, settle into adult life, and get to know herself a little more before getting married. Marin saw no reason to wait. Thirteen years and three children later, Marin is still happily married and had this to say: "I am glad that I married Erik—he is still the only one for me. But . . . I do wish I had listened to my family and married him later. We really struggled for the first several years and despite truly being in love, our frequent fights put a big strain on our relationship. When, in our late twenties, we began to develop different interests and goals for our lives, we had to go to counseling to get some help. All this time, we were struggling with infertility. In retrospect, I don't think we were old enough to handle such big life issues. We got through everything and stayed together, but it would have been easier to handle if we had been older when we got married."

RORY

The first time Rory slipped on that white satin gown, she knew it was the one. She was only six at the time, trying on Halloween costumes in the aisle at Walmart. Thus began Rory's love affair with all things bridal. She always expected that she would get married right out of high school, but because she wasn't dating anyone by graduation, she went on to college. By the time her senior year rolled around, Rory began to panic. Her boyfriend of a year, Bobby, wasn't on board with her plans of having a "ring by spring," so she gave him an ultimatum. He caved, and they got married that fall.

"I always wanted to be a young mom and was convinced that my eggs would shrivel up if I didn't have a baby by the time I turned twenty-four. I had Nathan just three days after our one-year anniversary. What should have been a happy time in our marriage ended up being awful. Bobby and I fought constantly. He always wanted to go out with his friends, but expected me to just stay home and take care of Nathan. I never got to have any fun. Money was always a big problem, too, mostly because Bobby was happy working part-time at Best Buy and spent most of his free time playing video games. I finally realized how completely different we are and that we want very different things out of life. Unfortunately I got so caught up in my goal to get married, I hadn't thought past the finish line. Bobby and I ended up getting a divorce, and Nathan and I are now living with my parents. Not exactly how I had imagined my life would be. My biggest regret is that my son is going to grow up in a broken home."

Vanessa, Marin, and Rory all echo the regretful refrains we've heard from the women who have sat with us crying their way through boxes of tissue: "I don't know what I was thinking." "I didn't even know myself when I got married." "I changed so much in my twenties; I would have chosen someone very different if I had waited to marry." "In my early twenties, I had no idea what I really wanted or needed in a husband." These married or divorced women, who ranged in age from twenty-four to sixty, were full of regret about the way they had spent their twenties. We asked them to complete the sentence "I wish I had taken time in my twenties to ______________________." Here are the most common responses:

finish my education
pursue my dream career
travel
figure out what I believed
deal with my family issues
get out of debt
live on my own
deepen my friendships
see a therapist

be more sexually responsible
feel better about myself

Through these conversations with our clients, a consistent theme emerged. Marrying young, before you know yourself and have a solid handle on your life, is a bad idea. We were both troubled to hear these frequent expressions of regret, especially because there wasn't much we could do to change the path these women had already chosen for themselves. That's when we realized that even though it was too late for these women, it isn't too late for millions of other young women. And it's not too late for you. Stay tuned . . .

But Everyone's Doing It

Hollywood celebrities are known for their whirlwind romances followed by intense proclamations of true love. In the last few years, there has been an epidemic of brief courtships between people in their young twenties, followed by extravagant weddings. These young celeb marriages have an average shelf life of around one to three years.

Jennifer Garner, movie star, married fellow actor Scott Foley when she was twenty-six. Jennifer was utterly effusive after her engagement: "He is a completely amazing human being!" she gushed. "I never imagined I could ever be this in love with another person. I'm giddy!" They were married for all of three years. A few years later, she married co-star Ben Affleck. Recently, when asked about the differences between the two marriages, this was her response:

> I don't have this fantasy about marriage anymore. Everyone says it takes hard work. Well, it kind of does—and I'm much more pragmatic about romance than I

> used to be. [With Scott] I wanted to see him as a white knight and was crushed whenever anything normal happened. I wanted to be the princess. Now I'm much more willing to see myself as human and flawed, and accept someone—the whole picture. My life is definitely changing for the better. I couldn't be happier or feel more comfortable with the direction it's going in.

Jennifer's reflections perfectly illustrate the difference between a twenty-something woman's perspective on marriage versus her perspective after thirty. You'll notice that she mentioned nothing about either of her husbands. She didn't say a word about which *guy* she felt the strongest chemistry with, or which *guy* made her laugh the most. It was her *own* perspective, expectations, and overall maturity that made all the difference between the two marriages.

And then there's actress Kate Hudson, who married rocker Chris Robinson at the age of twenty-two. She was obviously over the moon in love with her future hubby when she was quoted as saying, "We just kind of met and that was it. Every rule went out the window. We were telling each other we loved each other by the fourth day. I moved in a week later." Flash-forward to her admission shortly after her divorce from Robinson: "Looking back, it's pretty obvious that I married way too young. I'm such a different person now."

We're happy to report that some celebrities are actually getting it right. Here's what a recently married Beyoncé told *Seventeen* magazine about the importance of waiting to get married:

> I really don't believe that you will love the same thing when you're twenty as you do at thirty. So that was my rule: Before the age of twenty-five, I would never get married. . . . I feel like you have to get to know yourself, know what you want, spend some time by yourself

and be proud of who you are before you can share that with someone else.

Founder of eHarmony.com, psychologist Neil Warren concurs. After decades of working with engaged and married couples, Dr. Warren concluded that "Young people can't select a marriage partner very effectively if they they don't know themselves well. In this society, where adolescence often lasts until the middle twenties, identity formation is incomplete until individuals have emotionally separated from their parents and discovered the details of their own uniqueness."

This Is Your Brain. This Is Your Brain in Your Twenties.

According to a recent national survey by researchers at Rutgers University, 94 percent of singles stated that they wanted to marry their soul mate. But many of them admitted that they had no idea what they were looking for. Well, of course! Doesn't it make sense that you can't possibly identify a soul mate until you know your own soul? And did you know that the human brain isn't even fully developed until the age of twenty-four? Is it any wonder that choosing a spouse before then basically doubles your chances of divorcing?

We frequently see evidence of this immature thinking in young women.

Claire is twenty and a sophomore in college, engaged to be married next summer. "Tyler and I are just meant to be together. We've been dating for almost three years and are ready to get married. The plan is for me to move in with him and his roommate for now until one of us gets a job. It sucks that our parents are going to stop paying for school once we get married, but we'll just figure it out as we go along. Our parents keep telling us we're too young and we're going to change a lot in the next few years. But that's cool; we'll just grow up together."

Or take Robyn, the twenty-three-year-old newly married and pregnant woman who can't work because her doctor put her on bed rest. "Sure, it's tough financially right now, but it will all work out. John is working hard, and we will be able to pay off our credit card debt when I can work again—maybe in a few years when the baby is in school. We're not like those couples who have a baby and grow apart or fight when they don't have money—we just laugh about it."

One of the best qualities of youth is hope and a positive outlook on life and the world. Unfortunately, the flip side of that optimism is unrealistic expectations and naïveté regarding the realities of married life and the challenges it brings.

Getting to the Source

Are you feeling inundated by messages everywhere telling you that by your mid-twenties, you should be married and well on your way to having children? Or, is the pressure you feel coming from within? Maybe somewhere along the way, you created a time line for yourself that requires you to be married by, say, twenty-five and have kids by twenty-eight. This pressure can make you perpetually anxious about your future, and waste a lot of your precious time. We both lament the endless hours we frittered away in our twenties worrying about what our futures would look like. Where will I live? Who am I going to marry? Will I be able to have children? How many? Do I even want children? Part of that anxiety is simply human nature, but you can make a concerted effort to stop worrying about all that right now. In fact, we challenge you to completely put those concerns aside for the time being.

You'll have to stand strong. You'll be battling the message of most books, magazines, and popular Internet blogs that tell you that your twenties should be spent *finding* a man, *trapping* a man, and *marrying* a man. It's true, most of the books you're likely to encounter in the relationship section of your local bookstore focus on How to Hook a Guy in Ten Easy Steps, Land a Man in Thirty Days, Capture His Heart in Four Dates, and so on. The problem is, they're getting it all wrong. Your twenties shouldn't be spent finding a man; your twenties should be spent finding yourself.

If you're under the age of, say, twenty-seven, we want you to put those books down for a while. We're asking you to take a break from trying to figure out how to snag a great guy and instead spend some time becoming a great you. Yes, even if you are dating someone right now. We're not suggesting that you pick up the phone and break it off; just promise yourself that you won't make any rash decisions, such as getting married, before you've had a chance to reflect on the next twelve chapters.

Your Quarter-Life ~~Crisis~~ Challenge

If we've managed to convince you about what you *shouldn't* do in your twenties—get married or spend ridiculous amounts of time thinking and worrying about the future—you're probably wondering what your twenties *should* entail. For starters, let's acknowledge that your twenties is a time when your sense of self is seriously challenged. The hopes and dreams that you have been storing up are now bubbling up against reality as you face the real world. If you recently graduated from college, you're likely dealing with the pressure of finding your perfect job and facing the disappointment of realizing that the perfect job doesn't exist. You may be questioning whether your chosen career path is even right for you at all. You want to be financially independent but may be finding it difficult to break away from the security and safety net of Mom and Dad. For the first time in your life, you're responsible for your own decisions and might be struggling to define your values and identity apart from your family. You know you're supposed to be thankful for all the choices your generation has, but having so many options can be overwhelming.

In her book *20-Something, 20-Everything,* Christine Hassler explores the concept of a quarter-life crisis, which includes feelings of confusion, disappointment, a sense of being displaced, and general unhappiness. Hassler refers to a woman's twenties as a "Neverland between childhood and adulthood." We couldn't agree more that your twenties can be a confusing time, but we reject defining this decade as a crisis. A challenge, yes. A crisis, no. The good news is that while this decade will surely have more than its share of challenges, it can also be one of invaluable growth, inspiration, and self-knowledge. A time where the very foundation for your future is created—a foundation for a fulfilling marriage and family life.

If you spend your twenties learning how to be a fabulous, stable, independent, fulfilled single woman, it will naturally follow that you will choose a guy to marry who possesses these same wonderful qualities. You will lose your taste for the long-on-charisma and short-on-character guys whom you, in the flighty youth of your early twenties, found yourself drawn to like a moth to a flame. And you will have what it takes to be a great wife and partner in a lasting and loving marriage.

This book is not a guide on how to simply endure your twenties, but rather on how to embrace them. Chapters 3 through 12 each examine one of ten crucial aspects of your life and explore the importance of making good choices in these areas—choices that will eventually lead you to a place where you will be

- Able to decide if and when marriage is right for you.
- Capable of choosing a great husband.

- Empowered to make great choices for your life.
- Resolved to aim high and not settle.
- Enabled to have an exceptional and lasting marriage.
- Equipped to raise children who will go on to achieve all of the above in their own lives.

Based on the insights we've gained through our experiences of talking with hundreds of women over the years, and hearing their stories of marriages that have succeeded and many that have failed, we developed the Ten Keys to getting a fabulous single life now and an even better marriage later. Following these keys won't guarantee endless marital bliss, but they will go a long way in ensuring that you never end up in either of our offices.

As you delve into these ten areas in your own life and complete the exercises and quizzes found in each chapter, you will gain new insight and understanding about your past and about your hopes for the future. Simply reading the next twelve chapters will not change your life. But if you allow yourself the time to reflect on these ten areas and to be honest through the process, you *will* change your future.

Chapter 2

Ten Reasons Women Marry Too Young

Don't you dare marry young! Why not? You read this statistic in chapter 1, but it's worth repeating: According to the National Center for Health Statistics, your chances of staying married more than double if you get married after the age of twenty-five. Too many women marry too young and end up marrying the wrong person for the wrong reasons. Tragically, they choose a life partner before they even know who they are themselves. Before they know what they want or need—not only from a marriage, but even out of life.

So if marrying young doubles the likelihood of divorce, why do your twenty-something friends, cousins, and classmates insist on tying the knot now? We have spoken with hundreds of women, young and old, who have shared their stories of why they chose to marry at a young age. We've broken down those reasons into the ten most common *wrong* reasons women choose to marry young. You might relate to several of these ten reasons, so take the following quiz to see which type you most closely resemble.

The Ten Wrong Reasons to Marry Young Quiz

Are you Girl #1?

Y N Most of my friends my age are married.

Y N I can't wait to plan my wedding. I already know exactly how I want everything to be.

Y N *Brides* and *Martha Stewart Weddings* are my favorite magazines.

Y N I long for the day I get to register for all those fun new housewares.

Y N My friends spend a lot of time talking about getting married and how to "land a husband."

If you answered YES to two or more of these questions, you are the

"Always a Bridesmaid" Girl

You are the girl with a closetful of hideous bridesmaid dresses you would never be caught dead wearing again. You have dutifully stood by and watched many of your giddy friends walk straight off the graduation stage and down the wedding aisle. It's all so romantic and triggers your desire to have a doting husband of your own. When will it ever be your turn?

It's risky because: Many of you have dreamed about your wedding from the time you were a little girl. You already know what flowers you will have in your bouquet, the color of your bridesmaids' dresses, and what song will be playing as you float down the aisle. It's so easy to get caught up in the excitement of weddings and presents and bridal showers. These lucky brides even get to register for all new stuff—exquisite china, luxurious thousand-thread-count

Egyptian cotton sheets, four-slice toasters (our personal favorite), and everything a newly established household could desire. Appealing? Yes! Good reason to get married? No!

These days, a wedding date promises that the bride will be showered with attention. Anyone who has been around a bride knows that it is all about her. It is not just her day—it's her entire year! All the planning focuses on the bride—she gets every detail exactly as she wants it. Who doesn't love to be the center of attention, calling all the shots? It's intoxicating—you may have seen the popular reality show *Bridezillas,* which gives viewers an inside look into just how nasty entitled brides can be as they prepare for their big day. These girls are more concerned about getting their way and not letting anyone impede them than about their relationships with their mates, friends, or family. When did the wedding day cease being about two people becoming one and start being about one woman getting everything her spoiled heart desires? One of the show's bridezillas, Youmika, said it best: "It's my day—they all have to do whatever I want or they can walk!" And did you see the episode in which Lisa threw a tantrum (complete with fake tears and heaving shoulders) insisting childishly that her fiancé put up eighteen thousand dollars for first-class plane tickets to Bora Bora because it was the honeymoon she'd always imagined? No one was going to keep her from having her perfect honeymoon, not even her husband-to-be. What kind of partnership is that? What a dangerous precedent to establish even before the wedding! With all the perks of being the bride, it's no wonder that so many women report feeling disillusioned and disappointed in the first years of marriage, after the fantasy wedding day turns into the reality of day-to-day married life.

Every fairy tale ends with a wedding to a handsome prince and the words, "They lived happily ever after." No one tells the story of what happens next. Women prepare for months and years for their wedding day, without equal thought to the years of marriage that will follow the ever-important ceremony. But a life partnership requires more preparation than a wedding ceremony. If we put as much time and effort into creating our best selves as we put into creating the perfect wedding day, the divorce rate just might go down a percentage or two (or fifty).

What can I do to avoid being the "Always a Bridesmaid" Girl?

- If you crave the attention of being a bride, register for gifts with girlfriends just for the fun of it, ask for housewares for Christmas or your birthday or splurge on an espresso maker for yourself. You don't have to have a wedding to feel special or to set up house in a way that makes you feel legit.
- Find some new friends who are committed to getting a life before they say "I do." Log on to our website, www.LastOneDownTheAisleWins.com and chat with other young women who are interested in pursuing the same type of personal growth. Then, when your current friends start to mope about not being married yet, you can tell them about your vision for pursuing a fabulous single life instead of pursuing a willing groom. Chances are you'll discover that more and more of your friends will catch the vision and want to join you in your newfound quest.
- Watch 27 *Dresses* with some single girlfriends. Laugh at the uptight brides and admire the cool-headed, always-a-bridesmaid Katherine Heigl who ends up with her ideal man in the end.

Are you Girl #2?

Y N Love is all I need to be happy in marriage.

Y N We are in love, so we should get married regardless of how young we are.

Y N He is my soul mate, so why wait?

Y N I can't imagine life without him; I want to spend every minute with him, starting now.

Y N We will never get divorced, because we are more in love than other people.

If you answered YES to two or more of these questions, you are the

"All You Need Is Love" Girl

You are truly, madly, deeply in love with your Prince Charming. You are so good together that you feel sorry for other couples who think they know what love is, but only experience a small percentage of the connection you have. No one can convince you that your love could ever fade. It will cushion the blows of the world and cocoon you against any of the problems other couples face. Love is the most important factor in marriage, and you have it in spades, so let those wedding bells ring!

It's risky because: Love is by far the best feeling in the world. It is all-encompassing, makes you smile all the time, fills up the empty, lonely spaces inside you, and may even cause you to burst into spontaneous song. You realize that this feeling will probably not always be so intense, but you know that you will always be overwhelmingly and totally in love with this man. Unfortunately, love alone does not make marriage work. We've worked with many, many couples who began their young marriages very much in love—

only to discover later that marriage requires much more than strong emotion. As Sarah told us tearfully on the day she filed for divorce, "There's no doubt in my mind that I will always love Todd, but we had no business being married." Don't get us wrong—love is very important to a lasting marriage, but factors such as trust, selflessness, loyalty, character, integrity, respect, and common goals are even more important in keeping a couple strongly united in marriage.

Helen Fisher, a leading expert on the subject, divides the experience of love into three stages: lust, attraction, and attachment. *Lust* is the initial passionate sexual desire that draws you to a guy. You know the feeling: In the midst of the mind-crushing noise of a crowded bar, a hot guy walks by and brushes your arm. You look up, your eyes lock, and *bam,* electricity! Sparks! Lust! That intense animal magnetism can be mind-blowing, but as you may have noticed, this stage rarely lasts more than a few months. *Attraction* follows close on the heels of lust and is "the more individualized and romantic desire for a specific candidate for mating, which develops out of lust as commitment to an individual mate forms." That simply means that attraction develops when lust wears off and you begin to see potential for an actual commitment with this guy. Recent studies indicate that as people fall in love, the brain releases chemicals that resemble amphetamines, stimulating the pleasure center of the brain and leading to side effects such as increased heart rate, loss of sleep and appetite, and feelings of excitement. Did you catch that? Scientists have discovered that falling in love closely resembles being high on amphetamines! We call the hormones released in the attraction phase "love drugs." When you are in the beginning of a relationship, you are high on these love drugs. Whatever you do, don't make any big decisions until they begin to wear off—in about a year. Don't bother arguing the point. No matter how grounded you may think you are, you are high!

Since the lust and attraction stages are both temporary, a third stage is necessary if the relationship is going to go the distance. *Attachment* is the long-term bonding that enables relationships to last many years and even a lifetime. Couples in the attachment phase are linked together by their mutual commitment to marriage and children, and an emotional connection based on common interests and life values.

Here is a helpful visual of the three stages of love and their time line:

1. Lust (a few weeks/months)
2. Attraction (about a year)
3. Attachment (many years/decades)

The nature and intensity of young love, although intoxicating, actually serve to blind you to the realities of your man and the complexities of marriage. Shannon had a client whose "love" for her boyfriend was clearly blinding her to the realities of his true self. Anna was eager to have children, but her boyfriend, Paul, had gotten a vasectomy at age twenty-two out of a strong determination never to father children. She continued in therapy for a few sessions, vehemently resisting efforts to help remove her rose-colored glasses so that she could see the real picture of Paul as a potential husband. Instead, Anna married him. She returned to therapy a few years later in tears, saying, "Paul still refuses to reverse the vasectomy! He says he never wants to have kids! I can't believe this! What am I going to do?" Anna didn't wait for the giddy "love drugs" to wear off before getting married. But once they did, she was finally able to see her man for who he truly was. Paul didn't change after he and Anna married; she was just too high on love to see the real man to whom she pledged her love. Don't make the same mistake many young women make. Love is not enough.

As described in a 1940s guide to courtship, true, mature love is "an intelligent willingness to surrender self-will, to make sacrifices, to place fidelity, charity and duty above feelings, in behalf of a person whom one has found to be a good companion, a sturdy character, and a believer in the same purposes of life and marriage as oneself." The danger of basing a marriage on infatuation or strong emotions is that these feelings inevitably lessen in the first few years of marriage, leaving the couple to believe that they are no longer in love. We can't count the number of times we have heard women say they want a divorce because the couple "fell out of love." True love involves free will and commitment above and beyond just emotions.

What can I do to avoid being the "All You Need Is Love" Girl?

- Wait out some of the feelings of infatuation before making any major decisions about the relationship. The hormonal impact dissipates within about a year or two. Don't make a marriage decision within the first year of dating, no matter how old you are.
- Force yourself to make a list of how he rates on other important characteristics of a husband: trust, jealousy, integrity, loyalty, financial stability, and similar life goals?
- Ask your friends what they think of him—their brains are clear of the love hormones, so they'll hopefully be more objective. Encourage them to answer

honestly, and be prepared to really listen to what they say.

Are you Girl #3?

Y N If I sleep with a guy, I should probably consider marrying him.

Y N Sex could never be this good with anyone else.

Y N Sexual chemistry is one of the most important factors in choosing a husband.

Y N Not all guys are good in bed. If I find one who is, I should marry him.

Y N We are so hot for each other, we must be made for each other.

If you answered YES to two or more of these questions, you are the

"I Want Your Sex" Girl

You're the girl who is easily swayed by her libido. A good orgasm can practically launch you into wedding-planning mode. If the guy rocks your world in the sack, you think he must be The One. On the other hand, you might also be that girl (whose respectable numbers are dwindling) who believes that sex should be reserved for marriage. If you slipped up and had sex despite your convictions, you might decide to get married to "make it right" and believe that because you crossed the line with him, you must now commit yourself to him for the long haul. Either way, you are placing too much emphasis on sex when deciding to marry.

It's risky because: Sex and marriage go hand in hand—but sex is not the most critical factor in having a great marriage.

Don't misunderstand; sex is a vital part of a happy and lasting marriage. A good marriage involves lots of loving, hot, mutually pleasurable sex. But despite its power, sex alone is not a strong enough factor to hold a relationship together. It makes up only a small portion of your time (yes, even if you talk about it a lot or do it a lot). The truth is, marriage involves a lot of nonphysical communication, goal setting, compromise, and chores. To quote Dr. Harold Bessell, author of *The Love Test*, "Very few lasting relationships are made in bed. Fantasies may begin and end there; true love does not."

Another important thing to remember when it comes to sex and marriage is that after having sex with the same person for years, you will inevitably experience periods when it's less intense than others. Not to say the passion disappears, but it won't always rival the earth-shattering experiences of your first years together. If you mistakenly base your marriage on the strength of the chemistry, you are at risk of looking for sparks outside the marriage when the sexual flames cool a bit. If you confuse sexual attraction and excitement with love and commitment, you are a dangerous mate.

> *Getting married for sex is like buying a 747 for the free peanuts.*
>
> —*Jeff Foxworthy*

ALYSON

Alyson officially started dating when she was sixteen and never stopped. She had a string of boyfriends through high school, but was usually disappointed by how quickly the butterflies-in-your-stomach stage of the relationship wore off. Alyson had a test. If she no longer felt goose bumps when her guy kissed her, that was the sign. It was time for her to move on, which she usually did a few weeks or months into a relationship. That is, until she met Gavin. Their chemistry was immediate and mind blowing and like nothing she had ever experienced. Not only was Gavin absolutely gorgeous, but there was also something magnetic about him; she just couldn't get enough. Sex with Gavin was everything she had dreamed of, even rivaling the steamy scenes in those romance novels she loved so much.

After dating a few months, Alyson and Gavin started fighting about their many differences, from religion to politics to her plans for grad school. Luckily, their makeup sex was always so intense that Alyson would quickly forget why they were fighting in the first place. Gavin proposed and Alyson accepted. She knew there would be some issues to work through, like the fact that she wanted kids and he didn't, or that she wanted to live in the city and he was a true-blue country boy, but she believed their intense physical connection would carry them through whatever challenges they might face.

What can I do to avoid being the "I Want Your Sex" Girl?

- Think of a past relationship in which the sexual chemistry was the best part. Was it enough to keep the relationship strong? For how long? What did you do with your time when you weren't in the bedroom? What did you talk about? Did you let sexual attraction keep you in a relationship that was otherwise going nowhere? Good sex does not equal a good relationship.
- Stop having sex with your boyfriend for a set period of time and see how it goes. Do you have enough in common with him outside the bedroom to keep your relationship interesting?
- Read chapter 11, "Get a Sexy Life: Honor Your Sexuality" to gain a perspective on the importance of

honoring your sexuality in your single life and future marriage.

Are you Girl #4?

Y N I always imagined that I would get married before I turned twenty-five.

Y N I expect to have two or three children before I turn thirty.

Y N I assumed I would meet my husband in high school (or college).

Y N My parents got married right out of high school (or college), and it seemed to work out fine for them.

Y N I've been dating my boyfriend for a long time; so marriage is the next logical step.

If you answered YES to two or more of these questions, you are the

"Great Expectations" Girl

You always thought you would be married young; after all, your mom was married with two children by the time she was twenty-five. So now that you've been dating your sweetheart for the past four years, it seems like the next logical step is get married, right? Your expected time line for your life has always been as follows: graduate from high school, go to college, meet the love of your life, get married soon after graduation, have three children (a boy followed by identical twin girls) by the time you reach the ripe old age of twenty-six.

It's risky because: If you make assumptions about your future and the way life should unfold without a lot of soul-searching, you risk making a decision just because it worked for someone else. Don't simply do something because that is how your mom did it, or how you dreamed it would happen when you were a child. You are no longer a child. You are capable of thinking for yourself and exploring all your options. Do you really want to marry this guy, or is it just easier than breaking up or dealing with the constant questions about when you are going to get married? What would happen if you told him you wanted to wait a few years to get to know yourself better—would he wait, be excited about the prospect of marrying you as a more complete woman, or leave and find someone else? His reaction tells you a lot about his character and the potential you have for a lasting relationship.

> MARGE: *Homer, is this the way you pictured married life?*
>
> HOMER: *Yup, pretty much. Except we drove around in a van solving mysteries.*
>
> —The Simpsons

CLAUDIA

Claudia had dated her one and only boyfriend for seven years when he proposed. They were both twenty-two. "I couldn't say no to him. It would have broken his heart. Besides, I do love him, and marriage is the next step, right? It would be fun to go on one last trip with my girlfriends, though. I always wanted to go to Europe. I've also always been intrigued by the idea of living in a big city for a while. Whatever, it will be fun to be married and get on with real life." Claudia's mother was nineteen when she married her high school sweetheart, and Claudia had always expected she would meet her husband in high school, too. Claudia and her new husband will be living near her family in a rural town in central Idaho because that is what everyone else in her family does when they get married.

What can I do to avoid being the "Great Expectations" Girl?

- Decide on your own expectations for your marriage and figure out how to make that happen. For example, instead of "Get married at twenty-three" try "Make a solid decision about my mate only when I know who I am and what I want out of life."
- Complete this chart:

Current Expectations	True Desires	New Expectations
Get married at 25	Have a lifelong marriage	Get a life before "I do"
Have 3 kids (boy and twins)	Have a loving family	Marry right father/right time

Are you Girl #5?

Y N I want to be a mommy.
Y N My biological clock is ticking—loudly.
Y N I'm worried about infertility.
Y N I want a lot of children.
Y N I love babies!

If you answered YES to two or more questions, you are the

"Tick-Tock" Girl

When you were a little girl and people asked you what you wanted to be when you grew up, you always answered, "A mommy!" You were the best babysitter on the block by the time you were twelve. You became a teacher because it would help you be a better mom to your future children. You know exactly how many children you want and what their names are—you can almost picture their little faces. Your biggest goal in life is to have children, and you would be devastated if you couldn't. In fact, stories about infertility send you into a panic, and you fear that if you don't get married soon, you might never be able to have kids.

It's risky because: Wanting to have children is a marvelous desire—we each have three little ones of our own and are thrilled to be mothers. However, the fear of not being able to have children or the pressing urge to get pregnant soon is dangerous ground upon which to build a marriage. A *Cosmopolitan* magazine poll showed that "nearly 70 percent of women wouldn't consider having kids without a partner. But many of them *might* consider settling down with a less-than-ideal mate to beat the motherhood cutoff."

> *If you listen quietly, when all is silent, you can hear the gentle ticking of a clock. It's definitely a soft, quiet sound, but the fact that I can hear it means that it's getting louder.*
>
> —*Carlie, 28*

Answers to "Tick-Tock" Girl's Most Pressing Concerns

"My biological clock is ticking." The concept of the biological clock has been around for centuries and is rooted in biology. In *Baby Hunger,* Lois Leiderman

Davitz says, "The basic drive, the experienced desire, the urge to have a baby is innate, unlearned, and ultimately biologically based. But a woman's behavior, her emotions, and whether or not she decides to become pregnant depends at least in part on social factors in her life." The desire to have a baby, while natural, can take on a self-centered focus. *I* want a baby. *I* want to be a mother. Women who get married because they want to have a baby often choose a man who will suffice for their purpose, then end up divorced after they get what they wanted from the marriage—a child. Better to temper your baby craving and seriously consider whether a man would make a good mate as opposed to just a glorified sperm donor who happens to be willing to marry you when you long for a baby.

"If I marry later, shouldn't I be worried about infertility?" Not necessarily. How's that for definitive? Seriously, though, we know hundreds of women personally and professionally who have struggled with infertility. But this is key: Some of the women married at twenty-three, while others married at forty-three. If a woman is going to have fertility problems before her late thirties, it doesn't matter at what age she starts trying to conceive—she will still experience infertility. Meghan got married at twenty-four and began trying immediately to get pregnant. No one else in her family had ever experienced infertility, so she expected to get pregnant right away. After trying for a year, Meghan and her husband sought help from a fertility specialist and embarked upon a tough three-year process of taking fertility drugs and, eventually, in vitro fertilization. A set of twins and another baby boy later, Meghan says, "I never knew young women could suffer from infertility, too. I just thought I should have babies before my eggs got too old."

While it is true that a woman's fertility begins to decline at age thirty-five, the risk of infertility doesn't rise significantly until age forty. Data from the National Center for Health Statistics reveal that women between thirty-five and forty-four years old have a 78 percent chance of conceiving in a year. And don't believe all the hype in the media about the epidemic of infertility—in fact, the cases of infertility have declined since 1965. Back then, one in nine couples were considered infertile; in 1988, only one in thirteen couples were infertile. Nowadays, in fact, there are plenty of role models of mature motherhood: Nicole Kidman (41), Minnie Driver (38), Gillian Anderson (39), Juliana Margulies (41), Julia Roberts (39), Halle Berry (41). While we are not advocating waiting until you are forty to begin trying to have children, we do want to point out that it is not a definite cut-off age anymore.

"If I start having children later, I won't be able to have as many." How many kids do you plan to have between twenty-eight and forty? According to the Census Bureau in 1988, 48 percent of women age eighteen through thirty-four expected to have two children. Only 20 percent wanted three, and 9 percent wanted four or more. Unless you would like to have kids in the double digits, starting around thirty is just fine for most women. And better to have two children with a husband you chose wisely than to have four children you end up raising as a divorced single mother. Give your children the gift of a solid foundation: a lasting marriage with a great father and a mother who knows who she is and has a vast array of life experiences to draw from as she raises her children.

What can I do to avoid being the "Tick-Tock" Girl?

- Instead of focusing on your own desire to have a baby, think of what a baby will need from both parents. Make a list of all the most important qualities of a parent. Then honestly assess yourself in these areas. For example: *Consistency*—with all the drama in your life, do you really think you can provide consistency for a baby? *Wisdom*—Do you have the education and experience you need to lead a child?
- Get your baby fix by hanging out with actual babies. Offer to babysit for a neighbor or volunteer in the church nursery. You will have the opportunity to be around the object of your desire and gain a more realistic perspective on the demands (and screams and poopy diapers and spit-ups) of a real live child. You might just decide to put it off for a while after all.
- Laurie Nall, MD, gives the following advice to safeguard your fertility now:

See your doctor regularly. Discuss with her any menstrual irregularities or severe PMS symptoms. Sometimes thyroid disorders, PCOS (polycystic ovary syndrome), or other easily treatable hormonal imbalances could be at the root of your symptoms. It is important to get these symptoms under control before trying to conceive. Take advantage of these single years to get your body in gear.

Don't smoke. Women who smoke average up to twice as long to conceive as nonsmokers. According to the American Society for Reproductive Medicine, smoking damages your ovaries and eggs, and smokers reach menopause about two years earlier than nonsmokers.

Limit your sexual partners. The more sexual partners you have, the greater your risk of cervical cancer, which can significantly reduce your ability to have children.

Speaking of sex, make it safe. You already know that condoms help prevent pregnancy, but they don't protect you from all sexually transmitted infections. Did you know that chlamydia can lead to ectopic pregnancies and permanent scarring of the fallopian tubes? Screen annually for STIs—a leading cause of infertility in young women.

Are you Girl #6?

Y N I don't get along with one or more of my parents/stepparents.

Y N I want to get out of the house. I'm ready to feel like an adult.

Y N I feel trapped in my parents' house. I wish someone would rescue me.

Y N My parents still treat me like a child, even though I'm not!

Y N One or more of my parents, stepparents, or siblings is physically or verbally abusive.

If you answered YES to two or more questions, you are the

"Get Me Outta Here" Girl

You live with your parents in a less-than-ideal situation. You wish you could get out of the house, but you can't—not enough money, no job, too much debt, no friends to live with, and so on. Still, living there is driving you crazy. They don't treat you right. They are always yelling at you or treating you like a child or making you feel bad about yourself. If only someone would just take you away from all this!

It's risky because: You are in danger of settling for the first guy who offers a solution to your seemingly overwhelming problem. Any guy who would help you escape from that hellhole is automatically way more attractive than he should be. In fact, he looks a lot like a prince riding in on a white horse to rescue you, his fair maiden in distress. You are at risk for choosing a husband who is not *best* for you simply because he represents something *better. Better* is not *best,* or even good. Sure, once you're married, you'll be free from your parents, but soon after you'll realize that you're now stuck in a mediocre marriage. Talk about going from the frying pan into the fire! Now who will save you from *that*?

EMMA

Emma was sick of living at home. She had put up with her stepdad's put-downs and snide comments for long enough. But at eighteen, she didn't feel like she had any options. She worked at Subway and never planned to go to college because she had heard all her life how stupid she was—and she believed it. Mark was a customer who came in to get a sandwich one day. They dated for a month before they decided to run off to Las Vegas and get married. "I was so happy in that little chapel, even with its tacky plastic flowers and purple velvet pews. I finally got my first taste of freedom from my parents and it felt amazing! In hindsight, I can see that it wasn't really even about Mark at all. He was just my ticket out of that horrible house. I didn't realize that I was just trading one hell for another. Mark turned out to be a lot like my stepdad—he was critical of my weight, my hairstyle, my grammar, even my choice in music. It took me a while to grow up and realize that I didn't have to stand for that kind of treatment. I'm now divorced at twenty-eight with two children. Needless to say, my qualifications for a husband have changed a lot! I used to fantasize about meeting a man who would rescue me, but now that I can take care of myself, I am looking for a man who respects and adores me; the kind of guy who will be a great role model for my children."

What can I do to avoid being the "Get Me Outta Here" Girl?

- Come up with a plan to get out of your parents' house on your own. It will take a lot of determination and some long-term planning, but it will definitely be worth it. Seek out help from a friend or older sibling or relative who understands your situation. Read chapter 9, "Get an Independent Life: Establish Yourself Apart from Your Parents," for practical help with making the transition.
- Start thinking about the Big Picture—what you want to do with your life. This book is a great place to start. Any forward movement can be enough to build momentum and get you unstuck from your present rut.

Are you Girl #7?

Y N I feel lonely and sad when I don't have a boyfriend.

Y N There have been only a few short periods of time since high school when I was not in a relationship.

Y N Being in a relationship makes me feel happy in a way that I can't seem to feel when I am single.

Y N I get seriously depressed if a guy breaks up with me or doesn't call me back after a date.

Y N I feel loved and valuable only when I am in a committed relationship.

If you answered YES to two or more of these questions, you are the

"I Need a Man" Girl

You rely on a guy to provide the emotional security you crave. You are the girl who always has a boyfriend. You go from boyfriend to boyfriend like a monkey swinging on a tree branch, never letting go of one before you have a handle on the next. Any relationship is better than being alone, so you stay in a relationship long after you know you should have ended it. Having a boyfriend makes you feel pretty, happy, complete, desirable, and content. On the flip side, being single makes you feel unattractive, miserable, anxious, lonely, and sad.

It's risky because: If being alone makes you miserable, you might reason that marriage will make you ecstatic because you will never be alone again! It is always dangerous to count on another person to meet our emotional needs for security, acceptance, and personal well-being. People will always let us down—we guarantee that your husband (regardless of how old you are when you marry him) will let you down sometimes. Marriage is not a cure for loneliness. Many women have complained in our offices throughout the years that, "I feel more lonely in my marriage than I did when I was single." A warm body lying next to you in bed every night does not cure the emotional issues of loneliness and insecurity you may have. In fact, it may just make those feelings worse, especially if you go into a marriage expecting them to disappear.

MAYA

Maya was a pretty twenty-four-year-old who started dating when she turned twelve. Her parents were divorced when she was eight; she saw her dad only every other weekend and on Wednesday nights for pizza. She had a few close girlfriends, but quickly discovered that boys provided a nearly unlimited source of attention and affection. "I felt so special and cared for when I went out with a guy. They always made me feel pretty and wanted. I could always call a guy when I needed some company and they would come right over. My first long-term relationship lasted from my junior year of high school until my first week of college. I thought about breaking up with Tim sooner, but I felt so unsure about going away to school that it was comforting to know I had someone back home who cared about me. I met John at freshman orientation and fell head over heels. We couldn't stand to be apart, so I called my high school boyfriend and finally broke it off. John and I dated for about six months, but he was on the track team, and when he wasn't studying, he was at practice. I started spending time with Eric when John was busy. Eric knew how to treat a woman and I was pretty much over John, so we started going out. After Eric came Spence, then Trevor. Come to think of it, I've never *not* had a boyfriend. I tried being single once when my roommates dared me to go six months without dating anyone. I was like, 'Okay, no big deal. I don't need a man.' But it was tougher than I thought it would be. I didn't know what to do with myself. I got bored watching TV, I hated studying by myself, and hanging out with girls wasn't nearly as much fun as going out with a guy. I think I lasted about a month. Anyway, all that is behind me now. I'll never be alone again.

I'm engaged to the most amazing guy! We've been dating for the last six months. Adam and I are inseparable and he adores me! What more could I ask for?"

Cut to Maya in Shannon's therapy office four years later: "I thought that marriage would provide the security I was craving. Boy, was I wrong! It wasn't until Adam left that I realized that you can't build a solid relationship if you aren't a solid person. I understand now that my marriage was doomed from the start because I relied on Adam to prop me up emotionally and define my identity. I wish I had taken the time before I got married to get to know who I was inside, but I never even had the chance because I was never alone. I wish I hadn't tried so hard to avoid the loneliness of being single and instead figured out what I was so scared of. I'm finally taking the time now to get to know myself. I'm not sure I'll ever get married again, but if I do, it won't be because I need a man to complete me."

What can I do to avoid being the "I Need a Man" Girl?

- Read chapter 7, "Get an Emotionally Stable Life: Manage Your Emotions," and take the time to do each exercise. You need to get on the road to standing on your own two feet emotionally before you join with someone else.
- Try being single for six months. If that sounds impossible, it is absolutely necessary! Gather some friends to help you stick to it. Don't spend the time sitting idly by, fantasizing about your man, and texting your exes. Get to know yourself and figure out how to make yourself happy.

Are you Girl #8?

Y N I've never been good with money and don't think I ever will be.

Y N My husband will be in charge of our finances.
Y N I hate balancing my checkbook. What a pain!
Y N What's the use of pursuing a career? My future husband will support me.
Y N I'm a girl who likes expensive things, and a man should provide them for me.

If you answered YES to two or more of these questions, you are the

"Show Me the Money, Honey" Girl

You are confused, fearful, or downright ignorant about money matters. You long for a man to swoop in and solve all your financial woes. You believe that money is a man's business, and you fully expect that your husband will earn all the money and save for your future—after all, you'll be busy shopping.

It's risky because: Every woman should be financially savvy and able to take care of herself. If not, you risk marrying a man simply because he provides financial relief. That's not fair to you or to him. A man shouldn't be valued primarily for his ability to earn a living just as a woman shouldn't be valued primarily for how she looks. Besides, no matter how financially stable a man is when you marry him, there is no guarantee that this will always be the case. The job market is fickle. He could have a great job one day, only to be unemployed the next.

TRICIA

Tricia married her husband at thirty when he was a promising young engineer. Two years into their marriage, when she was pregnant with their first child, Brad lost his job and ended up unemployed for more than a year! Good thing Tricia had gotten her physical therapist license and had a lot of work experience—she quickly found a job and ended up supporting their family while Brad looked for another position. They would have been up a creek with a baby if Tricia had relied solely upon her husband's job without a backup plan and some solid work experience.

LUNA

Luna isn't so financially together as Tricia and admits to searching for a man to solve her financial woes. She's looking for a rich guy to take care of her so she can avoid taking responsibility for herself. In the meantime, she has racked up mountains of credit card debt because, in her words, "You gotta look good if you are going to land a millionaire." These stories never end well. Either Luna will marry a man for his money, disregarding more important qualities, or she will pass up a great match because he doesn't match up to her financial standards. Either way, Luna is risking her future happiness by refusing to take charge of her own finances.

Money is not quite as complicated as your parents' constant fights over it would lead you to believe. You are perfectly capable of managing your own money. Besides, there is nothing quite like the self-esteem boost that comes from taking care of yourself!

What can I do to avoid being the "Show Me the Money, Honey" Girl?

- Read chapter 6 "Get a Smart Financial Life: Take Charge of Your Money, Honey," and work through the exercises. You will learn the importance of creating healthy money habits that will benefit you for life.

- Remind yourself that you don't want to jump into a marriage solely based upon a man's ability to protect you from the painful realities of money. Getting a handle on your finances and learning to take care of yourself are important steps toward having a fabulous single life.
- Read the delightful book *The Importance of Being Married,* a novel by Gemma Townley, for a funny tale about a girl who tries desperately to marry for money—a lot of money.

Are you Girl #9?

Y N My parents just don't understand me.
Y N My parents never like my boyfriends.
Y N I tend to prove my independence by picking friends, boyfriends, and jobs my parents don't approve of.
Y N If my parents cautioned me against marrying someone I wanted to, I would just run off to Vegas.
Y N I know better than my parents. They just don't get it.

If you answered YES to two or more of these questions, you are the

"Rebel Yell" Girl

You make decisions just to tick off your parents. You derive secret satisfaction from doing anything that will make them mad. Your favorite time was when you brought that guy home who was covered from head to toe in tattoos and piercings—they flipped out! Ha! It served them right for thinking they had any right to shove their opinions down your throat. You can date or marry whomever the heck you want—it's your life!

It's risky because: In reality, you are *giving* your parents control by intentionally choosing someone because you think they won't approve. In actuality, you are allowing their opinion to determine whom you choose. It's a bad idea to make a decision as a knee-jerk reaction to your parents trying to control you. You may end up choosing someone who is not necessarily right for you, simply because he is wrong for them. Important decisions in life need to be made with your full awareness of your motives—in fact, choosing someone just to make your parents mad is a strong indication that you are not mature enough to make such a choice yet. A mature woman decides what is best for her based upon knowledge of herself, her needs, and desires—not as a way to get back at her parents. Someday you might even realize that your parents were right about that loser you dated in college. Heck, you might even go so far as to admit to them that they were right.

Your desire to choose someone your parents don't approve of could stem from a fear of having a marriage like your parents. You don't want to be like them, so maybe if you choose someone they don't like, you will end up with a different kind of relationship. Isn't their stamp of approval a predictor that he will end up like your dad and treat you like your mom? In reality, their disapproval doesn't guarantee that you will have a different relationship—you and your mate will determine how you maneuver through your marriage, and you will have to deal with the patterns you learned in your family, regardless of whom you choose.

What can I do to avoid being the "Rebel Yell" Girl?

- Get to know yourself and what you like apart from your parents' reactions. Do you like tattoos because they are interesting and artistic or because they make your parents crazy? Be honest with yourself and your reasons for making the choices you do.

- Remember that you are a different person from either of your parents, even if you believe in some of the same things. Do you agree with them on politics? Abortion? The plight of the poor? Whether education is important? Whether yellow is a good color on you? The sky is blue? Make a list of five things you agree with your parents about. If you choose a mate they approve of, that doesn't mean that you chose him for them; it just means that you happen to agree on something else important.

Are you Girl #10?

Y N Women in their late twenties to early thirties have a more difficult time getting married.

Y N It would be better to settle for a less-than-ideal mate than to be an Old Maid.

Y N If I were thirty and unmarried, I would feel like an Old Maid.

Y N I am afraid of growing old alone.

Y N The older I get, the less desirable or "marriable" I become.

If you answered YES to two or more of these questions, you are the

"Old Maid" Girl

You are terrified of becoming that old lady who never married—you know, the one who eats canned lentil soup every night and sleeps with her twenty-two cats she calls her "babies"? You can easily conjure up that image of yourself in your head. You want to snag a man while you still have your youth and your perky butt. You are glued to the daunting statistics that say women over thirty-five are less likely to get married than to get hit by lightning. (Who comes up with these lies, anyway? Dorky science guys who want women to settle for them out of fear of not finding anyone better? Shame on them!) You feel less marriable with each passing day.

It's risky because: Fear is no reason to get married. Take Zoe's story, for example:

ZOE

"I got married at twenty-four because I was determined to avoid becoming an Old Maid. In my hometown, everyone was married by twenty-three. When twenty-three came and went, I was afraid that if I didn't marry Cal, my college boyfriend, I would never find anyone else to love me enough to propose. I didn't want to pass up a sure thing and risk being old and alone. So we got married, had three kids and a decent marriage, I guess. We fought a lot. I certainly wasn't happy, but at least I was married. I figured out too late that it would be better to be single and happy than to be married to someone who wasn't the best match for me. That was when I met Brian—this great guy at work. He was everything Cal wasn't, and we connected on a soul level. I was so tempted to have an affair, but I didn't. I made my bed and I was going to lie in it. No need to make my kids' lives miserable just because I made a hasty decision when I was younger."

It was Nora Ephron who made famous the line that forty-year-old single college-educated women were more likely to be killed by a terrorist than to get married. In reality, statistics now prove that most of these women will eventually marry at some point in their lives.

LOLA

Our good friend Lola got married last year at age forty-two. She had wanted to marry younger and stood faithfully by as everyone in our circle of friends married and began to have children. She endured tons of setups and even joined eHarmony, but the one thing she didn't do was settle. "It was tough at times to be the only single woman among all of my married friends. And I'd be lying if I said that I never worried about becoming a spinster, but I always managed to banish the image of myself as a lonely old lady by replacing it with a mental picture of myself conquering my greatest fears by zooming down the autobahn in a super-charged Alfa Romeo. I know it sounds silly, but it helped to transform that negative image into a positive one. An important benefit of not getting married young was that I had the sad opportunity to see what didn't work in my friends' marriages. I watched their relationships go through ups and downs and even some that ended in divorce. Seeing the downside of marrying the wrong man, for the wrong reason, made me feel fortunate to be single and even more determined not to settle. When I met Mark, I knew that the wait had been worth it!"

What can I do to avoid being the "Old Maid" Girl?

- Look up these famous women who didn't get married until after thirty: Amanda Peet (34), Ali Larter (33), Claire Forlani (34), Marcia Cross (42), Ellen Pompeo (37), Kate Walsh (39), Sandra Bullock (40). Seeing their happy endings gives you a different vision for your thirties and forties—a far cry from old maids!
- Spend some time writing down the things you want to accomplish by the time you are thirty (or forty).

Focusing on what you want and what it's going to take to get there will lessen your fear of becoming an Old Maid. Besides, you won't have time to waste thinking about it!

Honorable Mentions

Those were the top ten reasons women marry young, but there are a few other regrettable reasons that deserve honorable mentions.

Culture

In your culture, women are encouraged to marry young. Everyone at your mosque/temple/synagogue/church tries to set you up with their son/nephew/cousin/coworker. Cultural imperatives are impossible to shift on your own, so don't try to convince your culture to change. Just know that you can still be a thriving part of your culture without bowing to all its expectations. Some cultures expect a woman to stay married to her husband even if he is unfaithful or abusive. Other cultures blame infertility on the sins of the mother or father. You can't choose your culture, but you can absolutely choose which parts of it you embrace and which you don't. Never bow to cultural pressure that could result in a miserable marriage that doesn't work for you. You are the one who is going to build a life with this person—make a choice that is right for you.

Fear of Going into the World Alone

You are about to graduate from college and you don't have a clue about what comes next. It's scary to go out on your own, and it sure would be nice to have a man around to make the important decisions, keep you safe, and rescue you from that exhausting and stressful dating scene. Gillian married at twenty-three to escape an uncertain future. "I had no idea how to support myself. I knew that if I didn't get married right away, I would be forced to be an accountant even though I hated the thought of the job. I was dating Josh at the time and knew that he was my only option if I wanted someone to take care of me. He was around when I needed security in an insincere after-college world. So I married him. Not the best reason to get married, I now realize, but I was afraid of the alternatives." Marriage does indeed provide a sense of security and belonging, but if you give yourself a chance, you will see that the world is not as scary as you fear it might be. Women who marry because they believe that they can't take care of themselves are much more likely to end up staying in an abusive relationship because they don't have any other options. Wouldn't you agree that that is even scarier than going it alone? Instead of *avoiding* maturing in the real world, embrace it! It will be intimidating at first, but college is like a cocoon—now is the time to spread your wings and fly. Find some like-minded, even eager, girlfriends to walk into this new adventure with you.

Pregnancy

They used to call weddings with a pregnant bride "shotgun weddings" because the dad would show up at the young baby-daddy's house with a mean-looking shotgun insisting that he marry the girl and "make an honest woman out of her." These days, celebrity couples who have children together but don't marry (Johnny Depp and Vanessa Paradis, Brad Pitt and Angelina Jolie) have done much to reduce the social stigma attached to out-of-wedlock pregnancy. While we wholeheartedly believe in marriage and the concept that children fare much better in a two-parent household, the statistics for marriages based solely upon an unplanned pregnancy are even more dismal than those for simply marrying young. If you are pregnant, there are better alternatives than getting stuck in a doomed marriage. Celeste has handled hundreds of adoption cases and has waiting lists of couples eager to adopt. If you strongly believe the father of the baby is the one for you, take some time to get some counseling and prepare for the realities of marriage. Once you get married, your parents won't help you as much with the child, you won't be eligible for the same government assistance, and you will have the added pressures of adjusting to a partner in a lifelong commitment.

Pressure

Parents are notorious for pressuring their daughters to get married. They brazenly ask about who you are dating, guilt you about not giving them grandchildren, and warn you with old wives' tales about Old Maids. Talk about relentless! You often let their calls go to voice mail because you can't stand the thought of more prying questions from your well-meaning mom about whether or not you have a date on Saturday night or whether that nice young man from work has called you lately. The pressure is enough to make you actually consider marriage just to get them off your back! Any marriage seems to offer peace compared with the constant haranguing of your parents. Resist the temptation to run down the aisle simply to pacify your nagging parents. Instead, inform your family that you want to be as prepared as possible for your future marriage and are taking the necessary steps to get there. Don't expect that your mom will stop nagging you right away, but stand your ground. You are the one who will have to be married to this guy, not your mom. Never make a momentous life decision to appease someone else. Besides, didn't your mom always teach you to stand up to peer pressure?

The Longing for Stability

You want to do it right, to create the family you never had as a child. Perhaps you are one of the millions of women who grew up in a divorced home and you always craved the stability you imagined an intact home would provide. You idealized marriage because your parents got divorced when you were very young and you had no actual experience with a happily married couple. You might even have vowed to yourself as a child that you would create the perfect, stable environment for your own children as soon as you could. This is risky because your image of marriage is a fairy tale, the musings of an unhappy little girl who desperately wants you to marry to create the stable family life she still wants so badly. No marriage can heal the pain from your unhappy childhood. That is too much pressure for a marriage to bear. Take a step back and work on healing the pain from your past before you bring your unrealistic expectations into a marriage. Chapter 4, "Get a Peaceful Family Life: Make Peace with Difficult Family Dynamics" will help you get started with this process.

The Low-Risk Equation: Maturity + Experience = Marriage Insurance

The young women who marry for the reasons we've talked about are basing their decisions on a skewed view of both marriage and themselves. Their perspective is skewed because they lack, by virtue of their age, the personal maturity and experience necessary to see clearly. A young woman who hasn't experienced life on her own—failure, joy, heartache, accomplishments, loneliness, and so much more simply hasn't benefitted from the self-knowledge and confidence that come from having to navigate life's ups and downs.

So if the rate of divorce is double for women who marry before twenty-five, what is so magical about the quarter-of-a-century mark and beyond? Certainly there is no mysterious maturity fairy that sneaks into our bedrooms on the eve of our twenty-fifth birthday and bestows upon us the ability to choose the right man and maintain a stable marriage. We only wish it were that simple! There are numerous factors that contribute to your improved ability to make good decisions about marriage as you get older. Think of how much you grew and changed from the time you were fourteen to the time you were twenty—you became such a different person in just six years. You went from being that gangly adolescent girl who loved reading Sweet Valley High books and dreaming of a life exactly like Elizabeth and Jessica's to a twenty-year-old young woman who now knows that real high school is nothing like Sweet Valley High. Your understanding of yourself evolved significantly. This personal evolution will continue in spades until you are in your late twenties. We guarantee that when you're looking back at your twenties, you will be astounded by how much your perspective on life has changed.

Some of what happens in that critical period from twenty to thirty is simple trial and error. The more you experience life and relationships, the more you understand how life works, how it doesn't work, and what you want out of it all. We believe that there is much you can do during this critical decade; things that will ensure a happier you and a happier marriage. Of course, we can't guarantee that your marriage will last forever if you postpone marriage and apply the Ten Keys. But we do guarantee that if you take the time in your twenties and early thirties to become your complete self, you will be able to avoid marrying for one of the ten wrong reasons and make a much better choice in a spouse. Becoming your best self isn't easy, but it is simple. We've broken it down into manageable steps in the following chapters. Get ready to seize the day, learn to stand on your two feet, and make empowering decisions about the rest of your life.

> *There are no shortcuts in the journey ahead, nor is there a turning back. . . . Development must be allowed to take its proper course.*
>
> —*I Ching*

Chapter 3

Key #1: Get a Connected Life

Invest in Friendships

Friendship? Yes, please.
—Charles Dickens

Friendship with other women can and should be a fabulous part of your life as a twentysomething. Girlfriends contribute to your life in unique and essential ways. They help shape who you are and who you have yet to become. If you choose well, you will find that your closest girlfriends understand you like no one else and can keep you sane, even when you feel like a certifiable woman on the verge. You'll hopefully marry a wonderfully sensitive guy who is in tune with your emotional needs, monthly cycles, and love for sample sales, but not even Mr. Wonderful will be able to take the place of girlfriends in your life.

Your twenties really is the perfect time to invest in friendships that will last a lifetime. You're finally (fin-a-lly!) moving past the unavoidable high school and college-sorority drama into a place of maturity, where you can develop true, solid friendships—friendships that you'll be able to count on throughout the pivotal moments of your life. Take it from us, you're going to need your girls! We're not talking about the kind of friendship that consists mainly of endless chatter about movies, makeup, Manolos, and McDreamy (although we appreciate all of the above), or the kind that is maintained by forwarding precious e-mails full of animated puppies, dancing hearts, and sappy poems. No, we're talking about the real-deal friends who care about you in both word and deed. Friends who are trustworthy and loyal. Friends who are happy for you when great things happen and who show up to be sad with you when tragedy strikes. True friends inspire you toward continual growth and self-discovery. True friends will be a source of stability and consistency throughout the coming years of inevitable change.

Experts Agree . . .

Scientists now suspect that friendship can literally counteract the inevitable stress that most of us experience on a daily basis. A landmark UCLA study suggests that women respond to stress with a cascade of brain chemicals that actually encourage them to make and maintain friendships with other women. According to the study's authors, Laura Cousin Klein, Ph.D., and Shelley E. Taylor, Ph.D., when a woman experiences stress, her body responds by releasing the hormone oxytocin, known as the bonding hormone. This hormone encourages her to gather and bond with other women, in contrast to the male response to stress, which is to tackle stress Lone Ranger style. When a woman does engage in befriending, she releases even more oxytocin, which then actually counters stress and produces a calming effect. This calming response does not occur in men, explains Dr. Klein, because testosterone (which men produce in high levels when they're under stress) seems to reduce the effects of oxytocin. Klein's theory about the connection between female friendship and stress may explain why women consistently outlive men, who suffer stress-related illnesses in higher numbers than women. "There's no doubt," concludes Dr. Klein, "friends are helping us live longer."

Study after study has also found that social ties reduce our risk of disease by lowering blood pressure, heart rate, and cholesterol. On the opposite end of the spectrum, researchers recently found that people who had *no* friends increased their risk of death, and that those who had the *most* friends over a nine-year period cut their risk of death by more than 60 percent. And that's not all. When the researchers looked at how well women functioned after the death of a spouse, they found that even in the face of this devastating life event, the women who had close friends were more likely to survive the experience without new health problems or permanent loss of vitality. Those without friends didn't fare so well.

The famed Nurses' Health Study from Harvard Medical School found that the more friends women had, the less likely they were to develop physical impairments as they aged, and the more likely they were to be leading a joyful life. In fact, the results were so significant, the researchers concluded that not having close friends or confidantes was as detrimental to your health as smoking or carrying extra weight. According to Dr. Robin Smith, Ph.D., a frequent contributor to *O* magazine and Oprah.com, "You cannot have self-esteem without true friendship—it is a vital ingredient in living your best life."

In fact, girlfriends are so important that there's even a day set aside in their honor. It's true! National Women's Friendship Day (NWFD), which was created by the Kappa Delta Sorority in 1998, is celebrated each year on the third Sunday in September and is currently endorsed by more than thirty states. According to Melanie Schild, executive director of Kappa Delta, "Our main goal is to encourage women to value and nurture their friendship with other women, something that is often taken for granted."

You already know how good you feel after a long heart-to-heart with a girlfriend, but now you have scientific proof that your girlfriends are good for your health and general well-being!

Why Now?

Your twenties and early thirties are the best time to get connected. These years offer you the opportunity to create and deepen friendships with other women. You have time *now* in ways that you won't as you get older. You also need your girlfriends *now*, more than ever, as you begin to make decisions that will have lasting consequences for your entire life. If you're not in a romantic relationship, friends can effectively fill that perceived void, as well as your need for emotional connection. True friendship can also teach you a ton about communication and commitment, both of which are vital to a healthy marriage.

The Gift of Time

When you're single, you have ample time to spend in long, late-night conversations with girlfriends. Conversations about anything and everything from whether you should go to graduate school, to why your ex was not the guy for you, to how your mom is driving you absolutely crazy, to whether or not the Prius really is as environment-friendly as it claims to be.

The fact is, once you're married, it will be more difficult to nurture female friendships. Your focus will naturally begin to shift. You'll be concentrating on maintaining and strengthening your marriage relationship, you'll likely be in a demanding stage in your career, and your energy will be channeled into

Personal Insight from Celeste

Some of my very best twentysomething memories are of sitting on the blue-striped couch in our apartment with my two roommates (who have remained two of my closest friends in the world), discussing in detail everything from intense family struggles to whether "the Rachel" really was a great haircut or not. We walked through first dates, broken engagements, law school graduations, and job changes by one another's sides. We also had our fair share of disagreements, hurt feelings, and ensuing tears. Thankfully, it wasn't all intensity and struggle. We also spent thousands of hours laughing and amassing a wealth of inside jokes and embarrassing moments. It was through my connection to these women and a few others during this time (you know who you are) that I was able to give shape to what I wanted and needed from life. These moments, years, and people left an indelible mark on me, for which I am deeply grateful. These friends saw me for who I was and loved me anyway. It was through their eyes that I was able to see a reflection of who I was, who I wanted to become, and what I needed in a husband.

creating a home. Once you have children, it becomes even more of a challenge to maintain your already-existing friendships, and you'll have limited time to pursue new ones. Sure, you'll gather new friends as you move through your thirties and forties, but there's just no substitute for friends who share your history and with whom you weathered your turbulent twenties. It is these friends who will remind you of who you used to be when you find yourself knee-deep in diapers and Disney character lunch boxes. It is these friends who will be there to celebrate who you've become ten, twenty, thirty years from now.

Friends Help You Figure It All Out

Real friendships provide support and counsel from people who understand you as you make significant decisions about school, work, relationships, and the direction your life will take. It's during your twenties that you more clearly define your moral and spiritual values and clarify what you want for your future. During your twenties, you'll face complicated family issues as you begin to separate from your parents. Who better to walk this journey with than girlfriends who love you, understand you, and will help you find answers to the questions they are grappling with as well?

"I Don't Need Girlfriends" and Other Ridiculous Myths

So if there are so many good reasons to have girlfriends and if now really is the best time to develop friendships, why don't you have better friends? Maybe you have fallen into the trap of believing one of the many myths about girlfriends.

Myth #1: I don't need girlfriends, because my future husband will meet all my emotional needs.

Mythbuster: Like it or not, your husband is *not* going to be able to tend to each and every one of your emotional needs. It will

Our Story—Shannon and Celeste

Throughout the years of our friendship, we had many conversations about things that really mattered to us. We debated whether or not Shannon should move to Costa Rica after grad school (yes), if Celeste should marry the dentist (no), if Shannon should get her own apartment (yes, but she didn't), if Celeste should have a dream wedding in Venice (absolutely!). One such memorable conversation took place the morning after a forgettable double date. It went something like this:

SHANNON: *Can you believe that guy tried to kiss me last night? Was he on the same date as me?*

CELESTE: *Can't blame a guy for trying. I'm out of your favorite tea. Will coffee do?*

S: *As long as it's not decaf. So, did you have fun with Paul last night?*

C: *Kind of, but I spent the whole time trying to figure out if I should break up with him. There have been some red flags, but I do really like him. The whole purpose of the double date was for you to see what you think of him, though. So? . . .*

S: *He's definitely cute! And he seems supersmart, but to be honest, kind of possessive. Like when I mentioned your ex and he made a joke about getting you to change your number—I don't think he was really joking. And I didn't get a chance to tell you this last night, but when you got up to go to the bathroom, he watched you like a hawk. While you were waiting, he said, "That guy is flirting with her. Excuse me, I gotta go take care of this," and he stormed off to collect you.*

C: *Seriously? Yikes! Well, I guess I should be surprised, but I'm not. That's not the first time he's acted like that. It's confusing because he's so sweet and attentive, but then it can get to be a little much. I got a little creeped out last week when he was at my apartment and kept checking my caller ID. I've been giving him the benefit of the doubt because he has a lot of qualities that I'm looking for, but I don't know, what do you think?*

S: *I think you should trust your gut on this one. You are such a free spirit and the most trustworthy person I know. It would be such a shame for you to be stifled in a relationship with a guy who questioned your every move. From what I've seen with guys like this, it only gets worse as time goes on. He's showing the typical signs of a guy who turns into a complete control freak. Obviously not a path you want to go down.*

Shortly after that conversation, Celeste thankfully ended the relationship with Mr. Controlling. After more than five years of close friendship, we trusted each other enough to be honest, and knew each other well enough to give advice based on personal insight into what made the other tick.

As we both now look back at the uncertainty and important decisions of our twentysomething years, we are grateful that we took the time to cultivate the kind of friendships that helped us figure it all out.

be patently unfair, not to mention disastrous, for you to expect him to do so. Even if your future husband is completely undying in his love for you and wants to meet all your needs for emotional intimacy, he cannot. It's a matter of wiring—his *and* yours. A man is just not wired to be able to give you all the emotional connection you, as a woman, are wired to need. So please, for both your sakes, release yourself from the romantic fantasy that once you get married you won't need girlfriends, because your husband is going to be dying to hear, for the fifth time, about your latest fight with your sister, how your cuticles just aren't as soft as they used to be, and why you absolutely adored the fourth *Twilight* book and can't wait for the movie to come out. If you make the effort to build close friendships with women now, you won't have to badger your husband until he agrees to paint your toenails. Instead of looking to your husband as the sole source of intimacy, you can pick up the phone or drop by a girlfriend's house when you need to dissect the conversation you had with your boss or are in a quandary over which age-defying cream to buy.

Myth #2: I need a man to keep me from being lonely.

Mythbuster: Friendship keeps loneliness at bay during your single years. When you're single, you can expect to battle feelings of loneliness from time to time. You're separated from your parents and siblings and may be in a new town without the comfort and familiarity of home. If you're not in a romantic relationship, it can seem as though everyone around you is in love and part of a blissfully happy "we." It's easy to start feeling like you're a loner, dwelling in a gap; you don't have the same childhood connection with your family of origin, but haven't yet created your own family.

We've all heard women say about a less-than-great relationship with a guy, "Well, at least I'm not alone." The danger in this thinking is that if you allow your loneliness to guide you, chances are you'll end up in a relationship that may meet your need for emotional or physical connection in the short term, but is basically a waste of your time, and his.

ALICIA

Alicia was sick to death of spending Saturday nights alone, roaming the aisles of Blockbuster only to find leftover flicks she'd already seen. She had moved to Dallas for work about a year ago and hadn't really made any friends since she'd been there. Work seemed to take up most of her time these days, and on the weekends she was reluctant to get out and meet new people. Each time she did manage to venture out, it seemed like everyone she saw looked happy and cohesive in their little couples and groups, oblivious of her aching loneliness. Alicia longed for human connection and actually looked forward to returning to work on Monday mornings so she could at least be around familiar faces.

In recent months, Alicia had gone on a few dates with her coworker Allen, who was fairly good-looking but talked about himself nonstop. Even though they'd spent hours together, Allen had yet to ask Alicia much of anything about herself. When she did manage to get a word in edgewise during their conversations, Allen's eyes would glaze over and he would start looking around distractedly. Charming! But good ol' Allen was nothing if not persistent, and before Alicia knew it, she and

Allen were in a full-blown dating relationship, spending most of their free time together. Unfortunately, the more time she spent with him, the more invisible and resentful she felt. Alicia knew the relationship was going nowhere, but couldn't bear the thought of spending her weekends solo, once again.

What's the answer to Alicia's dilemma? You guessed it! Girlfriends. Friendships with other women can help you fight the temptation to jump into a relationship with a guy who you know is not going to be a positive factor in your life. Most important, these friendships can also provide the emotional connection you need and supply an antidote to loneliness during your "gap-dwelling," twentysomething years.

Myth #3: I shouldn't waste my time investing in friendships if my end goal is to be married.

Mythbuster: Friendship is actually the perfect training ground for marriage. As philosopher Friedrich Nietzsche said, "It is not a lack of love, but a lack of friendship that makes unhappy marriages." If you think about it, marriage is just another type of friendship, albeit a lot more intense. Your experiences in cultivating and maintaining friendships is excellent hands-on training in how to establish a solid marriage relationship with your future spouse. Too many marriages suffer from lack of the basics: respect for the other person, ability to handle conflict, and ability to compromise. Investing in friendships now can teach you a ton about what it's going to take to be a loving wife and what qualities are going to be important as you choose your future husband/friend.

DESIREE

"I've lived with roommates and friends since college. I'm twenty-six now, and while my friendships with women certainly haven't taught me everything I'll need to know about my relationship with my future husband, they have taught me quite a bit. Through these friendships I've learned how to handle arguments, how to compromise, how to communicate, and how to stay committed, even when it gets rough."

You have an amazing opportunity during your twenties to put into practice what it means to be a good friend and to figure out how the notion of commitment gets played out in real life. It's during your single, twentysomething years that your friendships endure real-world realities such as work frustrations, financial problems, and significant time constraints for the first time. Maintaining friendships despite these stressors is the perfect way to prepare you for some of the challenges of marriage. If you commit the time and effort now building good friendships, you will later benefit two important ways: First, you will enjoy the love and support of those friendships for the coming decades; second, you will be equipped to enter your marriage relationship knowing what it means to love and be loved and how a relationship based on mutual respect should function.

Myth #4: I don't need girlfriends, because all my best friends are guys.

Mythbuster: While friendships with guys may *seem* less complicated, they are a poor substitute for the emotional connection and sisterhood you can experience with a girlfriend. You may have a guy friend who is a sympathetic listener, but only another woman can truly understand and relate to your experiences as a woman.

This myth is rooted in a long-standing history of tumultuous relationships between women throughout history, from Anne Boleyn to Lauren Conrad. Maybe you've been burned by a female friend in the past. Maybe you've been the wounded object of hurtful gossip or betrayal by one or more so-called girlfriends. We are always saddened when we hear the all-too-frequent lament of women, "I really don't have any girlfriends," but we also recognize that women can be downright vicious to each other. Women can be jealous and petty, and they can hold a grudge in a way that a man would never dream of! Honestly, it can be pretty scary to let your guard down after experiencing the pain that comes with the broken trust of a girlfriend.

If the above rings true for you, and you find yourself mostly hanging with the boys as a result, let us offer a little insight.

Personal Insight from Shannon

I can pinpoint the exact moment I decided that I preferred male friends to girlfriends. I was a junior in high school and had an established "bestie" named Sierra. We had been inseparable since freshman year drama class when I was Juliet to her Romeo. (No boys in the class would set foot on the stage.) We did the usual activities together, sitting in the quad talking about the cute senior boys who never looked our way, hanging out at the mall when our parents agreed to drop us off, and working on school projects together—we won the science competition with our groundbreaking experiment in rocket science involving baking soda, vinegar, and a balloon. Then Sierra did what we had previously only dreamed about and hoped for. . . . She got a boyfriend! I understood when she spent time with him instead of me at lunch. I even got it when she canceled our standing Friday-night movie tradition to hang with him. But it wasn't the boyfriend that bothered me.

It all started in second-period history when they made the announcement that I had won the election for Publicity Chair. I, of course, was ecstatic and rushed out of class to discover that Sierra had been very busy discounting my win in her Calculus class. "Sierra said the only reason you beat Maggie is because you stuffed the ballot boxes and that you were the one who changed Maggie's poster."

I was devastated. My very best friend, the one who knew me better than anyone else, had started vicious rumors about me! My first experience with painful betrayal by this jealous girlfriend set the stage for my subsequent disappointing relationships with women.

I entered college wounded by my high school experiences with Sierra and other so-called girlfriends, but hopeful that college women would be different. I jumped right into college life and joined a sorority, only to encounter more backstabbing women who jumped at opportunities to steal boyfriends, spread rumors and gossip about me and any other sorority sister who wasn't within earshot. I soon gave up trying to have meaningful relationships with women and fell into the easy routine of hanging out with guys.

It was in my mid-twenties, however, when I realized that my friendships with guys lacked the sisterhood I had always craved. I observed women who had great girl friendships and found myself longing for their unique connection. Seeing those friendships renewed my faith in the possibility that I could have healthy relationships with women. I resolved to make the leap and try again. But this time around, I was determined to choose my girlfriends more wisely. This time around, I would look for friends who were secure in themselves, who were willing to give, and for whom friendship was not an opportunity for competition. This time around, I would share myself tentatively at first, taking baby steps toward trusting as she proved to be trustworthy. That friend I chose so determinedly was none other than Celeste! And you can see how that worked out for me seventeen years later.

The most important thing you can do to change this pattern is to take a long, hard look at the kind of girlfriends you are attracting as well as the kind of friend you have been to the women in your life. We'll explore this in detail in the next section. If you don't make the effort to figure this out now, you will continue to attract the same kind of friends, and your bad experiences will only repeat themselves. In the meantime, we guarantee that while friendships with guys can be a lot easier and certainly a lot of fun, they can never replace the joy and depth that comes from intimate and lifelong friendships with other women.

Friendships with guys are inherently limited for three main reasons:

The Communication Chasm

In case you haven't noticed, men and women are wired very differently. Women are wired to establish intimacy and closeness with others through conversation. For men, talking is *not* the important part of the relationship. A guy would rather catch a movie or play tennis as a way of interacting than sit around and listen to you share your feelings, an essential component of female friendship. This simple but significant difference limits the degree of intimacy you can have with a guy friend. In a marriage, you commit yourself to building intimacy, despite these differences, in a way that you just can't within the context of a male friendship.

The Inevitable Shift

Once you're married, your friendships with men *will* change. It's a fact of life. Even if your husband becomes buds with your best guy friend, it's just not realistic to imagine that you will continue to spend one-on-one time with your guy friends in an effort to deepen those relationships. We're definitely not saying that friendships with your buddies can't continue and grow once you're married, but we *are* saying that the relationships are naturally going to change in a way that friendships between women don't have to. Your main man must be your husband; other friendships with men will naturally and necessarily be taken down a few notches.

And, of Course, the Sexual Tension

You remember the argument in *When Harry Met Sally*, right? That men and women can never be friends because sex always gets in the way? It's an age-old question. We say, there will always be sexual tension between men and women, whether you're willing to admit it or not. This assertion inevitably causes some uproar from the gallery of women in denial about their friendships with men. Here are the three main protests we commonly hear:

"But we're not attracted to each other!" You may not be *physically* attracted to him, but it only makes sense that if a guy and girl like to spend time together, it is because they are attracted to *something* about the other. Simply said, they *like* each other! So be honest with yourself. If you hang out all the time, have a lot of fun together, and really enjoy each other's company, chances are that at least one of you is looking for more than just friendship.

"Okay, he might have a crush on me, but he knows I don't feel the same way." You may be confident that you did an adequate job of sending him the just-friends vibe and that he received it loud and clear. But if he is still intent on spending time with you and playing the role of the attentive guy friend, it's obvious that he is harboring secret hopes of eventually winning you over.

"Yeah, he probably does want more, but he knows I have a boyfriend." You may be in a relationship, and your guy friend may respect the fact that you're off the market. Your status as "taken" may hold the sexual tension between you at bay, at least until a breakup occurs. We've all seen our fair share of romantic comedies where the best guy friend is waiting in the wings to comfort his brokenhearted friend and prove himself prime boyfriend material.

So what does this mean for you and the importance you place on guy friends? Friendships with guys can be great and may be a lot less complicated than ones with girls. But because of their inherent limitations, your friendships with guys will never be as secure, reciprocal, or rewarding as those with women.

Making It Happen: In Pursuit of True Girlfriends

Remember when your mom told you in the second grade, "Honey, if you want to have a friend, you have to be a friend?" Once again, Mom was right. These friendships born on the elementary playground were pretty straightforward: If you both liked hopscotch and strawberry lip gloss, you were friends. These days, your friendships are a bit more complicated.

When women complain about their friends or lack thereof, the first two questions we ask are: *What kind of friend are you?* and *What kind of friends do you choose?* Your answers to these two questions are crucial to creating and sustaining solid friendships. *You* can be the best, most loyal friend in the world, but if you are seeking out women who aren't good friend material because *they* lack character, are self-centered, or are so emotionally unstable that they can't maintain a healthy friendship, you are wasting your time and energy. On the other hand, you can pick great people as friends, but if *you* aren't giving to the friendship in a way that fosters depth and trust, you will not succeed in establishing a lasting friendship.

What Kind of Friend Are You?

While we all yearn for true friendship, it is not something that comes easily to most of us. Even if you grew up with a mom or other role model who was a great example of what it means to have deep friendships, it still requires a lot of work on your part as well as a willingness to take emotional risks.

When we asked women to describe the qualities they most

valued in their close friends and what distinguished these friendships from others, five qualities stood out. We call them the Five Be's of Friendship, and they are crucial to establishing friendships that will take you through your twenties and beyond; friendships that will be a source of joy and strength for the rest of your life.

Be: Transparent

A true friend is honest about her struggles. If the only details you are willing to reveal about yourself are your successes and happy moments, you won't be able to connect with others in a meaningful way. Why not? First, you aren't being honest. We all face challenges on a daily basis and we all struggle with insecurity, no matter how great our lives may appear to be on the outside. Second, when you're unwilling to let others see your shortcomings, you fail to create a safe place for your friend to reveal these same things about herself. No one wants to admit that she feels inadequate, when the girl across from her claims to be teeming with confidence at every turn. Third, if you insist on maintaining your airs of superiority and unflappability (which are probably just a mask for your insecurities), you are sure to stir up feelings of jealousy in others, which will quickly kill a friendship. Have you ever wondered why it is that some women in your life provoke feelings of envy while others—even very together and talented women—don't? This has everything to do with transparency. The more deeply we know another person's secret hopes and anguishes, and the more we can identify with her struggles, the less inclined we are to envy her and the more eager we are to see her succeed.

Be: Happy for Her

A true friend is sincerely happy when her friend accomplishes something wonderful or when something really terrific happens to her. Is that you? Or do you just pretend to be happy for her, all the while being overcome by the green-eyed monster of jealousy?

BETH

When Beth got to the restaurant where she and her good friend Kristin were meeting for an after-work drink, she was greeted by a very excited and breathless Kristin, who was just hanging up her cell phone. "Beth, I can't believe it! It happened!" said Kristin, almost shouting. Kristin went on to report that she just received a call from her boss at the television station where she had been slaving away for the past five years. He finally offered her the coveted on-camera reporter position, starting immediately! The job was everything Kristin had been working toward. "Wow," said Beth, "that is wonderful news." But just as the words were coming out of her mouth, Beth couldn't help but think of her own career achievements and how they stacked up against Kristin's. Instead of being happy for Kristin and ordering up a round of champagne, Beth sat there obsessing about why her own career had seemed to halt at the entry level and wondering if it would ever be *her* turn for a promotion. For the rest of the night, Beth pretended to be happy for Kristin, but was actually lost in thoughts of herself.

What should have been a time of celebration of Kristin's achievement turned into Beth's personal pity party. Like Beth, we all struggle at times with feeling like we don't measure up. Those feelings can easily get in the way of being truly happy for a friend when something great happens to her. But when you play the comparison game, your friendships can easily turn into a competition; and nobody can be genuinely happy for their rival. So stop focusing on how you stack up against your girlfriends and instead try being gracious for a change.

Be: Available

A true friend is there when you need her. One of the biggest challenges you will face going forward in your adult life is the shortage of time to invest in the things that are truly important to you. Pressure will come at you from every angle to challenge your priorities. One of the biggest tests will come when you are in a romantic relationship. Are you the girl who dumps her girlfriends at the first sight of Mr. Right Now? You can pay lip service to how much you care for a friend, but if you're *M-I-A* at the first sight of a cute *M-A-N*, it won't ring true.

STEPHANIE

"Teresa and I have been close since we were roommates in our senior year of college. She really is a great friend . . . when she's single. Since I've known her, each time she starts dating someone, I get pushed to the back burner. She's never around, doesn't return e-mails or phone calls, and is too busy to make plans. On the rare occasion when I do manage to catch up with her, there's only one subject she wants to discuss: the guy. I don't mean to sound pouty, but it happens every time."

You can claim that a certain friend is important to you, but unless you make an effort to spend time together, your friendship will inevitably begin to fade. Staying connected with your friends can be as easy as meeting for coffee or a drink every few weeks or connecting via e-mail or phone on a regular basis (poking someone on Facebook doesn't count), but if you want to have true friendships, you must carve out real time for each other.

Be: Honest

A true friend is courageous enough to be honest with you. At first glance, it may seem that a surefire way to gather hordes of friends around you is to hand out compliments like candy on Halloween. Sure, everyone loves a sycophant . . . for a while. The problem with being Little Miss Cheerleader is that it's simply not genuine, and eventually people figure that out. Of course, encouragement and spoken kindnesses are an important part of any close friendship, and we all need to hear words of admiration from those who know us best. However, if words of praise are all you're willing to offer for fear of "hurting her feelings," you are not a true friend. You are a true friend if you care enough to speak the truth *in love,* even if it means risking that your friend will be hurt or angry, or even threaten to end the friendship.

GINA

When Gina read Sydney's text, she felt a little sick to her stomach. "Call me! I have exciting news!" it said. Dialing Sydney's number, Gina already strongly suspected what the "exciting news" was. A brief conversation confirmed it: Heather was engaged to Ryan. And there was more. She wanted Gina to be her maid of honor. Gina feigned happiness for her friend and offered up the obligatory congratulations, but she really wasn't happy at all. For the past few weeks, Gina was afraid an engagement was in the future for Sydney. She wanted to tell Sydney that she was concerned about Ryan's excessive drinking and about how Ryan came on to her and constantly flirted with other women behind Sydney's back. She also wanted to tell Sydney that she thought it was plain stupid for her to marry Ryan after knowing him for less than six months. Gina knew she should sit Sydney down and just be honest with her, but . . . she didn't want to hurt her friend's feelings.

Was that really the reason Gina was keeping her mouth shut? No! Gina didn't want Sydney to be mad at her! She didn't want to ruin Sydney's happy day, even though it meant stuffing her feelings and watching her best friend make a lousy, life-altering decision. This certainly is not what true friendship is about. Of course, there's no guarantee that if you speak your mind to a friend she will see it your way, but if you want to hold the esteemed title of "friend," you have to be willing to speak up, despite the risks. In the end, if the friendship lasts, it will be even stronger because you cared enough to be honest.

Be: Loyal

A true friend is someone you can count on. When we asked women to define the meaning of true friendship, the word *loyalty* was on every woman's list. So what does it really mean to be a loyal friend? If you are a loyal friend, you will Show Up, Put Up, Roll Up, and Shut Up.

Show Up

A loyal friend shows up for others, even when it's not convenient. This means making the effort to attend important events in your friend's life, whether it's a graduation, a birthday party, or the marathon finish line. It can also mean showing up with orange juice and chicken noodle soup at the door of your friend who is down for the count with the flu.

Putting Up . . . Your Fists

A loyal friend knows how to defend. We're not suggesting that you take it to the mat, but if someone starts talking smack about one of your friends, you must be loyal enough to either address the gossip directly or, at the very least, calmly but firmly change the subject and refuse to be a part of the conversation.

Rolling Up . . . Your Sleeves

A loyal friend is willing to get dirty in order to be helpful. This may mean literally getting dirty by helping a friend move out of her apartment on a swettering August day. Or it may mean getting your hands dirty by spending your Friday night with your friend, making the twelve dozen cookies she forgot to make for her synagogue's bake sale.

Shut Up

A loyal friend always keeps her friend's secrets. Always. It can be so tempting to reveal something that a friend has told you in confidence. In the moment, it can make you feel important or powerful to show that you've been trusted with private information. Don't do it. Resist the temptation. Keep it in the vault.

Let's see how you rate on the Five Be's of Friendship.

The Five Be's Quiz

1. Check in with my friend via phone, text, or e-mail just to connect and find out how she's doing.
   I do this: NEVER SOMETIMES OFTEN
2. Speak up for my friend if others are saying anything unkind or untrue about her.
   I do this: NEVER SOMETIMES OFTEN
3. Plan an activity for my friend and me to do together (a walk, meeting for coffee or a manicure, catching a movie).
   I do this: NEVER SOMETIMES OFTEN
4. Share struggles with my friend and ask for feedback.
   I do this: NEVER SOMETIMES OFTEN
5. Offer practical help *without* being asked: For example, pick up her mail when she's out of town, take her to drop her car off at the mechanic, bring her a sugar-free Red Bull and a bag of chocolate-covered espresso beans when she's up late preparing for her presentation.
   I do this: NEVER SOMETIMES OFTEN

6. Make it a point to celebrate with my friend when something good happens to her.
   I do this: NEVER SOMETIMES OFTEN
7. Tell my friend when she has hurt my feelings or upset me.
   I do this: NEVER SOMETIMES OFTEN
8. Tell others about my friend's successes.
   I do this: NEVER SOMETIMES OFTEN
9. Tell my friend when I think the guy she has a crush on isn't interested in her or good for her.
   I do this: NEVER SOMETIMES OFTEN
10. Tell my friend when I am feeling unsure of myself or insecure about something.
    I do this: NEVER SOMETIMES OFTEN

How'd you score? Count up your number of OFTEN answers:

8–10: Congratulations! You've mastered the Five Be's. But don't get lazy! Keep up the good work and enjoy the rewards of true friendship.

5–7: You're on the right track, but are probably letting your friends down in ways you may not realize. Work the Five Be's to become a better friend.

4–0: You are missing out on the rich rewards of true friendship. The good news is that growing in the Five Be's will help you deepen and solidify your relationships in new and lasting ways.

No matter how you scored, there's always room for improvement. Everyone wants to be a good friend, but the constraints we face each day can leave us wondering how it's possible. We get busy with work and other demands on our time and end up pushing our friends to the back burner. Work pressures are real, even overwhelming at times, and must be given high priority.

But while we need to make money to fuel all the practical aspects of our lives, we don't have to sacrifice our friendships in order do it. Unfortunately, when we get stressed, we sometimes fail to give our friendships the attention they deserve, reasoning that we just don't have enough time and, besides, our friends will understand.

While your true friends will usually cut you some slack and give you the space you need when life gets overwhelming, there are consequences to neglecting your friends. Even if you've been friends for years, if you fail to nurture your friendship, it will begin to erode, just as a muscle that isn't used will begin to atrophy. Sure, you may have a decade's worth of shared memories with your best friend, but if you don't continue to create new experiences and connect in the *here and now,* your friendship will end up as nothing more than a shared bond based on the past and a scrapbook full of lovely memories. Also, if you give your friendships the short shrift during your times of busyness and stress, you are cheating yourself out of the invigoration that comes from even a brief connection with a close friend. In fact, it is precisely during these times of stress that we most need the support and rejuvenation that friendship can uniquely provide.

We challenge you to stop making excuses as to why you just can't seem to find the time for your friends, and instead try one of the following low-effort–big-impact ways to nurture your friendship. It will be worth your effort.

- Put pen to paper. Send her a card (requiring you to put down your PDA and grab actual paper and a writing instrument) for no particular reason, just to tell her that you are thinking about her and are thankful for her friendship. In this high-tech world we live in, taking the time to send a handwritten note sends a thoughtful message.

- Acknowledge important occasions such as work promotions or personal accomplishments. Call or send an e-mail to say, "Way to go!"
- Keep in regular contact. If you don't live close to one another, don't let more than a month or two go by without being in touch.
- Schedule a pre- or post-work hike, walk, or run together.
- Pursue a common interest by taking a class together. Flower arranging, sushi making, scuba diving anyone?
- Make a standing breakfast or lunch appointment with each other and keep it just as you would any other important appointment.
- If you live far away, plan an annual get-together at a halfway point or take turns hosting each other. Split the cost of the airfare. Check out MeetWays.com, a helpful site that makes it easier for you to meet up with your beloved friends. You tell them where each person is coming from, and they'll tell you the best places to meet. Love it!

What Kind of Friends Do You Choose?

Chances are that if you are the kind of friend who strives to follow the Five Be's of Friendship, you're going to seek out friends that aspire to do the same. Unfortunately, that's not always the case. Just as we all know fabulous, together women who always seem to end up dating the jerks of the world, you can have the ability and desire to be a great friend but end up choosing friends who fall way short of the Five Be's. If this is the case for you, it's time to step back, think about why this is happening, and start taking measures to change this pattern in your life. Take a moment to make a list of your three closest friends. Now go back and read through the Five Be's. Are you attracting the kinds of friends who demonstrate these qualities? As Samuel Johnson said, "True happiness consists not in the multitude of friends, but in their worth and choice."

Time to Disconnect! Cutting Ties with a Toxic Friend

Have you ever hung up the phone with a friend and in a moment of exasperation asked yourself, *Why in the world am I friends with her?* We've all encountered the toxic friend at one time or another; many of you may be struggling to deal with a difficult friendship right now. You know the type: high-maintenance, self-absorbed, and thrives on never-ending *d-r-a-m-a*. The time you spend with this particular friend is never enough for her, and although you do your best to give her good advice, you're quite sure she never takes it.

The prevalence of less-than-great friendships is painfully illustrated by popularity of the book *Friend or Frenemy?*, which purports to be a guide to evaluating whether your "bestie" is true blue or an enemy to be avoided like the plague. Yikes! The fact that there's a whole book dedicated to answering this question is a good clue that our standards and expectations for friendship are in need of a serious overhaul.

AMBER

Amber had finally reached her limit. She knew she had to find a way out of her friendship with Natalie, but she didn't know how to escape. She felt trapped. Amber and Natalie had met just after college and had been friends for five years. During that time, Amber had spent countless hours listening to Natalie's relationship and family dramas, work problems, and personal struggles. Every time they saw each other, Natalie unleashed a new drama onto the ever-attentive Amber. If it wasn't a boyfriend issue, it was an ongoing conflict with a coworker or a detailed recounting of an argument with her dad. The problem was that there was no reciprocity in the friendship. When Natalie did finally get around to asking Amber about *her* life, Amber was too exhausted from enduring Natalie's endless monologues to share anything about herself, which was just fine with Natalie. To make matters worse, Natalie was never satisfied with the time that Amber spent with her. If Amber wasn't available to talk when Natalie called her crying at 3 A.M. because her boyfriend hadn't responded to her text message, Natalie would become sulky and punish Amber with the silent treatment for days. Amber wanted out of the one-sided friendship, but she worried that Natalie needed her and would have nowhere else to turn.

Just as healthy friendships can bring intense joy and fulfillment to our lives, toxic friendships can be a source of great stress and anxiety. Friendships don't always have to be 50/50, and even good ones experience periods of imbalance, but a healthy friendship should make you *both* feel as though your needs are getting met. We're not suggesting that you should keep score of who's doing what and when, but you cannot have a true friendship when one person is doing all or most of the "heavy lifting." If you suspect that one of you isn't living up to her end of the bargain, take this quiz to find out where your friendship stands. Think of a friend you suspect might be a toxic friend, and then take a look at this list below and put a check by anything that is true of her.

Toxic Friend Checklist

____ She is my friend only when it's convenient for her.

____ She doesn't seem happy for me when good things happen.

___ She talks about herself more than listening to me.
___ I feel exhausted after talking to her.
___ She is a source of stress.
___ She constantly asks for my advice but never takes it.
___ She tries to make me feel guilty.
___ What I give never seems to be enough for her.
___ She disappears whenever there's a new guy in her life.
___ I always pay for her or clean up after her.
___ I feel like I give more to the relationship than she does.

How'd she do? More checkmarks than not? If so, it might be time to end the friendship or at least take drastic steps to change the relationship dynamic. We know from personal experience that ending an unhealthy friendship is a very difficult thing to do, but sometimes it's necessary. Too often we hold on to a toxic friend—out of either our own misplaced guilt or our need to be needed. Deep down you may also feel like you don't deserve any better than a friend who constantly overlooks your needs. Whatever the reason, the truth is that your so-called friendship is not a friendship at all. A relationship that isn't based on honesty or reciprocity has no real future (*aka* a waste of your time). By continuing an imbalanced friendship, you are hurting yourself—and you aren't doing your friend any favors, either.

One Way = Do Not Enter

So what should you do with a toxic friend? The first thing you've got to do is take responsibility for your part in creating the situation. If you're in a toxic friendship, it's because *you* chose a toxic friend or created one by allowing her to do all the taking and never calling her out. Your next step is to start setting better boundaries for yourself. If your friend asks you for something that you don't want to give, say no. Speak up when she is mean or overly critical toward you. Next, before taking the step to end the friendship, try to talk it out. Tell your friend how her behavior is affecting you and ask her to change her ways. Finally, if her toxic patterns continue, it's simply time to end the relationship and instead focus on friendships that are actually worthy of your investment.

Is It Time to Thin the Herd?

Now that you've examined the quality of your friendships, it's time to think about quantity. Since there's a limited amount of time every day to juggle the demands of work, social lives, and errands, you'll need to be intentional about committing to a small collection of friends, preferably one you can count on one hand (*aka* Your Fab Five). You can't possibly have ten best friends. You don't have enough time or emotional energy. If you persist in stretching yourself too thin in the friends department, you will surely end up letting your friends down. Socrates, in his great wisdom, once said, "A friend to all is a friend to none." Better to focus on a small handful and be a *great* friend, a Five Be's friend, than try to be a "friend to all" but come up short.

Sometimes this process of "thinning the herd" can be clear, such as in the above case of getting rid of toxic friends, but other times it can be a bit murky. Over time, as your friendships are tested and your values become more defined, you'll begin to clearly discern which of your friends are the Keepers—the ones who are trustworthy, generous of spirit, and challenge you to be the best version of yourself. The wonderful benefit of choosing depth over breadth is that you end up with friends who will walk beside you for a lifetime. Our Fab Fives are just as fabulous as they were in our twenties. Only now, instead of catching up over a glass of bubbly at the cool new wine bar, we catch up over juice boxes and bubble-blowing at the neighborhood park.

Or Is It Time for a Friend Round-Up?

Are you finding it difficult to find new friends? As you may have noticed, your twenties are a time of transition. Maybe you're living in a new city, surrounded by strangers, or maybe your close friends have moved away to start jobs or graduate school. Perhaps recent changes in your life have caused you to grow apart from your old friends. For the first time in your life, you may find yourself needing to make a conscious effort to make new friends.

In high school and college, you're surrounded by friends. You're sharing similar experiences with everyone around you. Making friends is easy. In fact, it's practically impossible not to. But when you leave the comforts of college life, you can find yourself struggling to make friends.

As Marcy shared with us, "It was easy to have tons of friends in college. I guess I didn't realize how much that was going to change after I graduated and moved to Seattle for my first job. At first I wasn't concerned about making friends, because it was always something that came so easily. That's not the case anymore. Gone are the days of just bumping into friends on campus or out on Thursday night. Now if I want a social life, I have to actually work at it."

If you're feeling less than flush in the friends department, it's time to reach out and get connected. Here are a few simple and practical ways to reach out and make new real-world friends, despite your busy life.

- **Mix business and pleasure.** Just because you already spend a minimum of forty hours per week with these people doesn't mean you can't log some off-the-clock hours with them as well. You obviously have work interests in common, which is a good start. Remember, they, too, have a circle of friends that they will introduce you to, and so on and so on. . . .

- **Remember your alma mater.** Most colleges and universities have alumni organizations that plan regular get-togethers with local alumni. You are already connected to these fellow alums through your shared school experience and may have friends in common, which is a great basis for friendship.
- **Go clubbing.** Do you like to run? Do you speak a little French? Kayaking your thing? Knitting? Whatever interests and hobbies you have, chances are that there is a club or local organization full of people who share your passion. Your mutual interest is a great jumping-off point for a new friendship. Check out meetup.com, a site that connects you with established groups in your area that match your interest. We love their motto: "Use the Internet to get off the Internet."
- **Give a little.** Regardless of where you live, you can always find a place to give back to the community through a local outreach organization. These opportunities include soup kitchens, tutoring programs, animal rescue shelters, and local hospitals. Chances are the people you meet are dedicated to causes other than themselves and how they look in their two-hundred-dollar jeans, which can translate into promising friend material.
- **Say a prayer.** If your faith is important to you, there's obviously no better place to connect with people than a local church or synagogue. Most worship centers have specific groups for twentysomethings and can be a great place to connect with others who share your religious beliefs. (Just watch out for the occasional forty-year-old guy trolling for fresh young twentysomethings!)

Friendship is a vital ingredient to having a fabulous single life. Friendship teaches you what it means to commit to another human being despite all her faults and foibles. Friendship also teaches you how to give and receive unconditional love from someone who really knows you. What better way to prepare yourself for marriage? The friendships you choose to invest in now will be a source of encouragement, strength, and joy throughout your twenties and all the chapters of your life that lie ahead.

Chapter 4

Key #2: Get a Peaceful Family Life

Make Peace with Difficult Family Dynamics

Insanity runs in many families. In mine, it gallops.
—Cary Grant in *Arsenic and Old Lace, 1944*

So you and your friends are sitting around, playing a fierce game of Taboo. You have to convey the word *psychologist*—what do you do? You sit down and imperiously cross your legs, saying "Tell me about your childhood. . . ." Instantly, everyone in the room gets it. There is a reason that therapists place so much importance on childhood experiences and family relationships: They affect how we view the world, relate to others, and generally think and behave. Your family relationships, especially with your parents, set the stage for every other important relationship you will ever have. With that in mind, you can imagine how important it is now, *before you marry,* to recognize your childhood influences, identify unhealthy patterns in your family, and accept the truth about the limitations of those relationships.

As if you don't already have enough on your plate! That sounds like a lot of work, as well as a lot of digging up old emotional wounds and facing more than a few unpleasant memories. Is it really necessary? It's not like you can do anything about the past, right?

Wrong.

While it's true you can't change the past, if you're willing to commit some time and energy to understanding how your upbringing shaped you as a human being, you'll be on the path to discovering new ways of relating to others and yourself, as well as to laying a healthy foundation for your future marriage and family.

Understanding Your Past

While families can take many forms, the one thing they all have in common is their immutable power to shape our subconscious beliefs, expectations, and emotional lives. Whether you experienced serious childhood trauma, garden-variety family dysfunction, or something in between, the truth is that we all enter our twenties with a certain degree of the proverbial emotional baggage stemming from our family relationships.

Psychologists estimate that you receive 50 percent of your emotional hardwiring between birth and five years old. You are programmed with an additional 30 percent between five and eight years old. This means that 80 percent of your psychological foundation is established by the time you are eight years old! The crazy thing is that most of us don't even remember a whole lot about that critical time in our lives. It hardly seems fair that so much of what governs our current decision-making process has already been determined for us.

But wait. There is some good news. These unconscious factors don't have to maintain control over your life. If you are brave enough to take the necessary steps, you can finally understand some of your more perplexing actions, reactions, and interactions and make an active decision to change your behavior, and along with it the very course of your life.

Professional Insight from Shannon

Kari came into my office with a look of defeat. She was an attractive girl in her early twenties with long dark hair pulled into a careless ponytail and wearing little makeup. "I'm confused. Are all men selfish pigs? Aren't there any good guys out there?" Through therapy, Kari revealed that her parents fought constantly during her growing-up years. "My mother was cold and unaffectionate. Nothing I did was good enough for her. I remember proudly showing her my eighth-grade report card and all she said was 'Why an A-minus? What is the minus for? Your brother got all A's! You must not have tried hard enough.' My older brother was the light of her life, and she constantly compared me with him."

When I asked about her father, Kari teared up and haltingly said, "He was the opposite of my mother." In time, she revealed how her father, from the time she was eight, would tell her he loved her, and then molest her. She hated it, but at the same time craved his attention.

"I knew it was wrong," she told me, "and I always felt guilty, but I didn't know how to make it stop." In her early teen years, Kari's life became a vicious cycle of promiscuity, feelings of guilt and emptiness, followed by abusing alcohol to hide from the pain of her past and her destructive choices. This cycle continued for years until she attempted suicide at her parents' house. After months of exploring how Kari's early abuse by her father and emotional distance from her mother created the subconscious foundation for her choices, a light went on. "I never realized that my childhood still had such a hold on me. I knew that I was making the wrong decisions about men, but I never put it all together until now. I was choosing controlling men who used me for sex because it felt familiar to me. I was programmed to associate attention and value with sex."

Once Kari became aware of how her past was impacting her current behavior—that she made decisions based upon childhood pain—she could begin the work of making changes and better choices for her life. We made a pact that she would stop dating entirely for a period of six months and then abstain from sex until she was in a committed relationship. This time proved invaluable for Kari. She was able to use it to face (without distraction) the pain she'd experienced as a child, and to finally reach a point where she could really change her behavior.

Understanding Your Family Patterns

There are some types of emotional programming that continue through generations, such as alcoholism, out-of-control anger, depression, adultery, and the pain of divorce. For these types of generational issues, it is helpful to look at familial patterns across time.

Professional Insight from Shannon

Jamie came to see me because she wanted advice on how to help her alcoholic boyfriend who verbally abused her. "I just want to help him get back on his feet, but he spends all his money and a good deal of mine on partying. I don't blame him, though, he just lost his job and he seems pretty depressed. I'm worried about him, but I'm starting to feel like he's taking advantage of me. I sometimes even come home from work during the day to check on him and make sure he's okay. My boss is getting pretty fed up with all of the missed work and I'm stressed out all the time. I've thought about leaving the relationship, but I just couldn't do that to him. He needs me."

Of course he needs her! That was the very reason she chose him in the first place. You see, as it turned out, Jamie's father was also an alcoholic. Knowing that alcoholism is usually a pattern in families, I suggested to Jamie that we complete a genogram, which is a detailed family tree that examines relational and behavioral patterns across generations. "I know that alcoholism is genetic, so I never drink because I'd probably become an alcoholic, too." I explained to Jamie that we were not looking for the genetic predisposition for alcoholism. We were looking for the pattern of the women in her family who chose to marry alcoholic men.

Sure enough, once we completed this in-depth look at her family tree, Jamie was floored by the obvious patterns that emerged. All the men on her father's side of the family were alcoholics, which spoke to the genetic component, but most of the daughters who did not become alcoholics themselves chose to marry alcoholic men. "Wouldn't you think that they would make different choices after the pain of growing up under an alcoholic father?" she asked incredulously. On a conscious level, yes, but the more powerful subconscious programming taught these women to seek the familiar. The programming they received at a young age taught them that their worth was in their ability to take care of Dad. These girls felt valuable because they were needed. Sound familiar? That's exactly what Jamie said about her loser boyfriend!

These daughters of alcoholics learned that pointing out the elephant in the room would only lead to anger and acts of violence. Better to just lie low and pick up after Daddy. These women, by watching Mom, had learned to make excuses for Dad when his office called to find out why he hadn't shown up that day. They learned to make excuses for Dad when teachers asked about bruises on their little-girl arms. They learned to continue making excuses for the men in their lives well into their young adulthood. These girls were trained to be codependent—to need to be needed. If we leave decisions to our subconscious minds, we will, for better or worse, always end up with something that feels like home to us.

Tracking Family Patterns: Create a Genogram

Okay, now this might take a bit of work to complete, but the results are well worth it. Think of the genogram as a detailed family tree that will tell you the important historical patterns of your family. The more detailed you are, the better you will be able to identify harmful patterns and consciously avoid the same pitfalls. So here we go.

Get out a blank sheet of paper. For step-by-step guidance on completing your genogram, go to our website, LastOneDowntheAisleWins.com. Once you have a pretty solid family skeleton, it's time to find the skeletons in the closets!

Start filling in all the juicy details: divorce, angry relationships, ages at marriage and divorce. Also note abuse, alcohol and drug use, and any other interesting characteristics such as well-educated women, family pressure regarding career choice, financial irresponsibility or instability, high-conflict marriage, infidelity, mama's boys, matriarch-ruled household, emotionally dependent parent–child relationships, unemployment, and so on.

Are you all done? Whew! Good job. That was quite a project. Now for your observations: What did you notice about your family patterns? Anything good that you are proud of? Which pattern do you want to break so you don't pass it on to your own children? Our website also has examples of completed genograms and helpful tips for understanding your own. As with all the exercises, make sure to seek professional help if you want to understand more or if you discover some troubling patterns that are stressing you out.

Kari and Jamie are extreme examples of how your childhood hurt can result in disastrous choices for your future.

To clarify, while we are all responsible for our own decisions, in order for us to avoid repeating harmful familial patterns, we must acknowledge our natural tendencies.

Further Insight from Shannen

So what happened with Jamie? Upon further examination of Jamie's genogram, we discovered that she had a great-aunt who broke the destructive cycle of marrying substance abusers and instead married an emotionally healthy man who treated her well. Jamie's assignment was to set up a time to meet with this aunt and ask her how she came to make the choices that she had.

The following week in my office, Jamie shared with me her aunt's secret to avoiding the familial trap of marrying an alcoholic. "Aunt Sharon told me that she learned about alcoholism in nursing school and determined that not only would she never risk becoming addicted, but she would prevent her future children from having to struggle with the disease. As a nurse, she was trained to help people, and she said that she prioritized marrying a good father for her children." I noted to Jamie that Sharon still had a desire to be needed, but she channeled her energy into helping sick people who actually benefited from her help. With the positive role model of emotional health in her own family, Jamie was encouraged that it was possible to break the pattern and make healthy choices for her future family.

Getting to the Core

Granted, you may not have grown up in a home where abuse or addictions were present. You may have even been fortunate enough to grow up in a loving, stable family environment.

Regardless, because we were all raised by other flawed human beings (*aka* Mom and Dad), there's no doubt that your childhood was riddled with experiences that, left unchecked, will impair your ability to make the best choices for your future relationships.

The good news is that while we are *influenced* by our pasts, we don't have to be *controlled* by them. The first step to wresting control is to identify the incidents, attitudes, and experiences that created our specific unspoken beliefs about relationships, the world, and ourselves. Cognitive-behavioral therapists call these "core beliefs." Your core beliefs have a direct impact on your present feelings and future actions.

Let's break it down: Say you had a mother who was very fearful and seemed to be fixated on all the terrible things that might happen. This is the *experience* that impacts your *core belief* that life is dangerous and that risks are to be avoided. This core belief leads to depression when you are unable to pursue your dreams with courage. This belief and related feeling can also lead to the *action* of continuously choosing men whose major offering is that they take care of you and keep you safe, when you should instead be focused on overcoming the irrational fears that you were programmed to believe as a child. Consider the following real-life examples of how experiences with our parents shape our core beliefs and result in poor choices:

- **The perfectionist mother.** Tracy's mom was never satisfied with second best. Their home was a showpiece, Mom's appearance and manners were pristine, and no matter how hard she tried, Tracy never felt as though her mom was satisfied with her. As a result, Tracy developed the core belief that she could never be good enough for her mother, or for anyone else, for that matter. This feeling of "never good enough" followed Tracy through her teen years as she struggled with anorexia and into her young adulthood when she married a hypercritical man who is never satisfied with her—from her appearance, to her housekeeping, to how the kids are performing in school.

- **The workaholic parents.** Laila's parents were both high-powered attorneys in New York. Ambition ruled and they were rarely home before 10 P.M. Laila had every tangible luxury a girl could desire, but never had the luxury of spending a lazy Saturday at the park with her dad or returning from a date to debrief with her mom. Instead, she was raised by a succession of well-meaning and efficient nannies. As a result, Laila developed the core belief that her needs and desires were not as valuable as those of others. She married a career-focused man who provided a lavish living but never shared her intimate emotions.
- **The sexist father.** Katrina's dad had always wanted a son, so when her little brother was born, Katrina became all but invisible. Weekends were spent tagging along to brother's sporting events. Dad made it clear that Katrina's accomplishments paled in comparison with her brother's athletic abilities. Katrina's dad encouraged her brother to go to medical school but dismissed her own dream of becoming a landscape architect as a waste of time and money. As a result, Katrina developed the core belief that women are not as valuable or capable as men and married a male chauvinist who became combative on the rare occasions when Katrina tried to assert herself in their relationship.
- **The ambush divorce.** Kim had never heard her parents fight, so you can imagine her surprise when, at age twelve, her parents informed her that they had "fallen out of love" and were getting a divorce. As a result, Kim

developed the core belief that the success or failure of a marriage was arbitrary and not within her control. She was terrified of commitment, concluding that since marriage was not likely to last forever, why risk it?

- **The money-troubled marriage.** Whitney grew up constantly hearing her parents fight about money. Her mother frequently expressed disappointment in Whitney's father for not providing better financially for the family. As a result, Whitney developed the core belief that money was the key to a harmonious marriage. Whitney made wealth her number one criterion in a potential husband and ended up marrying a guy who was wealthy but who lacked other qualities that truly mattered to her.
- **The absentee father.** Kaylee never knew her father. He split when Kaylee was five, leaving her to be raised by a single mother. Like most children of divorce, Kaylee believed that her father's leaving was her fault. As a result, she was convinced that she was unworthy of love and deserved rejection. Her fear of abandonment led her to marry a chronically unemployed man with a gambling problem who treated her badly but was too dependent on her to ever leave her.
- **The disdainful mother.** Renee's mom criticized everything her dad did, from his parenting to his politics to how he tapped his fingers when he was nervous. He could do nothing right in Mom's eyes. As a result, Renee developed the core belief that men were, at best, bumbling idiots, and at worst expendable. She married a long-suffering man with many faults that she never tires of pointing out, belittling him in front of her own daughters and setting a harsh example for them to follow into the next generation.
- **The raging dad.** Rebecca grew up under a constant barrage of rage from her father. The smallest thing would set

off a blowup at her mom, Rebecca, and her siblings, the cable guy, and anyone else unfortunate enough to be standing nearby. Rebecca's mom usually justified his violent behavior with "Your dad has a really stressful job" or "He's right. It *was* stupid of me to forget to pick up the dry cleaning." As a result, Rebecca developed the core belief that anger was indeed uncontrollable and certain actions warranted loud displays of rage and even violence. Rebecca married a weak man who excused her frequent outbursts of anger and stood by silently as she victimized her children.

- **The parentified child.** Cici came home from school anxious to tell her mom about the argument she had with her best friend, only to have her mother open the door in tears, gushing on about how insensitive Cici's dad was and how she was so hurt by his lack of caring. When her mom finally wound down an hour later and asked Cici about her day, "Fine" was her muted reply. After all, Cici learned that her mother's emotional pain was much more important and meaningful than simple high school squabbles. As a result of becoming her mother's confidante, Cici developed the core belief that her own emotions were not as important as others'. Cici married a self-absorbed narcissistic man who talked more and more as Cici grew more and more emotionally shut down, distant, and quietly resentful.

My Core Beliefs

Take some time now to examine some of your own core beliefs and how they impact your behavior and decisions. Be as specific as you can, and allow yourself some time and space to complete this exercise. Most people are surprised and even shocked when they see the impact of their childhood experiences in black-and-white.

The first part of this exercise is called the Downward Arrow Technique.

First, think of a situation that elicited intense feelings. For example:

SITUATION:

Sarah didn't call me back last night.
What does this say or mean about me?

↓

Whenever I am vulnerable with people and share my feelings, people don't like me.
What does this say or mean about me?

↓

I'll never have a close relationship with anybody.
What does this say or mean about me?

↓

I'm unlikeable = Core Belief

It's your turn. Just keep asking yourself what it "says about" you until you get to a fixed statement that seems absolute and unchangeable; that is your core belief.

Now that you have discovered a core belief about yourself, let's see if we can figure out where it came from. You can usually trace it back to something your mom or dad said to you or how they treated you. For the example above, whenever she would show her emotions as a child, her dad would shut her down by saying, "Nobody likes a cry baby." Take some time to sit quietly and just write down any childhood experiences that contributed to your core belief.

If this exercise is too difficult emotionally, or you draw a blank and can't seem to remember anything, this is a red flag. Don't be too hard on yourself. Your inability to remember difficult events in your past can serve as a necessary protection against overwhelming pain. Your mind has a wonderful defensive capability and is extremely sensitive to how much you can take. Don't push it. Instead, designate a trusted friend or maybe even a licensed therapist to walk through this process with you. This process takes work and may be painful at times, but dealing with it now will prevent a lifetime of greater pain.

Core Belief Record

Core beliefs are not easily changed—they have been lying quietly in your subconscious determining many of your emotions and actions completely unbeknownst to you for much of your life. That doesn't mean that you have no control over them; it will just take a bit longer to change them for good. Start by keeping track of all the evidence that suggests that your core belief is not 100 percent true. Use a record like this:

Core Belief: *I'm unlikeable.*

Evidence that shows that this is not true all the time:

1. My best friend from kindergarten still keeps in touch.
2. I have lots of friends on Facebook and MySpace.
3. My coworker Ben asked for my opinion about his project at work.
4. Lucy asked me to go shopping with her.

The more you challenge the validity of your core beliefs, the less control they wield over your life. For further help on core beliefs, read *Mind over Mood* by Dennis Greenberger and Christine A. Padesky.

Acceptance: It's Time to Give Up "Hope"

Now that you have gained insight into how to change your actions by becoming more conscious of your core beliefs, it's time to learn how to change your parents' actions, right? Unfortunately, it doesn't work that way. People waste a lot of time, effort, and tears waiting and pushing their family members to change their bothersome behaviors. If you base your happiness on any other person having to alter themselves in any way, you will be utterly frustrated and disappointed. This is an important lesson to learn before you choose a mate because we women are notorious for marrying a man with "potential" and then nagging, begging, and praying for him to change. Once you have a realistic view of your inability to change others, you will be able to accept your parents' shortcomings, thus saving yourself a lot of pain and disappointment. Only then can you choose a husband for who he is rather than for who you hope he will become, thus saving yourself from future heartache and divorce court.

Giving up hope doesn't mean you have to abandon your relationship with your parents. It's not an all-or-nothing proposition. But you do have to abandon your fantasy of "what could be" and accept "what is." In her book *Bad Childhood—Good Life*, Dr. Laura Schlessinger states it perfectly: "If you have a Doberman and you want him to turn into a Chihuahua, he will not turn into a Chihuahua, no matter how nicely you treat him or how much you hope it were true." In Juliana's case, acceptance meant approaching the relationship with her mother in a completely different way. Instead of obsessing over what she wasn't getting from her mother, Juliana started expecting less from her, thereby freeing herself from the incredibly negative, almost daily influence her mother had on her. Now

Professional Insight from Shannon

Juliana came to see me about the problems she was having in her marriage and at work. When I asked her specific questions about these issues, she would veer off into long teary explanations about how her mother was never there for her and how disappointed and saddened she was by that. Juliana explained that she had tried for years to have a loving relationship with her mother and just couldn't understand why her mother wasn't interested in reciprocating. To the contrary, Juliana's mother was emotionally distant, self-centered, and critical toward Juliana, as she had been throughout Juliana's entire life. After several sessions of covering this same ground, I finally asked Juliana why on earth she continued to be surprised by her mother's behavior. "Well," she responded, "I suppose I just keep hoping that she'll change." I explained to Juliana that the likelihood of that ever happening was very small and suggested that it was time to give up the hope of having a loving, caring mother if she wanted to move forward in her life.

when she calls her mom, she does so to see how her day is going, talk about the weather or about how well her tomatoes are growing. Juliana now has pleasant, albeit less substantive conversations with her mom, but she's taking what she can get. And she's finally stopped banging her head against the wall.

This process of acceptance requires you to see your mom or

dad as individuals from yourself—people with their struggles, childhood pain, and limitations.

JENNA

Jenna's father grew up with emotionally distant parents. There wasn't much warmth in their relationship, and he never ever heard the words *I love you* from either of them. The only emotions expressed in his household were anger and disappointment. Remarkably, Jenna's dad grew into a kind, loving man who deeply desired to have a family of his own. Jenna's dad loved her and expressed his love by being supportive of her pursuits. When Jenna was little, he drove her to soccer practice and coached her team. As she got older, he helped her with school projects, helped her fix her car, and was always in the front row during her frequent school plays. Jenna knew her dad loved her, but struggled with the fact that he never verbally expressed any emotion toward her. How she longed to hear him say *I love you* or *I'm so proud of you*.

During the past few years, Jenna had become fixated on her father's lack of verbal expression. She voiced her complaints to her father, but not much changed. She pouted, but to no avail, and then finally threatened to curtail their relationship. Jenna was distraught by her father's seeming refusal to change, which she interpreted as his lack of love for her. Jenna's husband was frustrated by Jenna's constant need to talk about her father, her depression, and her inability to recognize the pain she was causing her own children and husband by her ongoing "suffering." Eventually, Jenna's blind spot disappeared as she began to realize that her father's lack of emotional expression was not directed at her. He simply lacked the ability to put his feelings into words. Through some difficult conversations with her mother, Jenna discovered that this dynamic also existed between her parents and had been a source of frustration for her mom throughout their marriage. Her father's shortcoming in the verbal-expression department was something that Jenna came to accept; she learned instead to be grateful for all the ways that her father *does* show his love for her.

The Sometimes-It's-Okay-to-Give-Up-Hope Experience

In this exercise, you will literally be giving up your unrealistic hopes that your parents will change significantly. This one takes a bit of footwork, but will be worth the effort.

First, write your wishes for your parents down on a three-by-five card, one wish per card. For example: "I wish my mom would show an interest in my life."

Next card: "I wish my dad would tell me he loved me."

Next card: "I wish my mom would stop criticizing my appearance."

Write as many cards as you need to. Tie each card to a helium-filled balloon and go to a serene location—a park, the beach, your own backyard. Pick a card and say out loud "I am letting go of my wish that . . ." Then read the card and let the balloon go.

As you watch the balloon float out of sight, really focus on letting your wish disappear with it. Pay attention to how light you feel right now. The burden of those unfulfilled hopes was heavier than you ever realized. Now, whenever you find yourself hoping for something you wrote on one of those cards, take a minute, close your eyes, and remember the image of releasing that hope and the freedom you felt in that moment.

Now is the time for you to decide that despite past or present challenges with your family, your future is yours for the creating. You are not doomed to repeat the negative patterns; nor can you assume that the positives of your upbringing will repeat themselves automatically in your own future family. Now is the time for you to understand how your childhood impacts your present core beliefs, and that once they're identified and understood, those core beliefs *can* be changed. Seeing your family as they truly are can be tough, and true understanding and acceptance can take a lifetime. Now that you have gained a deeper understanding of your family dynamics, you are equipped to change unhealthy patterns, make conscious life choices, and create better relationships with your parents and future spouse.

Chapter 5

Key #3: Get a Fulfilling Work Life

Figure Out What You Want to Be When You Grow Up

> *Your profession is not what brings home your paycheck. Your profession is what you were put on earth to do. With such passion and intensity that it becomes spiritual in calling.*
>
> *—Virgil*

Your twenties is the decade in your life when you have unfettered (read: unmarried and childless) time and freedom to find the answers you're going to need to create a sure foundation for your future career. This is the ideal time to figure out your passion and your purpose in life and then go for it! A reward of being intentional in your education and career choices during your twenties, before you get hitched, is that you will begin to experience an incredible maturity and refinement. You will learn new things about yourself as you challenge your limitations, expand your professional capabilities, and build on your strengths. And where will all this lead you? Into a place of confidence, clear purpose, and a strong sense of self—all of which you will bring into your future marriage.

Regardless of whether you have absolutely no clue about your future plans or have the next twenty years mapped out (down to the fabulous suit you'll be wearing when you accept your dream promotion), you are likely dealing with a lot of questions and anxiety about your future career. If you're like most women in their twenties, you've spent a good deal of time asking yourself, *What do I want to be when I grow up?* In order to make it easier to answer this all-important question, we've broken it down into the Four C's of your working future—Calling, Continuing Education, Choices, and Career. You may be wondering:

- *Calling:* What is my purpose in life? Where do my strengths and passion lie? Will my career be fulfilling?
- *Continuing Education:* Do I need more education to get where I want to go? How will I put this hard-earned education of mine to use?
- *Choices:* What factors should I consider in making job choices? Do I have to choose between being a mom and having a career?
- *Career:* How do I make the career of my dreams a reality? What specific steps should I take?

Calling

May you be blessed with passion and may you follow it all your life.

—*Sister Helen Prejean*

Are you determined to find a career that fulfills your sense of passion and purpose? Or have you resigned yourself to the notion that passion and work are two completely separate concepts? Not only can passion and purpose coexist in your work, but they should both be nonnegotiable as well.

Working on Purpose

You shouldn't sign on to a career path, no matter how respectable it sounds or how much job security you think it will offer, unless you truly enjoy most of what that career demands. Take the law, for example. We know too many lawyers who really don't like their job; in fact, they're miserable. They went to law school because they didn't know what else to do, or because their parents wanted them to, or because they didn't have any interest in going to medical school. After a few years of practicing law, they either quit altogether and start over in an unrelated field or resign themselves to the next thirty-plus years of working in a job they're not passionate about.

Although drive and discipline are important, they will take you only so far. You must, *must* find a career where you feel a sense of excitement and purpose in your work. The great news is that you live in a country where that is, without question, yours for the taking. We're talking about the "take the bull by the horns" kind of taking, which requires a lot of commitment, enthusiasm, and determination and can require many years of navigating a winding path before you discover something you love.

Identifying Your Strengths

If you want to find your calling, you need to identify your passions as well as your strengths. It's important to recognize that these things need to be evaluated together. For example, you

Personal Insight from Celeste

Thankfully, I love being a lawyer. I believe that my legal career fits my skill set, interests, and passions perfectly. I truly view my practice of law as a calling and wouldn't want any other job, unless of course I could score a gig as a well-paid travel critic in search of the perfect island vacation. Does that mean that I don't sometimes view my work as drudgery? No way! There are plenty of times when I am flat-out resistant to diving into a task that requires a great deal of attention to detail and minutiae. Without passion for my work, I would avoid, delay, and procrastinate until doing the work would be an act of pure discipline, fueled by a sense of fear of what would happen if I didn't get it done. But it's the bigger picture of what I am accomplishing for the client that drives me to get after the task at hand.

can be very passionate about the idea of making a living by creating pottery in a little studio behind your California bungalow. But if you find that you have little or no natural ability behind the potter's wheel and know deep down that your pottery-making skills were arrested in the third grade when you made that misshapen ashtray for your dad, you should probably keep searching. Or you may love the idea of being a nurse and helping people in their time of physical need. But if the thought of taking a blood sample makes you woozy, continue in the search for your calling.

SARAH

Sarah is a tremendous classical pianist. Even though she's barely twenty-eight, she has already performed to great acclaim before some of the toughest music critics around. A few years ago, Sarah became disillusioned with how commercialized the music industry had become. She decided to bid adieu to the music world and become a real estate agent. She reasoned that since she loves architecture and old homes, selling houses would be a perfect expression of her passion. When Sarah told her family about her plans for a career change, they carefully asked questions about why she thought her strengths were a good fit for real estate, knowing full well that those same sensitivities that made Sarah such an amazing musician would surely be a liability in the often dog-eat-dog world of real estate sales. Sarah couldn't pinpoint any specific strengths she possessed that would predict success in real estate, but decided that her love of architecture would make up for her lack of sales experience. She's been at it for a few years now, and things haven't gone that well for her. While Sarah enjoys exploring the vintage homes and the cool architecture, she detests the business part of the job and really hates having to sell herself to clients and potential buyers.

Sarah's story illustrates perfectly how important it is to take an honest self-inventory before embarking on a career path. And don't try to go it alone. We're not usually the best ones to identify our own strengths, because it can feel like bragging. It's also tough to be objective about yourself. That's why you need to involve your friends and family in the next exercise. You need objective opinions, and who better to help you with this than the people who know you best?

Ask Around

Choose five people who know you well: one or more of your parents, friends, maybe a pastor or rabbi, a teacher or professor, or a supervisor. It's most helpful to get opinions from people of different age groups because they will have significantly different perspectives. Ask each of them to answer the following questions, and encourage them to be honest.

1. What would you say are my top three personality strengths?
2. What are my weaknesses that could negatively impact my career?
3. What would you say are the three things that I am good at?
4. Name three professions that you think I would do well in.
5. Name two professional areas that you don't think would be the best fit for me.
6. What do you consider to be my best quality?

It can be truly enlightening to get the insight of others who know you well. Many times, people around us don't offer their insight simply because we don't ask.

Passion: Will I Know It When I Feel It?

Finding your passion will require you to take a look inside and begin to articulate what excites you, what inspires and drives you. Answer these questions quickly to get to your gut feelings and passions. If you hesitate and think too long, your brain will get too involved and you'll probably end up writing what you *think* your passions *should* be. Remember, passion is what's in your heart, not in your head!

My Passion Inventory

What inspires me?
What are the three things I value most in life?

What makes me happiest?

What makes me cry?

What is my favorite subject to read about?

What is my favorite kind of TV show—drama, comedy, cooking, fashion, competition?

What activities, projects, groups, volunteer opportunities have I spent time on?

What intrigues me?

What gives me energy?

When do I feel most fulfilled?

Now that you are in tune with your heart, your passion mode, apply it to your career desires. Think of what jobs excite you. Don't think practically yet; stay in the passion mind-set for this exercise.

Does the idea of working in the movie industry thrill you? Does working with children fulfill your desire to give back to your community in a meaningful way? Do other cultures and languages intrigue you? Are you inspired most when you are creating? Does the intensity and energy of Wall Street draw you?

Complete the sentences:

I feel most like myself when I'm ______________________.

My perfect working environment would be________________.

I would like to be remembered as the person who__________.

My favorite subjects in school were ____________________.

My dream job is ______________________________________.

How do you feel right now? Most women tell us that they feel invigorated after completing these exercises. When you give your passions a voice, you are tapping into endless reserves of energy and excitement. Remember how you feel right now, and don't fall into the trap of choosing a career path based on a "head" decision only. Of course you have to make money, but don't abandon your passions or you will be miserable and heartsick in your work.

Figure It Out

There are a ton of great resources available to help you along the way as you seek answers to the burning questions: What is my purpose? What is my passion? What are my strengths? Here are some of our favorites:

StrengthsFinder 2.0 by Tom Rath. A new and upgraded edition of the online test from Gallup's *Now, Discover Your Strengths,* which gives you access to an online self-assessment tool, the result of which is a comprehensive description of your five personal strengths.

What Color Is Your Parachute? by Richard Nelson Bolles. The hands-down bestselling job-hunting book in the world. To quote *Fortune* magazine, "the gold standard of career guides."

Do What You Are by Barbara Barron and Paul Tieger. This is a great book that helps you plot your career based on your own specific temperament. It encourages the idea that you should find a job and career that suit who you really are at your core.

Queendom.com: A website chock-full of tests, including some great career tests that can help you learn about your aptitudes and evaluate whether you are on the right path.

If you need more help figuring out your calling, seek out a career counselor who can sit with you and help you zero in on your optimal career choices. Most important, take your time and promise yourself, right now, that you will choose your career path from inspiration and not from fear; that instead of ending up in a dead-end passionless career, you won't stop until you find the one that puts bread on your table *and* a fire in your belly.

Continuing Your Education

Graduate School: Escape Hatch or Logical Next Step?

There are certain practical decisions that you will need to make as you move toward your ideal career. Graduate studies can be a great career-enhancer, giving you a competitive edge in your current field or creating a brand-new opportunity. For many, going to graduate school is a great choice, but it's definitely not the right path for everyone. Most graduate programs take between two and five years to complete and even longer to reach the doctorate level. Graduate school can be stressful and demanding, and it also usually comes with a hefty price tag. If you're up for the challenges, the decision to go to graduate school may be a very smart move.

Even if your chosen career does not require a graduate degree, you still may want to consider some of the other benefits of earning one.

- A graduate degree can help you begin your career without having to start at an entry-level position.
- People with graduate degrees statistically earn higher salaries than those without them.
- Some professions automatically pay you more just for having a graduate degree.
- In many fields, you can be promoted only so far without a graduate degree.

Graduate training can also help you keep your job or find a new one. Many jobs require you to stay up to date on changing industries, and earning a graduate degree can show your employer that you are on the cutting edge of your profession. If you want to start a new career, graduate school can offer the skills and knowledge necessary to transition into your chosen field.

Many professional careers require graduate work. If you're interested in becoming a teacher, doctor, lawyer, or social worker, you need at least a short stint in grad school. Some careers, such as those in finance, don't mandate a grad degree, but having an MBA in those jobs can go a long way. Many companies will even pay for promising employees to attend graduate school. At the very least, postgraduate education will give you a competitive edge, which is increasingly important these days.

So should you go? Will the benefit of getting a master's or doctoral degree outweigh the cost? As you decide, here are some important things to consider:

- Are you ready for graduate school, or would you be better off getting a few more years of work experience? Working for a while before going back to school allows you a chance to clarify your career goals, grow up a little, and maybe even save some money to help offset graduate school expenses. Having some life experience under your belt will also likely improve your chances of getting into graduate school.
- Are you willing and able to go back into serious student mode? Grad school programs are typically rigorous and demanding, requiring more hours than many full-time jobs.
- Are you willing to live like a poverty-stricken student again? This can be especially difficult if you've been working for a few years and gotten used to being able to afford good food and the more-than-occasional dinner out. Can you stomach the idea of returning to a steady diet of spaghetti and cereal?
- Are you willing to take the financial plunge? Do you know the total cost for your program and how you're going to find a way to pay for it all?
- Will your increased earning power outweigh the cost of getting your graduate degree?

These may sound like commonsense considerations, but you'd be surprised by how many graduate students we encounter who just dove into school with nothing more than a vague notion about why they were there. For both of us, attending a private graduate school was worth the pain of student loans that we'll be paying off well into our twilight years.

You must have a tangible and well-thought-out reason for wanting to go to graduate school. Perhaps the degree will help you advance in your career, or open more doors. Perhaps you are considering an academic career and want to get a master's degree to see what that might be like. Maybe it's as simple as loving to learn and wanting more. Just make sure you have a *good* reason for wanting to make this commitment—preferably one that has nothing to do with the fact that you want to stay in your grandfather's will, you can't bear the thought of enduring another week under the iron-fisted rule of your current boss, or you want to avoid the painful realities of the real world. If any of these three flimsy reasons rings even a little bit true, it's time to investigate some other options. Graduate school can be the exact ticket you need to get you where you want to go, but it's definitely *not* the easy way out of your career conundrum.

Choices

As you begin to unravel some of the questions about your life's calling and the type of education you'll need, there are other choices that will present themselves. Here are a few:

Will I Choose to Balance Career and Family?

What if you want to have children someday? Does that change things? If mommyhood is one of the roles you're hoping to land, does that mean you should lie low behind the sandwich counter, making pastramis on rye, dreaming of Lamaze classes and minivans until that glorious day when Mr. Prince Charming *aka* the Father of Your Children locks eyes with you across a crowded deli? Um, no. It doesn't.

Let's first deal with the obvious and practical reasons you shouldn't forgo making positive career choices in favor of waiting for the man of your dreams to come along. For starters, you may not get married, ever. Or, even if you do, you and your husband may decide for whatever reason, *you* are going to be the one who brings home the bacon. What if you get married and have children with the intention that your husband is going to be the primary breadwinner, but he becomes disabled or otherwise unable to work? Or, despite waiting to get married, following the Ten Keys, and making a seemingly good choice in a husband, you end up divorced and having to support your family? Life can be unexpected that way.

Even if you're relatively sure that children are part of your future plan and that like the majority of women, you will end up being the primary caretaker for those little cutie pies, that needn't change the fervor and commitment with which you pursue your career in your twenties. However, it *does* require you to give yourself permission to be flexible in the way you pursue your career goals after the kiddos come along.

We are both very thankful that we seized the opportunities in our twenties to establish careers, challenge ourselves professionally, and gain confidence that came from accomplishing these goals. We both had an entire decade to prove to ourselves that we could do well in very competitive fields. So when it finally came time in our thirties to scale back our work and begin the parenthood adventure, it was a lot easier in many ways than it would have been if we hadn't used our twenties to accomplish our career goals. The transition from work to home felt like less of a sacrifice and more of an opportunity, because we had already succeeded in the work world. While it wasn't easy to accept the fact that we would need to pull back and, in the process, lose some of the professional footing we'd gained, we both believed that the sacrifice was worth it and that we'd be able to return to our careers full-force in the future, if that's what we wanted or needed to do.

If you plan on having children someday, it makes sense to plan your education and your career with that future goal in mind and to pursue work that allows some flexibility down the road. Certain careers lend themselves to a better work–family balance because they are more forgiving of career interruptions. Doctors, lawyers, teachers, real estate professionals, and therapists, for instance, have more flexibility than corporate executives. Entrepreneurs have the most of all. You needn't flush your expensive degrees down the toilet and with them your years of work experience in order to have a family. Take some time to find out about women who have succeeded in the careers you're thinking about. If you find that the majority of women in these fields don't have time for children and you plan on being a mom, you may need to tweak your career goals. If you do find some moms who are doing the work you aspire to, try to spend some time with them and ask them how they do it. What tensions do they face between home and work responsibilities, and how do they reconcile them? How do they stay current in their field but still make time for their kids? How much control do they have over their work hours? How common is telecommuting or job-sharing in their industry? Looking back, would they have chosen a different career path? Thinking through these issues now, before you are married, will greatly benefit you later on when you face the challenge of creating balance between career and family.

It's nearly impossible to have a hard-charging career, harmonious marriage, secure children, and time for yourself all at once. Notice that we didn't say that it was impossible to be married, with children, a job, and regular workouts. It's the adjectives that make all the difference. We know plenty of women who left school buying the line, *You can do it all and have it all!* They went on to get married, have children, sign on to big mortgage, and buy a lot of stuff—all the while moving full speed ahead in their careers. The truth is, many of these women ended up unhappy in their marriages, perpetually on edge with their children, resentful of their career choices, and generally stressed out and frustrated with their lives. Can you blame them? Why do these women think that they can meet all those simultaneous demands? They are attempting to do everything a man has traditionally done while at the same time maintaining their sense of obligation to be the nurturer and caretaker of their home and family. These women were duped into taking on both roles and soon realized that there's not nearly enough time or energy in the day to do it all. Barbara Walters sums it up perfectly: "You can have it all, just not at the same time."

So what's a woman and mother-hopeful to do? Take advantage of the time you have *now,* in your twenties, to focus on your career. Take on challenges and develop your marketable skills. Use your twenties to get to a level in your career that will ensure you a place to come back to if you decide to ease off your corporate-ladder-climbing ways when the babies arrive. Sure, your career track might stall for a few years. But we promise you this: If you are a hardworking, talented professional in a field that you like, there will always be a place for you.

Will I Choose My Parents' Dreams or My Own?

Like it or not, your parents will strongly influence your career choices. Since the time you got the lead in the fourth-grade school play, your parents proclaimed your future as a movie star. Since the time you rescued that little birdie with a broken wing, you were destined to become a veterinarian. Since the time you were voted student body president, you were headed to the White House. If your career choices end up being a departure from what your parents have been quietly (or not so quietly) planning for you since you were five, you may have to contend with a little parental skepticism or even flat-out disappointment.

JULIE

Julie's earliest memory of her parents discussing her future as a schoolteacher was over breakfast the summer between seventh and eighth grade. "Well, she can always take a year or two after college and do the Teach for America program and *then* go back for her credential," said her father, as if Julie were invisible. Her parents were both second-generation educators who met in their early years of teaching and were now high-level administrators in a large school district. Whether intentionally or not, they often spoke to Julie as if her future teaching career were a foregone conclusion. Julie's parents regarded teaching as the ultimate act of service and the best method of giving back to society. So you can imagine the struggle Julie faced when it became very clear to her during her senior-year teaching internship that she absolutely, *positively* did not want to be a teacher. She wanted to be an industrial designer.

At first, Julie's parents remained unfazed, convinced that she would come to her senses with time and that the whole industrial design thing was nothing more than a fleeting notion. When Julie started applying to industrial design programs after college, they finally recognized that she was serious. Throughout those first few post-college years, Julie felt terribly guilty when the discussion of career and jobs came up. "My parents sacrificed a lot to help me pay for college," she explained. "I felt like a bad person when I decided not to pursue teaching. It is such a noble profession in so many ways. My parents are obviously disappointed in my career choice, but I'm hoping that once they see that I'm actually good at the whole ID thing and love going to work each day, they'll come around. Maybe it will just take time, but it sure has taken a toll on our relationship."

We don't share Julie's story to suggest that your parents' input regarding your career path should be ignored. Instead, Julie's experience with her parents is a reminder that if after a lot of soul-searching, practical evaluation, and good counsel, you decide to pursue a career that deviates from your parents' hopes for you, you must pursue it with honesty and perseverance. Just be willing to take the heat without losing your cool.

Your parents may try to steer you toward a prestigious or lucrative job simply so they can brag to their friends, succeed vicariously, or count on you as their fallback retirement plan. Before you assume that their guidance is rooted in selfishness, remember that deep down, most parents just want their children to be happy. While they will probably acknowledge that having a well-paying job doesn't guarantee fulfillment or happiness, they also know that having a little money makes life easier. Give your parents the benefit of the doubt they probably deserve, but don't let your desire for their approval influence your career choices to the extent that you end up starting down a career path you're not sold on. Respect your parents *and* yourself enough to communicate with them honestly about your interests and hopes for the future. If you don't, you'll end up resenting the heck out of them. If you do, you'll likely win their respect and confidence in your grown-up judgment.

Will I Choose to Pursue Fame or Excellence?

Eighty-one percent of eighteen- to twenty-five-year-olds surveyed in a Pew Research Center poll released in June 2008 said "being famous" is their generation's most important goal. This is troubling, but not really too surprising, given the overwhelming number of reality-based shows wherein people are becoming famous for, well, being their *under*whelming selves!

Of course, it's natural for humans to seek attention, but twenty-somethings seem to be making fame one of their chief aims, without regard for substance, character, or talent.

Being famous used to mean that you had distinguished yourself in some way. You became famous because you did something well, because you offered something unique that others perceived as having distinct value. Fame typically resulted from excellence. These days, however, you can become wildly famous for simply starring in a sex tape, a mug shot, and a crotch shot (not necessarily in that order). Or you can become famous by deluding yourself into thinking you can sing, dance, model, or cook and then appearing on national television to make a mockery of yourself. And if you didn't make it beyond the first or second round of auditions, don't worry . . . you can *still* be famous! All you have to do is post your video on YouTube or pose half-naked on MySpace or Facebook. It's just that easy. So what's the big deal? Is it so wrong to want to be famous?

Maybe not. But maybe there's something more here to think about. If your aim is fame, then that is where your focus is going to lie. Fame is then no longer the result of something amazing and unique that you've worked hard for, sacrificed for, and achieved. It's just an unearned and ultimately empty end.

How about being famous for doing something great? How about being famous for inspiring significant social change? Or how about setting aside the goal of fame altogether and instead making it your chief aim to be compassionate, excellent, and a woman who decided early on to use her talents and intellect to contribute to society in a meaningful way? How about that? And, if you become famous as a result? Congratulations! Enjoy your fame and use it to help others. Maria Shriver, newswoman, First Lady of California, and daughter of the late Eunice Kennedy Shriver, wrote a wonderful little book titled *Just Who Will You Be?* about the importance of knowing yourself and becoming who you were meant to be. She says this about fame:

Personal Insight from Shannon

I have received several e-mails in the last few years, asking how I came to be on TV and have my own show as a psychotherapist. Young women say to me, "I just graduated with my psychology degree and I want to be a TV therapist like you. How did you do it?" First of all, a TV therapist is Lorraine Bracco on *The Sopranos*. I'm a licensed psychotherapist in private practice for more than fifteen years. I went to school to be a therapist because I wanted to help people, I love to listen, and people fascinate me. Because of my expertise, I received requests to speak on various topics and a television career was born. I am proud that I am known for my experience and insight—not just for being seen on TV. I have a satisfying feeling after I've appeared on a show to discuss an important subject because I know that my message has reached hundreds of thousands of people who will never set foot inside a therapy office. Who wants to go to a therapist who is doing it for the fame? So how do I respond to those e-mails? I tell people to do what they love and get really good at it. People will take notice and want to hear what you have to say.

And if you are so lucky that the things that you do
attract you some fame? Well, "God Bless" to you!
But don't get confused and be clear-headed, too
You aren't your fame and your fame isn't you!
Fame's just a perception, an image, a role

But it isn't the truth and it isn't your soul.
Under the spotlight the shine fades real fast
And the fun of the fame never really does last.
There are folks who are famous but their lives are a mess
Because just being famous doesn't bring happiness.

Our advice? Forget about fame. Instead, seek to distinguish yourself because of your excellence. And always, *always*, wear your panties in public.

Will I Choose a Variety of Paths?

> *Your twenties are always an apprenticeship, but you don't always know what for.*
>
> —*Jan Houtema*

Now is the time to try as many new things as possible. You, Uncle Sam, and possibly Sallie Mae are the only ones you need to answer to. Once you're married, you can't just pick up and go to language school in Venezuela for a year. You can *now*. Once you're married, you can't as easily take a job with an international PR company in Beijing. You can *now*. Once you're established in your career, you can't take a job merely because it's interesting to you and you've always been curious about that field. By then, you'll have too much to lose and it will be more difficult to start all over again in another profession. When you're single, you can make the move from being a receptionist at a credit union in Toledo to being a receptionist in a museum in Paris. Now is the simplest time for you to take your teaching credential on the road, to San Francisco, Chicago, even Barcelona! You get the idea. Read *Delaying the Real World* by Colleen Kinder for some creative and practical ideas about how to craft adventures that will both pay the bills and offer an exciting alternative to a traditional job.

Along with a lot of really *wonderful* things, marriage brings with it increased financial responsibilities and children who are dependent on you for everything. Being married also requires serious collaboration with your husband when planning for the future. You can't just take off. You'll need to take into consideration your spouse's job constraints, opinions, and family relationships as well. We're certainly not saying that getting married means the end of interesting work experiences or trying new things. But the fact is that once you're married, you're no longer making decisions on your own.

Many Paths, Many Opportunities

According to the Bureau of Labor Statistics, most people have more than eight jobs between the ages of twenty and thirty. Daniel Gilbert, a Harvard psychologist, says that changing jobs frequently during those years is the right approach because we really don't know what we'll like until we try it. According to Gilbert, if you have several different jobs during your starting-out years, you'll be more equipped to decide what you ultimately want to do with the rest of your adult working years. As proud employees of at least eight different organizations each during our twenties, to Mr. Gilbert, we say, "Hear, hear!" How are you supposed to know much about various careers right out of college? Sure, you may be familiar with your parents' careers, and maybe you did an internship or two during your four years of college, but that's probably it. Hardly enough information to base a potentially forty-plus-year career on, don't you think?

Be forewarned. Not everyone agrees that job-hopping is good for your career. Most of the naysayers seem to be corporate human resource types who are worried that you'll be "here today, gone tomorrow," before the company is able to recoup the investment made in training you for the job. They will also warn that too many jobs on your résumé may cause you to come across as flaky and somewhat fickle. We'd argue that even if you end up having to do some fancy footwork to explain your "diverse employment history" to the HR gal behind the desk, job-hopping in your twenties is an excellent approach to really figuring out which jobs light your fire and which ones burn you out. Another positive of having several jobs as you're starting out is that you are able to build relationships with many more professionals than you would have if you'd stayed in one place for ten years. More relationships equals stronger professional network equals greater opportunities for the future. See how that works?

MEGAN

"I really had no clue what I wanted to do right out of college. I graduated with a liberal arts degree, so I wasn't really qualified to do anything special. I got a job at a bookstore to pay the bills, but I always knew that bigger things were in store for my career. One day, I was shelving books and came across the novel, *The Nanny Diaries*. I loved that book! Granted, the nanny's job seemed tough, but I thought I would much rather take care of an adorable child, even a spoiled one, than restock shelves all day. I looked on craigslist.org that very night and answered a few ads looking for a full-time nanny. I interviewed the following week and took a job in a Dallas suburb caring for two little girls whose mom was a clothing designer. I jumped into my new job with gusto! I was certain that I was now destined to become the owner of my very own nanny agency, after I had a chance to learn the ins and outs of the actual job, of course.

"After six months on the job, I was enjoying myself for the most part, but was starting to question my burning desire to make a long-term career out of this gig. To be honest, I was starting to feel antsy and a little bored. The kids were adorable, but the repetition of playing dress-up, going to swim lessons, and trekking back and forth to the park was becoming a bit mind-numbing. And then there was the whining. Whew! I had a newfound respect for parenthood. Maybe I could own the nanny agency without actually being around kids that often.

"Just days before I was planning on giving notice, my boss casually mentioned that her business was in the middle of an overseas expansion and she really needed an assistant. I had always been very interested in fashion design so I jumped at the chance to be considered for the job! That was two years ago. The business is doing amazingly well and I've been to Europe three times in the last year. More than ever, I'm a huge believer in being open to new opportunities and that you should be willing to try different career paths as they come your way. Having a plan is crucial, but sometimes doors will open when you least expect it."

So don't get discouraged if your career and whole life picture aren't what you imagined right away. Pursuing various career paths over the years is a process and an economic reality, so you might as well enjoy the excitement of change. A few rare individuals know exactly what they want and what they're good at from an early age, but for most of us, it takes time to calibrate our lives. That's precisely why it is *imperative* that you take this time during your twenties to experience that process, learning about the thousands of career choices that are available to you and which one is ultimately right for you.

Career

Now that you've gotten a bit of clarity about your career choices, there are certain things you can do to speed things along and establish a solid foundation for success in your chosen field. Defining your goals and always doing your best work are surefire ways to catapult you to professional stardom.

Getting from Here to There: The Importance of Measurable Goals

A goal without a plan is just a wish.
—*Antoine de Saint-Exupéry*

Whether or not New Year's Eve is right around the corner, there is no time like the present for making career resolutions. It's easy to become discouraged by the task of goal-setting because it's tough to know how to get started. If you don't lock down manageable and measurable ways to achieve your goals, they will feel more like wishes, out there somewhere, unattainable.

According to Ronnie Ferez, the man behind leading career advice site, YoungUrbanProfessionals.net, the most common problem with twentysomethings in the workforce is that they lack career goals and objectives, resulting in their willingness to jump on the first job offer that comes their way.

So how do you plan your career? How do you proceed? Ferez offers up four rock-solid steps to career planning:

1. ***Set SMART (Specific, Measurable, Attainable, Realistic, and Time-Bound) career goals.*** If you are currently a marketing assistant, consider making it your goal to become a marketing manager ten years from now. Then start pursuing the necessary incremental career objectives.
2. ***Build your core competencies.*** Your core competencies are special job skills and knowledge that make you effective and efficient in your job. Learn new technologies that will make you more competitive in your own field.
3. ***Expand your influence.*** Develop your leadership and people skills. Top jobs require these skills. Join pro-

fessional associations and networking organizations in your field of work.

4. *Plan your career.* Don't just take another job! Heed author and educator Laurence J. Peter's words of wisdom: "If you don't know where you are going, you will probably end up somewhere else!"

Now it's time to get practical in planning for your career future. Use the following guidelines to help you stay focused and increase your chances for success.

Determine What You Want

One person's goal might be to get a promotion and the corner office, while another might want to enjoy her job, make enough money to cover her bills, and be able to set her own schedule. Either way, the first step to goal-setting is determining what you actually want. Where do you see yourself professionally in the next five to ten years? When setting goals for your career, it's important to look ahead and not merely focus on immediate concerns. For example, if you're currently a junior high school math teacher (bless your heart), one of your immediate goals could be to have your lessons planned at least three weeks in advance. Perhaps a one-year goal would be to start a peer-counseling program at your school. A future three-year goal may be to get your master's degree, which would increase your pay.

Write down what you want to be doing one year from now. Three years from now. Five years. Ten years.

Set Specific Career Goals

After deciding on what you want to work toward, be specific when setting your goals. Instead of saying "I want to graduate and be successful," set your sights on "After graduation, I want to work as an accountant at one of the top eight accounting firms in Chicago." Make your career goal specific. If it's too vague, it will be hard to visualize, and you won't have anything concrete to work toward.

Look at your list of one-, three-, five-, and ten-year goals. Were you specific? Go back and rewrite your list as specific goals rather than vague wishes.

Set Measurable Career Goals

With your specific goal in mind, your next step is to decide how to accomplish it. Not being able to view your progress can cause your commitment to quickly wane. That's why it's important to set smaller shorter-term goals along the path to your long-term goal: to make your progress measurable. You will stay more motivated when you work toward your goal by taking baby steps rather than by attempting giant leaps. For example, setting a goal to attend at least one professional association event per month is just a stepping-stone toward the bigger, long-term goal of building a strong professional network.

Take your five-year goal—what steps do you need to take *now* to make that goal a reality? Keep breaking the steps down until you get monthly and weekly goals. Write these weekly and monthly goals in your daily planner and keep track of your progress.

Don't Set Yourself Up for Failure

As you pursue your career goals, set your sights, but be realistic. An unachievable goal only sets you up for failure and can be discouraging. Also, very rarely do things work out exactly how you plan. Be flexible when encountering roadblocks. Sometimes these barriers can force you to modify your goals to meet the current situation. Take a minute to brainstorm about some potential roadblocks and possible solutions. For example, "If I try unsuccessfully for three months to get a job in advertising, I could get a part-time internship or pursue a job in the related field of public relations."

What roadblocks might you encounter on the road to reaching your goals? What could you do to overcome those potential obstacles?

Thinking about what you want to achieve and setting an actual plan of action is a great start to successfully reaching your career objectives. Tracking your progress with short-term goals will keep the long-term goals well within your grasp. Consider the wisdom of Armand Hammer when he said: "Just think of something that would be 'wonderful' if it were only 'possible,' then set out to make it possible." Or the simple brilliance of Bill Murray in the '90s movie classic, *What About Bob?*: "Baby-steps onto the elevator, baby-steps into the elevator, I'm on the elevator."

Doing "A" Work Even if You Have a "C" Job (*aka* "Welcome to EntryLevelVille: Please Check Your Ego and Diplomas at the Door")

You've zeroed in on your career goals. You're ready to go. There's only one problem . . . you lack experience. Regardless of all your education, "willingness to learn," and optimism, you just don't have it. There's only one way to gain that experience and fill up all the blank space on your résumé: you gotta work. These days, in order to excel in just about any given field, you must immerse yourself in the work to gain day-to-day experience, even though that may mean taking up residence in your very own, very small, cubicle.

More likely than not, your work will involve a good deal of Tedious Drudgery. To make matters even more challenging, while you're busy trying to prove your worth and make your mark, your coworkers and superiors may treat you like an idiot, ignore you, and even dismiss your ideas as Silly Drivel of the Inexperienced. Some may be downright rude and condescending. Enduring that kind of treatment can be trying, to say the least. In fact, it might even make you cry from time to time. Welcome to your first real job.

While you're sitting at the front desk wearing that headset, remember that working for a few years as a receptionist, a file clerk, a glorified coffee fetcher, a customer service representative, or whatever entry-level job you currently have, does *not*

Personal Insight from Celeste

Fresh out of school and ready to take on the world, I had been offered a job at a large industrial company doing what was described in the ad as "general office work." Not exactly a position fitting of my newly inked political science degree, but, hey, my rent was due in three weeks. I showed up for work on that Monday morning, wearing the new suit I had purchased with graduation money and a killer pair of black patent leather heels. The department supervisor cheerfully greeted me, pointed out the bathroom, and led me down a maze of poorly lit corridors to a room at the end of the hall. "This is where you'll be spending most of your time," she said, opening the door. "Great!" I cheered to myself, "My own office!" I stepped into a huge room filled with boxes. Boxes everywhere, dozens of them. They must have been stacked six feet high. In the corner of the room was a wobbly card table, holding a small shredding machine. That's right, my job was to shred the contents of those boxes. Each and every document. That was my job. So, after more than a few minutes of indignance and feeling sorry for myself, I decided I could either storm out of there in all of my "I didn't go to college for this" glory, or I could determine to become the fastest and best damn paper shredder/college graduate that company had ever seen. In this moment of truth, I decided that I was going to do A work in a C—okay, D—job. To my relief, after two weeks of proving myself as a hard worker and Master Paper Shredder, I was rewarded with a promotion. You may not find this skill listed on my résumé, but it was this same work ethic that guided me to subsequent career successes.

condemn you to a permanent career in that position. It may take a year or two, but you certainly can transition into something else, something better, *if* you're willing to suck it up and do a good job in your current occupation.

Since the less-than-desirable entry-level jobs are virtually unavoidable when you have just finished college, you should use them to your advantage. If you have to be a receptionist/copy clerk/customer support rep for a year or two, make the most of it. Take a job in a field that interests you. Use your time there to get familiar with the jargon, attitudes, and everyday vibe of the field. Sure, you may have limited exposure, but every little bit counts.

Consider the following dual roles of these entry-level jobs:

- While you're answering phones for an event-planning company, you're also meeting people in the field who will be invaluable contacts later on when you start your own catering business.
- While you're transcribing dictation for a physician, you're learning medical terminology that will give you a leg up in nursing school.

- While you're numbering legal documents, you're seeing how a court case is organized, which is extremely helpful for a future attorney.
- While you're working as a production assistant, you're learning how a movie is made from the ground up—something every successful film producer needs to know.

Remember, you're not going to be in this job forever, probably not even more than a couple of years. Regardless of the specific tasks, you are setting your own standards for how you are going to approach your work, both now and in the future. Determine now that even if your job stinks and requires you to use only half your brain, you are going to do A work. You can use the other half of your brain to devise a plan for getting your next, more challenging, and better-paying job. Now get back into that cubicle. . . .

Note: Watch the cult favorite *Office Space* starring Jennifer Aniston and Ron Livingston for a novel take on a guy in a dull cubicle who turns the traditional office doldrums upside down. A true classic.

As you navigate down your career path, you will at times feel intimidated, incompetent, and unsure. But as you push forward, you will begin to feel your confidence building. You will surprise even yourself as you rise to meet new challenges and find the courage to step up and take risks when you would rather run and hide in your parents' basement. As scary as it can be, the reward will be your newfound self-assurance as your place in the world becomes more and more clear. Take the time now, while you are single, to carve out this fabulous place, allowing yourself the freedom to stop and start and to change course if you need to. Remember, your work does not define who you are now, or who you'll be twenty or thirty years from now, but it can be a wonderful opportunity to use your unique talents in ways that will benefit your future marriage and family, your community, and the world at large.

> *Shoot for the moon. Even if you miss, you'll land among the stars.*
>
> *—Les Brown*

Chapter 6

Key #4: Get a Smart Financial Life

Take Charge of Your Money, Honey

Money ranks with love as man's greatest source of joy and with death as his greatest source of anxiety.

—John Kenneth Galbraith

Okay, just take a deep breath. Some of you are breaking into a cold sweat at the mere thought of reading a chapter about money. Others of you are certain the last thing you need is another boring lecture on 401(k)s and the importance of saving for retirement. Many of you are tempted to skip this chapter altogether simply to avoid the stress that always accompanies thinking about your finances. Quick—before you move on to less painful chapters—take this true-or-false quiz to determine if this chapter is for you.

Financial Assessment Quiz

T F I am tempted to skip this chapter.
T F I feel nervous or uncomfortable when talking about money.
T F I feel stupid about financial matters.
T F I overspend.
T F I can't seem to save any money.
T F I grew up in a family with money problems, and I can't seem to break the cycle.
T F I have a lot of credit card debt.
T F I don't know my credit score.
T F I never seem to make any headway in paying off my credit cards.
T F I couldn't survive without my parents' financial support.
T F I worry about money.
T F I am afraid I won't have enough money to pay my monthly bills.
T F I avoid paying my bills until the last minute and often pay them late.
T F I don't know how much money I have in the bank.
T F I don't have much confidence in my ability to manage money.

If you answered TRUE to any of these questions, you must read on. Don't be dismayed. We promise that this exploration of financial matters will be unlike any other books you may have read in the past, or heated arguments you may have had with your parents. We won't give you a lecture about cutting down on your spending and keeping track of every cent, but we will give you the reasons and the tools to get smart about your money.

Money and Marriage

One of the best ways to prepare now for a successful marriage is to improve your current relationship with money. Money is one of the top two causes of divorce in America today, second only to infidelity. If you fail to take this time to figure out your underlying motivations and beliefs about money and take practical steps to take charge of your finances, you will remain financially blind and will put your future marriage at risk.

Seven Ways Financial Blindness Will Harm You and Your Future Marriage

1. **You're more likely to make a poor choice in a spouse.** If you believe you need a man to take care of you, you will be more likely to settle for the first guy who can wipe your financial slate clean and offer you financial stability. It can be tough to survive on your own these days, but if you truly believe that you are not capable of taking care of yourself, you are at risk for marrying a man simply because he's got a large stash of cash regardless of whether he fits other, more important criteria for a husband.
2. **You're more likely to unfairly put the burden of financial management on your husband.** If you insist on burying your head in the sand when it comes to money matters, you are not acting as an equal partner in your marriage. Not only is that irresponsible, it is also unfair to expect your husband to carry your financial deadweight. The task of managing a household and making sound financial decisions for a family is too much for one person to handle alone.

3. **You're more likely to put money before your man.** If you have an unhealthy attachment to money, and the most important things to you are a bigger house, a better wardrobe, and a more expensive car, your husband may begin to wonder whether you will ever be satisfied. Heaven forbid he loses his high-paying job or decides that he would rather teach high school. You could never abide such a change to your lifestyle. If your relationship with your husband becomes secondary to what he provides for you, you will end up with a resentful husband (or ex-husband).
4. **You're more likely to lose your husband's respect.** If you are a damsel in financial distress, it upsets the proper balance of the marriage relationship. If you are irresponsible with money, it creates a parent–child dynamic in the marriage in which your husband is the finger-wagging dad who doles out limited allowance to his irresponsible child. Here's how it goes: You overspend, he gets mad and tries to restrict your spending, you pout, he loses respect for you as a partner and a grown-up.
5. **You're more likely to find yourself trapped in a bad marriage.** If you are insecure about your ability to adequately handle finances, you will be more likely to remain in an unhappy, even abusive relationship. If you don't take the time to prove to yourself that you can slay the financial dragon now, you might later become its prisoner in a bad marriage.
6. **You're more likely to fall prey to Financial Infidelity.** That's just a catchy term for lying to your spouse about money, which is fast becoming an epidemic. If you avoid talking with your husband about money as a result of your own financial blind spots, you're setting yourselves up to be secretive about financial dealings. Financially unfaithful spouses make secret purchases, maintain hidden accounts, and/or lie about how much

they make. In a recent *Redbook* magazine survey, nearly one in four people interviewed said that openness about money is more important than fidelity. As one of the respondents put it, "It's one thing to fool around. It's another thing to fool around with my hard-earned cash!" If you and your husband can't talk openly and honestly about money, you will end up keeping each other in the dark about your financial choices, which can be devastating to your marriage.

7. **You're more likely to be unable to protect yourself in the event of divorce or death.** If you fail to educate yourself about money matters and leave them to your spouse to handle, you will be at a serious disadvantage if you end up divorced or widowed. Your husband might be the one who handles the checkbook in your marriage, but it's irresponsible, not to mention stupid, to hand over the financial reins completely. In the event of divorce or death, what you don't know *can* hurt you. In many divorces, women who let their husband completely control the finances often end up with less than their fair share of the marital assets because their husband was free to hide money and lie about his income in the midst of the divorce. Widows lose millions of dollars each year to unclaimed life insurance proceeds and unclaimed accounts. You may think that ignorance is bliss when it comes to money, but if you find yourself in divorce or probate court struggling to make sense of your marital financial picture, you will surely be feeling ignorant, but far from blissful.

Scary, huh? Our purpose in cautioning you about these risks is not to frighten you away from marriage, but to encourage you to do whatever it takes to remove your financial blinders so you can enter marriage financially savvy with your eyes wide open.

F-Words: Critical to Financial Success

Nobody denies that money is essential. As Zig Ziglar, financial guru says, "Money isn't the most important thing in life, but it's reasonably close to oxygen on the 'gotta have it' scale." If you believe that financial smart is simply a matter of budgeting, saving, and balancing your checkbook, you're mistaken. That's right, finances are not just about numbers. In fact, the most significant factors of your financial life are your attitudes, feelings, fears, and expectations. No wonder money is a leading cause of marital strife—it is *emotional*! We all have specific, often subconscious emotional associations with money, so until you figure out your emotional relationship with money, you will never get a handle on your finances. In order to get smart about money, you have to explore three fundamental F-Words (no, not *that* F-word) of financial success:

- Family: How your upbringing caused you to feel the way you do about money.
- Feelings: How your subconscious views about finances affect your current financial state.
- Financial Plan: What you can do to get smart about money in order to protect yourself and your future marriage from emotional/financial entanglements.

Family

Where Did My Attitudes, Beliefs, and Expectations about Money Come From?

Yep, you guessed it . . . your parents! We don't want to fall into the trap of blaming everything bad on your parents, but as you read in chapter 4, you can't deny the indelible influence they have over every aspect of your life. Money is no exception. From the time you got your first piggy bank, your parents were shaping your views about money. You heard them argue about how much to spend, whether or not to save, and how in the world they were going to afford to pay your tuition. Each one of us inherits attitudes and behaviors about money.

Most of us, though, are not aware of our subconscious beliefs about money. Many of us come from homes where money was never discussed in front of the children because our parents considered it improper. Whether they vocalized their opinions about it or not, the way your parents handled money spoke volumes. As a child, you were a sponge, soaking in the information, attitudes, and actions you witnessed. Even when you were too young to put words to your impressions, you were receiving messages. Those messages now make up your unspoken, unidentified motives, fears, and attitudes about money. Most of us have to do some sleuthing to figure out the underlying messages we received about finances as a child. It's like finding puzzle pieces and fitting them together to get a more complete picture of our "money mind." So let's get started piecing together your personal puzzle, shall we?

Your Money Mind

Answer the following questions as honestly as you can to identify some of the ways your parents have influenced your beliefs about money. Don't worry about writing in complete sentences; just jot down whatever comes to mind. If you remember a story or situation, write down as much of it as you remember.

How did your parents handle money?
Which one paid the bills? Which one made more money?
What were their attitudes toward money?
Did they live beyond, within, or below their means?

What did they fight about most regarding finances?
Who spent the most money?
Was money a problem in their marriage?
Did they fight about it a lot?
Did they have separate bank accounts?
Did they have a lot of money or never enough?
Did they teach you the importance of budgeting? Saving? Investing? Giving?
Did they hide money or purchases from each other or lie about spending?
Did you earn an allowance or did they give you money when you wanted it? Or both?

Now do you see where some of your beliefs about money originated? Our earliest beliefs, feelings, and fears about money are shaped by our experiences. The following stories are examples of how parents impact our financial beliefs in sometimes unpredictable ways.

CANDACE

Candace grew up in a large Victorian home in Tennessee. She went to the best private school, rode horses on the weekend, and always dressed in the latest fashions. Her father worked at a bank and her mother considered herself a socialite (that simply meant she didn't have to work). Candace's father drove a new Cadillac, and her mother refused to drive anywhere because it wasn't becoming of a socialite. At least once a month, her mother found a reason to host an elaborate dinner party at their house. She was involved in several charities and foundations, so it was never a problem to find someone who wanted her to host a benefit. Candace seemed to have it all, so she should have no issues with money, right? Not quite.

On the outside, it appeared that Candace's parents had no struggles with money, but upon closer inspection, the problems were crystal clear. Candace's family was all about outward appearances, but the reality was that each month, they were going deeper into debt to support the image of success they had created. Candace heard her parents argue frequently about how much money her mom spent on clothes and entertaining. Her dad wanted his wife to get a job, but she vehemently refused, saying it was improper for a woman of her status to work.

When Candace was in seventh grade, one of the families from the club was basically ostracized when the father lost his job and could no longer afford private school tuition or country club dues. Through that experience, Candace learned that money, or at least the nice things it affords, provides a place for you in society. It doesn't actually buy friends, but it buys you status among them.

So how do you think Candace managed her money when she went out on her own? Do you think she saw how risky it was to pretend to have money and spend what you don't have? Do you think she refused to buy on credit, choosing instead to live within her means and insist on having friends who liked her for who she was? Unfortunately, Candace ended up following in her parents' deeply ingrained footsteps. After graduating from college, she rented a gorgeous apartment that cost more than 50 percent of her monthly income and maxed out her shiny new Visa card to fill up her brand-new closet. After all, as her mom always said, "Honey, only spend money on the important things . . . things that make you look important and feel important."

Candace explains away her overspending with an emotional response: "I only feel good about myself when I have nice things. When I buy expensive things, people look at me differently and I like that feeling, the feeling that I matter."

MEADOW

Meadow grew up in a simple home with her parents and older sister. She always wore hand-me-down clothes that her sister had outgrown; they grew most of their own vegetables and watched an old nineteen-inch TV with a foil-covered rabbit-ear antenna on top. Meadow's parents were both highly educated physicians who chose to work in nonprofit clinics because they were passionate about helping the poor. They equated wealth with greed and never passed up an opportunity to illustrate this important truth to Meadow and her sister. Meadow loved and respected her parents, but she also loved watching *The O.C.* with her sister and daydreaming about beach houses, designer clothes, and rich boyfriends who drove fast cars.

Did Meadow follow in her parents' footsteps as Candace did? Did she eschew a life of luxury in order to serve the underserved? Not exactly, but she did carry a burdensome legacy of her parents' beliefs about money. . . .

When Meadow graduated from law school, she withstood her parents' pressure to work for a nonprofit, choosing instead to work for a large law firm that offered a huge salary. She wanted to buy all the things she'd never had as a child and longed to fit in with the other attorneys in their designer suits and new BMWs. Why, then, did she seem stuck in a financial rut, unable to afford any of the nice things she hoped for? Deeply ingrained in Meadow's subconscious was still the belief *Wealth=Greed*. Something inside her resisted success in her career because she didn't want to be greedy. She turned down promotions, gave credit for her work to other attorneys, and always undercharged for her services. She sabotaged her own financial success because of the firmly entrenched beliefs she inherited from her parents.

BROOKE

Brooke describes her childhood as "really tough." Her mom was a single mother of three who worked two jobs to support her family. Brooke's mother was a smart and diligent woman who worked her way up from hostess at TGIFriday's to waitress, then to manager. She taught her children the value of money, the importance of saving, and how effort is rewarded. Brooke recalls playing with her brothers at the park when her mom commented, "Look at those moms with their manicures and nannies. They've probably never worked a day in their lives. Lucky snobs don't even know how good they have it." Brooke knew her mom longed for a husband who would give her a break and help support the family. Brooke explained, "Mom didn't complain a lot, but it was pretty obvious that she was jealous of other moms who were married and didn't have to work much."

Brooke had a great example of a strong, capable woman and grew up with a true understanding of the value of money. Did she have an easy transition to financial independence? Did Brooke move into her twenties with confidence in her ability to support herself as a competent single woman? Nope. Brooke was terrified of ending up with a life similar to her mother's, and was determined to instead find a man to take care of her. After high school, she became obsessed with getting married. Brooke found a guy with a steady job who loved her more than she loved him. Assured that he would never leave her, she married him shortly after her twenty-second birthday. Now when she goes to the park with her baby to get away from her stifling marriage, she suspects that her mother might not have had it so bad.

SHAYLA

Shayla was a rich daddy's girl from Atlanta, Georgia. Her family was loaded, and she had everything a girl could desire. Shayla always had the best stories to tell when the teacher asked, "What did you do during summer break?" She brought photos of the beachfront villa on Maui, gold nuggets panned in a mine in California, and an exotic bowl carved from indigenous Guatemalan wood. Shayla didn't earn an allowance but had only to ask for money to see the latest movie, update her wardrobe, or buy the latest techno gadget. She never had a summer job, because her family was always too busy traveling. Her mom spent a lot of time with Shayla, teaching her manners and proper etiquette. She taught her how to arrange flowers, cook an exquisite pork loin roast with baby potatoes, and decorate using feng shui. The one skill Shayla's mother didn't teach her was how to manage money. It simply didn't occur to her that it would be necessary.

Did Shayla marry a rich man because she didn't know how to provide for herself? Did she make the most of her entertaining skills to become the next Martha Stewart? Actually, Shayla moved to New York to pursue her dreams of becoming a literary agent. She is now twenty-seven, single, and freaking out. Although she is making a decent living, she never expected to be single at this point in her life. She always expected that she would be married to a man who would provide for her financially, just as Daddy did. She still gets a lot of financial help from her dad because she's convinced herself that there's no way she'll be able to make it in the world without a man to provide for her.

My Story

Take some time now to identify the unspoken messages you received about money as a child. What role does money play in your family? How will you be tempted to end your story? Are you determined to avoid your parents' financial difficulties or will you relive their mistakes?

> I grew up in a ________________ [wealthy, poor, middle-class, struggling . . .] family. My ____________ [mom, dad, stepdad/mom] earned most of the money. We bought ______________________________ [dinners, IRAs, vacations, education . . .] with our money. Our financial situation made me feel ______________________ [comfortable, anxious, secure]. We were ______________ [wealthier, poorer, same financial status] as my friends and

neighbors. My parents often said this about money: "Always ____, and never ____."

Now that you have a head start, continue your own story in a separate journal and predict how it will impact your financial decisions and attitudes.

Feelings

How Do My Feelings about Money Impact My Current Money Problems?

"Dealing with money makes me want to cry!" We hear this from twenty- (and thirty-, forty-, and fifty-) something women all the time. Money is a very emotional issue. Most people don't realize just how much their feelings impact their financial lives, because they avoid examining those emotions. It's just too uncomfortable. The simplest test of whether your emotions are keeping you from being smart about money is to note your reaction to the subject. If you space out, fog up, stress out, or find it impossible to learn and apply new financial information, you can be sure that it is your *feelings* about money that are causing your block.

As Barbara Stanny says in her aptly titled financial book *Prince Charming Isn't Coming,* "There is a colossal psychological component that casts a dark shadow over our financial dealings. For many of us, getting smart with money is as much about conquering fear and overcoming resistance as about learning facts and managing assets." When dealing with money, fear can be paralyzing and keep you from making good financial decisions. Until you figure out what you are actually afraid of, you can't make any headway in the financial department. If you want to know where your fear comes from, answer the following questions:

What Are My Financial Fears?

Are you afraid of failure?
Are you afraid you don't have what it takes to be a financial success?
Are you afraid people won't like you unless you buy them things?
Are you afraid people will judge you for not having nice stuff?
Are you afraid that you will be poor?
Are you afraid that you will let your parents down if you aren't financially successful?
Are you afraid that you will never achieve the life you imagined for yourself?
Are you afraid you'll never get out of debt?

Now that you've identified some of your specific fears about money, let's examine them even more closely.

Core Fears Exercise

Sometimes your fears may seem irrational or out of proportion to reality. That's because you have subconscious beliefs that fuel your fears. Identifying this underlying core fear is the first step to overcoming it.

First, think of a financial situation that elicits intense feelings. For example: I just received a credit card statement in the mail and broke into a cold sweat.

Belief	**Feeling**
What am I afraid this means for my future? I'll never be able to get myself out of debt.	*How does it make me feel?* Disappointed in myself for overspending Out of control

Belief	Feeling
What am I afraid will happen next? I'll have to ask my parents to bail me out.	*How will it make me feel?* Stupid, like a kid Embarrassed
What am I afraid will happen next? I'll have bad credit.	*How will it make me feel?* Like a failure
What am I afraid will happen next? I'll never be able to buy a car or house.	*How will it make me feel?* Inferior
What am I afraid will happen next? No one will want to marry me.	*How will it make me feel?* Unlovable
What am I afraid will happen next? I'll die alone.	*How will it make me feel?* Despairing and hopeless

In this example, the core fear is that you will die alone. At first glance, your intense reaction to the credit card balance seems irrational. But now that you're aware of the core fear buried in your subconscious, it makes perfect sense. A cold sweat is not an irrational reaction to the thought that you will die alone. Try this exercise yourself to discover how your current feelings about money are impacted by your core fear.

Financial situation that elicited intense feelings:

____

Belief	Feeling
What am I afraid this means for my future?	*How does it make me feel?*
What am I afraid will happen next?	*How will it make me feel?*
What am I afraid will happen next?	*How will it make me feel?*
What am I afraid will happen next?	*How will it make me feel?*
What am I afraid will happen next?	*How will it make me feel?*
What am I afraid will happen next?	*How will it make me feel?*

My Core Fear is ______________________________.

Fear is the most common general reaction to dealing with money, but it usually leads to one or more of the following emotional reactions about money.

Denial and Avoidance

Never underestimate the power of denial.

—American Beauty

Somewhere deep in the recesses of your intelligent brain is a stupid reaction to your fears about money—you simply refuse to address it at all.

Denial and avoidance are dangerous. They lead to bad credit scores, debt, and no financial cushion in case of emergency.

Personal Insight from Shannon

I struggled with denial about money throughout much of my twenties. I thought that if I didn't balance my checkbook, I wouldn't have to address the painfully low balance in my account. I could pretend I had enough to spend on new clothes as long as I didn't see the single-digit balance staring back at me. I had a limited income, so I reasoned that looking at how much money I didn't have wasn't going to magically create more money. Yet at the same time, I irrationally believed that if ignored it, it would miraculously take care of itself. I even spent extra money each month to pay for overdraft protection to protect myself from my own bank statements!

As often happens with the cycle of fear/denial/depression, whenever I was confronted with my dire financial straits, I would become depressed and lose hope—feeling completely out of control and overwhelmed. No wonder I avoided it like the plague! Confronting it only made me feel bad and never did any good. It was only years later, when someone gave me a budget worksheet, that I was able to catch a vision for how empowered I could be by managing my money. I'd still rather spend more than I have, but I know how much I have and I've worked too hard rebuilding my credit score to let it all go for a trip down denial lane in my new designer shoes.

People in denial often find themselves with late fees and poor credit because they put off paying bills. If you have read this far, you are probably feeling yourself slowly being pulled out of your denial. In the "Financial Plan" section of this chapter, we will give you practical tools to wipe out your avoidance for good. Having a great plan will give you a sense of control, and by taking even small steps, you will gain confidence in your money-management skills. These newfound skills will enable you to control your money, not the other way around.

Misplaced Hope

Someday my Prince will come. . . .

—Snow White

You try to keep a positive attitude about money, hoping for the day when someone (preferably a fabulously wealthy man with a steady job, generous heart, and a healthy retirement account) will save you from your money woes and high credit card balances. Despite strongly feminist beliefs about work, independence, and competence, many women still admit to a secret wish that a man will come along and take care of them. This misplaced hope cripples them as it stunts their financial growth. As Barbara Stanny says, "We will never become truly smart about money, no matter how hard we try, until we explicitly decide: *No one is going to take care of my money for me; that responsibility falls on my shoulders.*" Try saying that aloud right now. Were you convincing? Now, look in the mirror and say it again like you really believe it. By making this statement out loud, you are actively shifting your perspective and reassigning that misplaced hope. You're putting the responsibility back where it belongs—on your own capable shoulders. Make that statement of responsibility your personal mantra as you begin to tackle your finances and gain confidence in your abilities.

Anxiety

Worry is a cycle of inefficient thoughts whirling around a center of fear.

—Corrie Ten Boom, author and Holocaust survivor

Thinking about money makes many women nervous. It can inspire actual physical signs of anxiety, such as sweaty palms, pounding heart, shaky hands, racing thoughts, dry mouth, and tight chest. Some people even report having anxiety attacks when faced with money issues. All these reactions can be traced back to our fears about money. The core fear you uncovered in the earlier exercise is the source of your anxiety. For example, if your core fear is that you will be unlovable if you lose all your money, of course you feel anxious at the thought of going into debt!

The most common way people express their anxiety is through worry. Worry is debilitating. People who wallow in worry describe themselves like this: "I obsess about money but never seem to make any progress." "I worry about money all the time—it even keeps me awake at night. I have to take a sleeping pill sometimes just to turn my mind off." If you allow yourself to sit and worry, you will be stuck whirling in an endless cycle of fear and anxiety without ever taking steps to get out. What's the greatest cure for anxiety? Action! Do something about your finances! Resist the temptation to waste your energy worrying and instead channel that energy into action steps that will ease your anxiety. The more action you take, the less you will have to worry about.

Despair

Do not despair of your life. You have force enough to overcome your obstacles.

—Henry David Thoreau

If you frequently feel helpless or hopeless about your financial situation or your inability to resurrect it, you are not alone. Tara, twenty-six, describes her feelings of despair like this: "I feel so hopeless when it comes to money. It always seems like no matter what I do, I cannot pull myself out of the hole I've dug. I know I have no one but myself to blame, and I think that's what is so depressing. It's not like someone stole my credit card or forced me to buy all that stuff against my will."

If you are in a financial mess and can't seem to get yourself out of it, you may begin to despair. Being in a financial mess can mean different things for different people. Cindy makes a decent living, but because she can't seem to figure out where her paycheck disappears to every month, she despairs that she will never be able to gain control of her finances. Elena makes an entry-level salary, but because she relies on credit cards each month to cover her basic needs, she despairs that she will never get out from under her growing debt. Becca just got a pay raise, but because she can still only manage to save one hundred dollars a month, she despairs that she will never be able to put away enough money for a down payment on a car.

Getting a handle on your finances may seem like an impossible battle. You, like many women, might believe that you don't possess the necessary intelligence, skills, or brain cells to figure it all out. Some women believe the rubbish that they are not as good at math as men and therefore inherently unable to understand money. What a load of crap (and a really weak excuse)! There are hordes of successful female bankers, financial planners, accountants, money managers, personal investors, and chief financial officers of large corporations. You are *not* hopeless in matters of money. You are probably just inexperienced and fearful. As you work through the Financial Plan section, you will gain skills that will replace your despair with hope and lay the foundation for a solid financial future.

The Dangers of Emotional Spending

> *Whoever said money can't buy happiness, simply didn't know where to go shopping.*
>
> —*Bo Derek*

Now that you understand your fears about money and all the accompanying emotions, it's time to examine how spending money impacts your feelings. If you spend money to alter your feelings, mask your feelings, or avoid dealing with your feelings, you are likely engaging in the dangerous habit of emotional spending.

It starts out innocently enough. You're feeling down and getting a mani/pedi cheers you up. Purchases have the power to make us feel sexy (stilettos), organized (colorful filing system), comfortable (Egyptian cotton robe), powerful (personal training sessions with celebrity fitness trainer), skinny (spray tan and seaweed cellulite wrap), nurtured (chocolate lava cake), and so much more. The problem with spending to make yourself feel better, is that you begin to use spending like a drug. And just as with drug abuse, there are three dangerous consequences:

- **Tolerance.** Whereas you first used emotional spending sparingly, as your budget allowed, over time you find yourself needing to spend more and more to get the same emotional fix. Think of the alcoholic who builds tolerance to alcohol: pretty soon one drink doesn't cut it anymore. You used to be able to instantly boost your mood with a one-dollar Wet n Wild lipstick, but now you've moved on to the hard stuff—Chanel at thirty bucks a pop. But as anyone who has suffered through morning-after hangovers can attest, the buzz always wears off.
- **Dependence.** Once, you were able to manage your feelings by dealing with them head-on, but as life has gotten

more complicated, you now find yourself craving trips to the mall to quell your difficult emotions. It's so much simpler to ease your sadness by buying a new pair of earrings than to dig in and resolve an argument with your best friend. Treating yourself to the newest iPhone seems like the perfect way to soothe your feelings of humiliation after bombing your presentation at work. Soon, however, you'll find that you have all but lost the ability to deal with your emotions in a healthy way. Just like a junkie looking for her next fix, you can begin to feel anxious and even shaky if you are made to confront tough emotions without your credit card.

- **Disconnected relationships.** If you turn to money when you're feeling down instead of to your friends or family, you will never be fully engaged in those relationships. Healthy relationships are based on mutual dependency and intimacy, which can be pretty scary, especially if you have a tough time dealing with your own feelings. Whereas emotional spending doesn't require you to be emotionally vulnerable, it is ultimately a poor substitute for human connection, and will always leave you feeling empty. If you allow yourself to turn to money instead of your loved ones in times of stress, you will lose both.

To an emotional spender, developing a financial plan can feel like death. A budget takes away your feel-good spending drug, causing you to feel punished, restricted, and anxious. Withdrawal, anyone? In order to deal with your negative feelings, you will be tempted to spend money, but resist the temptation. As with any addiction, it will take time to regain control. Your first step is to make a plan that not only gets you back on financial track but also allows you a little spending leeway so you don't have to go cold turkey.

Financial Plan

You gots to get yo' money right.

—*Chris Rock*

Now that you've got a clearer picture of your emotions about money, you're in a position to gain control of your finances. First things first: Let's identify your Financial Personality and illuminate your Financial Blind Spots. This quiz will reveal the value you place on money and the purpose it serves in your life.

Financial Personality Quiz

1. Money means:
   a. No more worrying.
   b. Fabulous shoes and fun trips.
   c. Security and stability.
   d. Respect and admiration.
   e. Things will always work out.
   f. I can take care of others.
2. At my worst, when it comes to money I
   a. Feel anxious and fearful.
   b. Am impulsive and spend on things that make me happy or bring me pleasure.
   c. Am thrifty and extremely disciplined, rarely spending anything on myself.
   d. Use it to get attention, respect, and admiration.
   e. Avoid thinking or talking about it and hope for the best.
   f. Give it away, even if I can't really afford it.
3. My financial motto is:
   a. "Sure, things are fine right now, but you never know what disaster is right around the corner."

b. "You can't take it with you, so spend it on something that makes you smile."
c. "A penny saved is a penny earned."
d. "Everybody loves the rich girl."
e. "If I don't think about it, it can't get that bad."
f. "It's better to give than to receive."

4. What I have to show financially is:
   a. A fully funded 401(k) and savings account.
   b. A closet full of designer duds and a wall full of photos of me in exotic locales.
   c. A solid investment portfolio.
   d. Fancy car, time-share in Aspen, gorgeous condo in the best neighborhood.
   e. Nothing, unless you count my credit card debt.
   f. Needy friends and family, as well as orphans in third-world countries, who are better off because of my generosity.
5. Your personalized license plate would read:
   a. CAWSHUN
   b. BYITNOW
   c. SAVEMOR
   d. ICANBYU
   e. BLIND2$
   f. GOT2GIV

If you chose mostly ***a***, you are WORRYING WANDA: You are fearful of losing your money, so you never take risks. No matter how much you make, you are always afraid that you will not have enough to pay your bills or save for retirement. Thinking about money makes you feel anxious because you fear the future and never believe that you will be able to provide for yourself. ***Family***: You likely grew up in a family that suffered financial hardship, or a well-to-do family that lost it all through divorce, job loss, or death. *Financial Blind Spots:* Your fear of not having money is getting in the way of enjoying the money you do have. As you create your financial plan, it's especially important for you to keep your eyes open for opportunities to break out of your comfort zone and make your money work for you. If you continue to hold on to your money so tightly, it will never be free to make you more money in interest from wise investments.

If you chose mostly ***b***, you are PLEASURE-SEEKING POLLY: *Save* is a four-letter word to you. You see money as a tool to get the things and experiences you enjoy. You spend your money on things that make you feel good in the moment and don't save, because it lacks the instant gratification you adore. ***Family***: You likely came from a family with easy access to money and you always had the latest and greatest clothes, trips, cars, and the like. Or, on the other end of the spectrum, you might have grown up without any nice things. You always vowed to yourself that you would buy whatever you wanted when you grew up and had your own money. ***Financial Blind Spots***: You are voted the financial type Most Likely to Be in Debt. Because you crave immediate gratification, you resist any type of restriction on your spending. As you create your financial plan, it's especially important for you to start slowly at first so that you aren't tempted to give up the budget altogether and make a run for the nearest Banana Republic or international airport terminal. It will be crucial for you, more so than for the other types, to make sure that your budget includes at least some fun spending money. You'll probably find it easier to cut back on things that other types would take for granted like electricity (you can always wear that new cashmere sweater and keep the thermostat at 50 degrees) just so you don't feel overly restricted in the personal spending arena. When you stick to a budget, you'll find that it's very gratifying to see your debt get smaller and smaller.

If you chose mostly *c*, you are SUSIE SAVER: Unlike Pleasure-Seeking Polly, *save* is your favorite word. Las Vegas is your idea of hell. You clip coupons and would never even consider buying anything at full price. You often miss out on fun activities with your friends because you don't want to spend money on "frivolous fun." You keep a meticulous budget and spend only on necessities, socking a generous portion of your check away in savings, your 401(k), and low-risk investments. You are happiest when gazing at your fat savings account balance. ***Family***: You likely grew up in a home where thriftiness and saving money were a fact of life. Extravagance and luxury were considered wasteful and selfish pursuits. You were raised to feel guilty about spending money and now find that you can't buy anything without feeling stupid, depressed, or ashamed of yourself. ***Financial Blind Spots***: You are great at planning for the future but need some work on living in the present. As you create your financial plan, it is especially important for you to spend some of your money on yourself now instead of hoarding it all for the future. It will be a challenge for you to allow yourself to enjoy spending some of the money you have worked so hard to earn. Whereas most people need to figure out a budget to rein in their spending and figure out a savings plan, you need to budget some money each month for f-u-n.

If you chose mostly ***d***, you are VIP VALERIE. You use money to get respect and maybe even friends. Money creates your wealthy image and makes you feel valuable and sophisticated. You like how it feels when people look at you with admiration as you pick up the tab. You work hard to pay for the compliments you receive on your professionally decorated dream condo or your perfectly polished ensemble straight out of the latest issue of *InStyle* magazine. You relish feeling important and money affords you that feeling. You might earn enough to cover your grand expenditures or you might be going deeper and deeper into debt each month, but regardless of your financial status, you always appear to have it all. ***Family***: Your family was likely one of two extremes: either very image conscious, or poor to the extent that you were judged harshly and looked down upon by your peers. You determined early on that money could buy you respect, friends, and even an inflated sense of self-worth. ***Financial Blind Spots***: Your challenge is to find out who you are apart from your possessions. As you create your financial plan, it is especially important for you to focus on establishing a solid savings and investment schedule. Let's face it, 401(k)s are far from glamorous, so you'll need to muster the discipline to include them in your plan.

If you chose mostly ***e***, you are AVOIDANT ANNIE: You avoid discussing money, rarely look at your bank balance, and barely skim your credit card statements. You pay extra for overdraft protection just to protect yourself from having to keep track of your finances. There's nothing like a big fat cell phone bill to plunge you into the depths of despair and hopelessness. You have learned that if you can avoid thinking and dealing with everything related to money, you feel better—at least for the time being. By now, you might suspect that burying your head in the sand actually creates more problems than it solves, but the thought of figuring out your finances just feels too overwhelming. ***Family***: You likely come from a family in which one or more of your parents were free-spirited and hated to be limited by a budget. In such families, the carefree parent is continually happy until reined in by the financially aware parent, which causes many fights. You learned that avoiding money issues seems to be a happier way to go and budgeting never solves anything anyway. You might also be the product of a parent who was devastated emotionally by finances, becoming depressed. You have seen how money changes people's moods and impacts children when parents can't function due to excessive anxiety or depression related to money. In order to avoid those negative feelings, you avoid the cause of them altogether: money. ***Financial Blind Spots***: To be honest, we are a bit amazed, and very impressed, that you even got this far into this chapter. Good for you! You are well on your way to removing the financial blinders you have worked so hard to keep firmly in place. As you create your financial plan, it is especially important for you to be patient with yourself and take small, manageable steps. Because you tend to feel overwhelmed easily by financial matters, one practical step that may be particularly helpful for you is to find a Money Buddy to help you with your plan. Look for somebody you trust who's good with his or her own money. A peer is better than a parent. Sit down with your Money Buddy at least once a month and work through each step of your financial plan. The friendly support will be comforting and provide necessary accountability so you have a better chance of sticking to the plan.

If you chose mostly *f*, you are GENEROUS GENEVIEVE: You thrive on giving your money and time to charitable causes. You have a big heart and feel that the greatest thing money can buy is the satisfaction you receive from helping others less fortunate than you. Taking care of others is as much second nature as taking care of yourself. You give even when it is painful or you have to sacrifice your own comfort. ***Family***: You likely grew up in a family that modeled giving. Maybe your parents opened their home to travelers and readily shared with people who needed help. You might have memories of many family dinners in which there were unfamiliar faces around the table. On the other hand, you might be the product of a family who was always in need. You help others because you remember the look on your mother's face when someone helped your own family. ***Financial Blind Spots***: You might think that you have nothing to work on in the financial arena. After all, everyone loves a cheerful giver, right? True, but don't forget to give to *yourself*. Think of yourself as a pitcher of water, constantly pouring into other people's glasses; if you allow yourself to become empty, you won't have anything else to give. As you create your financial plan, it is especially important for you to focus on the savings/investment section to ensure that you are taking care of your own financial future.

Now that you are familiar with your financial personality and blind spots, you can begin to construct the financial plan that's best for you. There are endless books, magazines, and Internet articles dedicated to managing your money. We've narrowed down the information overload into three basic areas of money management: Budget, Credit Cards and Debt, and Saving.

Budget

It's clearly a budget. It's got a lot of numbers in it.

—George W. Bush

While your twenties and early thirties is the right time to establish a healthy relationship with the green stuff, now is also the time to treat yourself, discover your personal style, and have some fun before you take on the responsibility of a mortgage and a family. Having a good, realistic budget can help you do it all.

When it comes to budgeting, some of the best advice we've ever received is this: "Don't spend more than you make. A selfish expenditure today equals a personal sacrifice tomorrow." Even if you stop reading right now (please don't), if you put that advice into practice (please do) you will be light-years ahead of most people, financially speaking. It is so simple, yet so many of us struggle to keep our spending in line with our income. If you are determined to keep yourself out of debt and on top of your monthly expenditures, you must keep a budget in order to know exactly where your money is going each month.

This budget is not a magic formula for getting control of your spending. As author William Feather wisely said, "A budget tells us what we can't afford, but it doesn't keep us from buying it." Nor is this budget a ball and chain that will keep you from having any fun. A balanced budget is not merely one in which all your money is accounted for. A balanced budget means your money is allocated in a balanced and realistic way—covering necessities and frivolities, daily grind and weekend fun. A balanced budget maintains the needs of everyday life while providing for expenditures that make you feel alive. When we put it that way, it doesn't sound so bad, does it?

Let's give this budget thing a try, shall we?

The Practically Pain-Free Budget

There are several online budget calculators, but our budget exercise is a little different from the typical ones you've probably seen already. Every budget we've ever seen requires you to keep receipts for two to three months before you even touch the actual budget. While we agree that you have to know where your money is going before you decide how much should go where, we've taken a slightly different approach with our budget exercise. First we want you to get an understanding of where you *think* your money is going. Then we want you to *know* where it is actually going. Estimating how much you spend in each area is revealing. For example, you may estimate that you spend fifty dollars a month on meeting friends for cocktails, but come to find out that you actually spend over double that! The mystery of the disappearing sixty dollars per month has been solved. You may find that your estimate indicates that you should have several hundred dollars left over at the end of each month, yet you find yourself broke. This means that you don't have a realistic handle on how much money you spend on under-the-radar expenses such as lattes, gum, movies, parking fees, greeting cards, iTunes, and the like. Others of you may not have even considered some of the sections before looking at the worksheet: "I forgot that I automatically pay ten dollars/month for my Netflix account." The "Estimated" column of this budget will reveal your spending blind spots.

The next step is to keep all your receipts from stores and ATMs for two months in a row. Then, go back and complete the

"Actual" column with the accurate totals for each month. (Note: If an expense is not a recurring monthly expense, just add up what you spend annually and divide by twelve to get your monthly average, as for a vacation or car insurance.) Go right now to your computer and log on to LastOneDowntheAisle-Wins.com. Click on the Practically Pain-Free Budget and get started.

Rein It In: Here's How

There are only two ways to balance a budget: decrease spending or increase earning. Unless you plan to go out and get a second job or ask for a raise, you've got to figure out how to reduce your spending. Housing expenses, student-loan payments, and health insurance payments are fairly static, but every other area can withstand some cutbacks without too much discomfort. But take note that if your housing costs accounts for more than 30 percent of your income, you will have a tough time making ends meet. Here are a few practically pain-free ways to save some cash. Pick one of the following ideas each week and see how much you can save in just one month:

Coffee: We love our tall, nonfat, sugar-free vanilla latte just as much as the next gal, but do you know that a Starbucks latte costs about a hundred times more than home-brewed coffee? Brew your own and save $25/week, which translates to a whopping $1,300/year! Don't want to give up your espresso habit? How about investing in an espresso maker for home? You can get an excellent quality one for about $200, still saving you more than $1,000 per year.

Cable TV: Dropping premium channels saves an average of $30/month or $360/year. Or drop cable altogether and save $780/year. See chapter 9 for all kinds of ways to use your newfound free time.

Mani/pedi: Save it for a special occasion with the girls or before a big event. Doing your own nails weekly saves up to $1,650/year.

Bottled water: Save the environment while you save money. Save $25–$40 per month on delivered bottled water. The latest filter pitchers from Brita or Pūr work just as well and will cost you a one-time $50 fee.

Clothes: If you must have something for the new season, forgo the name brand and buy knockoffs at places like H&M, Forever 21, Zara, or even Target. The clothes may not last forever, but you'll be on to the next trend by the time they wear out.

Cell phone: Consider using your cell as your only phone and get rid of your landline. Also log on to billshrink.com, and they will analyze one monthly statement for free and recommend the best package for you. You could save up to $40/month. That's a whopping $480 a year!.

Cigarettes: As if you needed another reason to quit smoking, a pack-a-day habit costs you at least $900/year! And that doesn't include the hefty cost of a lung transplant.

Travel: Check airfare trends before you buy a ticket. Log on to farecast.com and type in your destination and travel dates. The site will let you know if the fare is due to go up or down over the next week.

Other helpful ways to get control of your spending:

Go on a cash-only diet: It's harder to part with your hard-earned Benjamins than to whip out a convenient piece of plastic. When you use credit cards, you don't see your bank balance going down and you can remain in denial until your statement arrives in the mail. Spending with only cash will help keep you honest.

Splurge on some things; save on others: Farnoosh Torabi, author of *You're So Money* recommends, "Take your steady out for that $350 dinner after the big promotion. You might just have to eat PB&J for a week to make it happen." If you increase your spending in one category of your budget, you just have to tighten your belt in another area.

Keep track of what you spend each day: Just as dieters keep a daily food diary to track their calorie intake, you need to keep a log of your purchases. Mint.com can also help you track all your purchases each day. The site will even send you texts if you exceed your budget. It's like your very own budget babysitter!

Learn to distinguish needs from wants: Our needs are few: shelter, food, clothing, and transportation. Ask yourself, *Do I really need this item? Can I live without it? Will the less expensive version or current version I already have suffice for now?* Put your wants on a list at the end of your budget and save up for them. Chances are, when you realize how hard you had to work for it, you may decide that it's not such a need after all.

Justifications for Overspending=D.E.B.T.

We want to caution you against three common justifications for engaging in Downright Egregious Budget Transgressions (D.E.B.T.):

"But I can afford it." We recently met a friend for lunch at her law firm in downtown Los Angeles. As we pulled into the parking lot, we noticed a hard-to-miss lineup of Porsches, BMWs, and Mercedes, many of them so new as to not yet have license plates. When we pointed this out to our friend, she told us that most of the newest vehicles actually belonged to the first-year associates. After nineteen years of being students, and for many of them, eating more than their fair share of Top Ramen, these young professionals were collecting paychecks bigger than they had ever imagined. Many of them responded by signing leases on pricey beach apartments, becoming regulars on the Wolfgang Puck restaurant circuit, and trading in their grandmother's hand-me-down Nissan Sentra for a shiny new convertible.

Now, there's nothing wrong in the least about rewarding yourself for years of hard work and accomplishment. The danger lies in the fact that once you become locked into financial commitments such as expensive cars and apartments and you get used to a certain lifestyle, it is really, truly hard to go back. Down the road, if you decide that you don't want to work so many hours, or that you want to transition into working for your favorite nonprofit, it will be nearly impossible to adjust your lifestyle to the extent you'll need to.

Personal Insight from Celeste

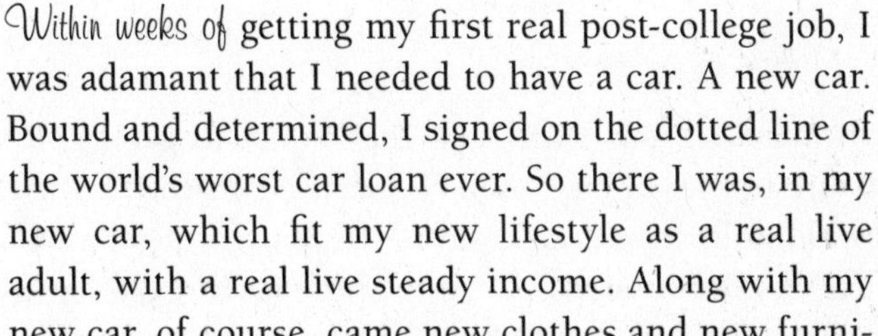

Within weeks of getting my first real post-college job, I was adamant that I needed to have a car. A new car. Bound and determined, I signed on the dotted line of the world's worst car loan ever. So there I was, in my new car, which fit my new lifestyle as a real live adult, with a real live steady income. Along with my new car, of course, came new clothes and new furniture for my apartment. After all, I was a professional with a career and I had to look the part, right? Wrong. As you can imagine, my new outward accoutrements didn't necessarily reflect the reality of my bank account, or my salary. My first few Visa bills made it pretty clear that the things I considered needs were actually nothing more than a bunch of stuff I wanted.

"But I deserve it." You do! You've worked hard! You got the job, or the promotion, or the raise! But do you know what else you deserve? The peace of mind that comes from knowing that you can pay your Visa bill in full when it comes in the mail or that you can join your girlfriends on a last-minute weekend road trip, even if payday isn't until next week. We're not suggesting that you should deprive yourself of enjoying the perks that come from earning your own living, but the "reward" really isn't a reward when it ends up costing you your peace of mind.

"But I need it." Sure, you're going to need some new work clothes and a couch for your apartment. But you don't need everything at once. Focus on one big purchase and save up for it. Enjoy the couch for a while before you start eyeing that matching chair. Go slow. Make do. You'll be glad you did.

Credit Cards and Debt

Debt is the slavery of the free.

—*Publilius Syrus*

Although it may seem that they're out to get you, credit cards are not inherently evil. When used correctly, they can help you build good credit and may even score you a free airline ticket once in a while. There are myriad books out there full of good information about managing credit cards. Here are a few of the most helpful tips we've found:

- Limit the number of credit cards you have. No one needs more than one or two. You should have a Visa, your ATM card, and maybe an American Express card. And never apply for store credit cards. Their interest rates are usually exorbitant.
- Shop around for the best interest rates. Look out for teaser rates that lure you in only to skyrocket in a few

months. Find a card with a low rate that lasts at least a year or a slightly higher rate for the life of the credit card. To help you figure out the best deal for you (higher interest rate/no annual fee or lower interest rate/annual fee/perks) check out the credit card calculator on LeadFusion.com. We know it's tedious, but if you are going to use credit cards, it's imperative that you educate yourself on the fine print.

- Consider the perks, but don't overlook the annual fees associated with airline mile or percentage-back cards. *Money* magazine prints a list of the best credit card deals every month.
- Pay the bill the day it arrives, whenever possible. Early payments raise your credit score, and because interest accrues daily, you'll end up paying less.
- Know your credit score. You're entitled to access your credit report from the three credit reporting agencies—TransUnion, Experian, and Equifax. There are also several websites that will give you immediate access to your score. These sites are full of helpful information about how to improve your score as well.

Five Steps to Digging Yourself Out of the Debt Hole

The average U.S. consumer has *nine thousand* dollars in credit card debt. And in the troubled economy, that average is steadily climbing. The average interest rate for these cards is 14 percent with some as high as 29.8 percent! If you are caught in the debt trap, the absolute first step is to stop using your credit cards. Just put them away and pretend they don't exist. If that doesn't work, get out the kitchen shears and chop, chop.

The second step is to sit down and face the facts. Make a list of the cards and their balances. For each card, list the interest rate and the minimum monthly payment. Step three is to call each credit card and request a lower interest rate. Even a slightly lower rate on one card can equal a significant savings. Tell them you are considering transferring your balance to a lower interest credit card. That will usually do the trick. The fourth step is to create a payoff plan in which you pay off the card with the highest interest rate first, while continuing to make minimum monthly payments on the other cards. Fifth step is to avoid late fees like the plague. Late fees will kill you. How stupid do you feel whenever you have to pay a thirty-five-dollar late fee on your hundred-dollar payment? You can change your payment due date to correspond with your payday so you will have available cash to make that payment on time. Another way to ensure on-time payments is to arrange automatic pay from your checking account.

Saving

> *In the old days a man who saved money was a miser; nowadays he's a wonder.*
>
> —*Author unknown*

Many of you wonder how in the world you can possibly save money when you struggle to make ends meet as it is. In order to get on board with the concept of saving, you need to first figure out your long-term financial goals:

What does financial security mean to you?
When would you like to retire?
If you don't get married first, when would you like to buy a house?
What are your hopes for your financial future? (Note: "Marry a rich man" is not an acceptable answer. Haven't you been paying attention?)

Based on your answers to these questions, make a list of your top five long-term financial goals. Now take the quiz below to determine what steps you are already taking to achieve these goals and make long-term financial security a reality.

Steps to Financial Security

- Y N I have a savings account.
- Y N I contribute to my company's 401(k) plan.
- Y N I have one or more investment accounts.
- Y N I have met with a financial planner.
- Y N I have a plan for retirement.
- Y N I have financial goals.
- Y N I know the difference between a mutual fund, a bond, and a stock investment.

Go back and put a star by all the questions you answered *no* to. Congratulations: You now have your long-term financial security To-Do List.

See? That wasn't so bad. Now that you have a better idea of the role of your family and your feelings in your financial attitudes and a rockin' financial plan, you are ready to get control of your money. When you determine to get smart about money, you are giving yourself a better shot at *not* being part of a couple who fight about money, lie about money, and eventually break up over money. You now see that rather than being an unbearable burden, getting a handle on your finances is actually incredibly freeing. Once you are in control of your finances, you will be free to make a better choice in a spouse, free to look at your bills each month with confidence, free to spend within your budget, free to envision a future of financial security.

Chapter 7

Key #5: Get an Emotionally Stable Life

Manage Your Emotions

> *Little emotions are the great captains of our lives and we obey them without realizing it.*
>
> *—Vincent van Gogh*

Emotions are the passions that drive our lives. They keep life from getting boring, but they can also complicate everything if we don't figure out how to keep them in check. Taking the time now to untangle the confusing web of your emotions will have a huge positive impact on your future marriage and family. Getting a handle on your emotional life will allow you to experience your feelings without fear of harming relationships, losing control, or hurting the people you love. You'll be able to give and receive love without reservation. Doesn't that sound great?

Everybody wants to feel the positive emotions: happiness, contentment, joy, delight. It's human nature to avoid the negative ones: anger, fear, sadness, guilt. Many of us were taught to stuff our emotions, to view certain feelings as good and others as bad or unacceptable. But the truth is, the only thing that makes an emotion bad is if we respond to it by acting badly. If you let yourself honestly experience your feelings, while keeping your actions in check, you can learn a lot about yourself and what's important to you. The way we experience our emotions will literally determine the quality of our lives. Pretty heavy, right?

So Many Emotions, So Little Time

Underline the words that describe how you feel right now.

Irritable Optimistic Angry Easygoing Content Responsive Drained Energized Adventurous Vain Tired Affectionate Sulky Kindhearted Unsuccessful Envious Excitable Threatened Bored Restless Disorganized Pessimistic Frumpy Grateful Rushed Lighthearted Relaxed Overextended Inefficient Uncoordinated Weary Impulsive Lusty Depressed Pouty Persuasive Carefree Worthless Frustrated Nervous Inhibited Gracious Creative Self-conscious Indecisive Apathetic Anxious Argumentative Vengeful Disillusioned Tense Overwhelmed Empty Fulfilled Worried Joyful Fearful Moody Grumpy Sociable Humiliated Ashamed Driven Scared Guilty Needy Disappointed Aimless Powerful Stressed Panicky Frazzled Embarrassed Unstable Sad Mad Happy Motivated Reserved Calm Shy

Now go back and circle the feelings you would most like to experience. We've all heard messages from childhood leading us to believe that expressions of emotion are bad and should be avoided. "Big girls/boys don't cry." "Calm down, it's not that bad." "Stop crying or I'll give you something to cry about." Stuff it, deny it, suck it up. We were trained to keep our emotions under control, lest they make a fool of us. But attempts to control emotions by denying them only lead to increased frustration. The thing about emotions is that they are like water in a balloon—if you squeeze one end of the balloon, the water will just flow to the other end. When you deny your anger, for example, you might notice that your stomach hurts and that you're irritable with a stranger. Your anger didn't go away; it just came out someplace else. Sometimes these misplaced emotions disguise themselves. You're upset with your roommate for bouncing a rent check, but instead of expressing your anger directly to her, you later make a sarcastic comment about her "astute money-management skills" in front of her friends. Until you can readily identify and manage your emotions, you are at their mercy and they will wreak havoc in your life and relationships.

There are many ways your emotions can be destructive when you let them get out of control. Once you can begin to see clearly where your emotional sensitivities lie, you can start figuring out how to deal with these emotional fireballs in a healthy, nondestructive way. And once you've got a better handle on them, you can prevent these emotional reactions from harming or even ruining your relationships. If you think about it (and if you're honest), your out-of-control emotions may have already been the culprit in previous breakups, fights, and broken friendships. That's normal, but thankfully, it's preventable. You never have to be a victim of your emotions. Take charge, learn from them, and let them enhance your life. When you get a handle on your emotions, they can bring you joy, make you more compassionate, and help you forgive both yourself and others.

The Five Emotional Pitfalls

We've identified five of the most common Emotional Pitfalls: anger, anxiety, insecurity, depression, and fear of failure. Even if you consider yourself to be emotionally stable and even-tempered, you should be able to identify yourself in *each* of these areas. Take the true/false quiz at the beginning of each section to begin to recognize ways in which your emotions impact your daily life.

Emotional Pitfall #1 Anger (*aka*: resentment, bitterness, vengefulness, sarcasm, entitlement, aggression, intolerance, impatience)

> *Holding on to anger is like grasping a hot coal with the intent of throwing it at someone else; you are the one who gets burned.*
>
> *—Buddha*

- T F I sometimes say things in the heat of an argument that I regret later.
- T F I usually keep my mouth shut even if I'm upset.
- T F I am often irritated, annoyed, or bugged.
- T F I often feel uncomfortable expressing my anger.
- T F I tell it like it is, even if it means yelling or screaming.

MONICA

"My father was pretty mean to me and my brother. Whenever I would do something wrong, he would fly off the handle and go on and on about how useless I was and how I would never amount to anything. As I got older, I just tried to stay out of his way. I learned from a young age that anger was scary, mean, and dangerous. I avoided conflict like the plague because I never wanted to make anyone mad. I swore I'd never marry a man like my dad. By nineteen, I was desperate to get out of his house and away from him, so I made the worst mistake of my life and got married. And guess who my husband was exactly like? That's right, my dad. It's taken me ten years and a divorce to learn that you can be angry but not act out of control. I always thought there were two choices when you were angry: You could either shove it down or you could explode. Since my divorce (and after a lot of therapy), I now know that when you express anger in the *right* way, it's *not* scary and can actually help two people understand each other better."

How Will I Recognize My Anger?

Anger is a normal, even healthy emotion, but the way we choose to express or suppress it can cause huge problems. Many people assume the only way to express anger is through yelling or screaming. But there are actually three ways that people deal with anger: They express it aggressively, suppress it, or assertively communicate it.

Letting it all out: People who express their anger aggressively yell, cuss, humiliate, and are basically out of control. They don't consider the consequences of their words or actions. They lack self-control and simply express their unbridled emotions as they experience them. Aggressive expressions of anger include out-of-control rage and physical or verbal violence. Aggression is disrespectful of others and the most destructive way of expressing anger.

Keeping it all in: People who suppress their anger ignore their anger and deny it, even to themselves. If you were taught that all verbal expression of anger was wrong, keeping your anger inside might seem like the best way to deal with it. But when anger isn't recognized and expressed, it either turns inward, causing depression or physical illness, or seeps out in the form of sarcasm or misplaced anger toward an undeserving person.

Doing it the right way: People who manage their anger well express it assertively by acknowledging their feelings and then communicating their frustrations respectfully. They can calm themselves down enough to see clearly, then make their needs known without harming others. This is the healthiest way of dealing with anger.

What Does My Anger Tell Me about Myself?

Anger can be very revealing. Because it's often a gut reaction, our anger is the voice of our unfiltered emotions. If you are willing to look deeper at your anger, you stand to gain invaluable insight into your true self. As psychiatrist Carl Jung taught, "Everything that irritates us about others can lead to an understanding of ourselves."

One of the first things you can learn from your anger is what messages you received as a child. People who are easily angered usually come from families that were full of chaos and poor communication. If one of your parents expressed his or her anger aggressively, you probably learned to mimic that behavior or to fear anger so much that you end up suppressing it altogether. On the other hand, your parents might have been the suppressive types who taught you that it was okay to feel sad, happy, or anxious, but never okay to feel angry.

We all have specific things that trigger our anger. These "hot buttons" give us important insight into our sensitivities. Are you irritated when your friend keeps you waiting? You're triggered by feeling disrespected. Are you annoyed by people who question your different political viewpoints? You're triggered by feeling judged. Are you upset when you hear someone being rude to a store clerk? You're triggered by injustice.

If your anger is out of proportion to the situation, it's an indication that you have suppressed anger from the past. You might have a pattern of suppressing your anger until the pressure and frustration build up to an intolerable level. Think of the saying, *It was the straw that broke the camel's back.* If you have ignored all the annoying straws building up, eventually it will take only a small incident to make you snap into a rage.

If you are easily annoyed, it might tell you that you are experiencing what we call the Princess Complex. Are you angered when you have to wait in line for more than two or three minutes? Do you often feel as though you deserve to be treated better? Are you easily frustrated by "stupid" people? Do you get mad when people don't take your advice or value your opinions? Your sense of entitlement may be at the root of your anger. You take pride in getting what you want because after all, you deserve it. A woman with the Princess Complex was probably spoiled as child and taught to believe that the world revolves around her. Woe to anyone who threatens to dislodge her tiara!

What Does My Anger Look Like in Friendships?

You lose friends after exploding at them when things don't go your way. You find yourself constantly apologizing for fights and trying to justify your behavior. You are easily irritated, and your anger usually escalates into arguments that you readily blame on your friend. If suppressing anger is more your style, you might find yourself slowly building up resentment toward your friends until the relationships fade away.

What Does It Look Like at Work?

You often feel like you're treated unfairly. You are frequently annoyed by coworkers. You often complain that you aren't paid enough or appreciated for the work you do. You are resentful when a coworker is acknowledged for her good work.

You are impatient with customers and have difficulty maintaining a professional tone. You may have even lost a job because you lost your temper. If you are angry at a coworker for arriving late to your meeting, you might become too distracted by your suppressed anger to maintain your focus on your presentation.

What Will It Look Like in Marriage?

If you are explosively angry, you will have frequent intense conflicts with your husband. You don't fight fair. Yelling, name-calling, and profanity are your verbal weapons of choice. You justify being mean to him because, after all, it's *his* fault for making you so mad. If you are the suppressing type, your unexpressed anger will grow, along with your resentment. You will inevitably grow more and more emotionally distant from him. When he asks you "What's wrong?" you'll lie through clenched teeth, "Nothing!"

One of the biggest factors in divorce is not how *often* you fight, but *how* you fight. If you call your partner names, humiliate him, and use profanity when you are angry at him, statistics forecast that you are headed for divorce court. Of course, all married couples get angry with each other from time to time, and there's no doubt that it's better to express your anger than to hide it or ignore it. But if you don't learn to channel your anger into appropriate conflict resolution, your marriage will be doomed. In fact, a couple's ability to resolve conflict in a healthy way is the number one predictor that the marriage will succeed. It's that important.

How Can I Keep My Anger in Check?

You can't get rid of anger altogether; nor should you try. Anger is our best indicator that we are being taken advantage of, manipulated, or disrespected. You can't control the fact that people will let you down and the world will be full of frustrations and disappointments, but you *can* change the way you react to these unavoidable situations.

Relax. When you feel the wave of anger coming on, try some relaxation techniques such as deep breathing, counting to twenty, or picturing a tranquil setting.

Talk to yourself. When you are angry, you usually think in drastic terms: *What a freakin' idiot! Everything's ruined! I'll never be able to recover from this!* Replace the extreme language with more realistic assessments of the situation: *This is frustrating, but I can fix it. Getting upset isn't going to help anyway.*

Ask for it. Suppressors stew in their anger and expect others to read their minds. Anger expressers tend to make demands rather than requests. Be clear about your desires, but state them with respect: *Please pay the electric bill on time from now on* rather than, *You're so irresponsible! Why can't you get your act together?*

Listen up. The best thing to do in a heated argument is to stop, listen, and consider the other person's position. Escalating a conflict doesn't do anybody any good. It's natural to get defensive in an argument, but try to listen carefully to the other person's perspective on the conflict.

Give yourself a break. If an argument is quickly spinning out of control, take a time-out. Let the person know you need some time to cool off and set a time when you will both return to continue a clearheaded discussion.

Do I Need Therapy?

If your anger feels out of control and it's negatively impacting your relationships or work, it might be time to seek professional help. If you have ever been violent or flown into a serious rage, you definitely could benefit from therapy. A licensed mental health professional can help you understand and manage your anger. You may also consider seeking out an anger-management group.

Emotional Pitfall #2 Anxiety (*aka* nervousness, worry, edginess, sleeplessness)

What, me worry?

—Alfred E. Neuman (Mad *magazine)*

T F I worry a lot.
T F I feel stressed out.
T F I'm under a lot of pressure at work.
T F My friends often tell me I need to relax.
T F I obsess over things.

LYNNE

"I've been married for four years and I would have to say that the biggest issue in our marriage is my stress level. I'm stressed out all the time. I worry about work, so I end up staying late at the office a lot. My husband, Dan, calls me a workaholic and doesn't understand why I can't relax and spend time with him. It's not that I love to work, I'm just terrified of what will happen if I fail to meet the demands of my job. If I'm honest, I guess I've always been a worrier. I worry that my husband will fall out of love with me. I worry that I will get cancer. I'm worried that we won't be able to have kids when we start to try. I'm worried that people will think I'm a bad neighbor or friend. I know I'm a worrywart, but I can't help it. Dan is always telling me to loosen up and have some fun and that I'm starting to stress him out, too. I'm worried that if I don't get a handle on my anxiety, he will leave me for someone more fun and easygoing."

How Will I Recognize My Anxiety?

Anxiety ranges from general worry and nervousness to extreme anxiety and debilitating panic attacks. You can usually identify anxiety by its physical symptoms: heart palpitations, tense muscles, headache, butterflies in the stomach, trembling hands, nausea, sweaty palms, and difficulty sleeping.

Anxiety can tie you up in knots inside. Worriers tend to imagine the worst and dwell on the bad things that *might* happen. You let fear worm its way into your thoughts and grow roots, developing into full-blown worry. Your tendency to worry doesn't usually discriminate between the serious and the trivial. You may worry just as much about whether you'll be on time to a movie as you do about whether you're going to get that raise at work.

If you let anxiety go unchecked for too long, the very outcome you fear becomes reality—sort of like self-hypnosis. Take, for example, the dialogue that might go on in your head before going out with someone you really like. *What if he doesn't like me? I just know he won't like me. Why should he like me? He won't.* If you tell yourself that over and over, you'll psych yourself out to the point that you won't be yourself during the date, proving yourself right . . . he won't like you! Because you don't believe that he'll like you, you won't end up being likable.

What Does My Anxiety Tell Me about Myself?

Anxiety tells you that you're pressuring yourself to be perfect, keep up an image, or be something you know you are not. When your outside doesn't reflect your true self, you fear you won't be able to keep up the pretense and that eventually your real, imperfect self will come out. For example, you are nervous that your apartment won't be spotless when your friends come over, ruining their image of you as the perfect hostess.

When you lack confidence in your ability to handle unexpected situations, you develop fears about the future. You feel anxious about the possibility of being called on to speak in meetings because you don't feel confident in your ability to think on your feet.

Your tendencies to worry may have originated in your

family. If your mother was a worrier, you learned to obsess about the future rather than to plan for it. Her worry shaped your feelings about the world and led you to believe it was a dangerous place. She spent a great deal of energy worrying about what *might* happen, even though her fears rarely came true. These fears limited your experiences because she discouraged you from taking risks.

What Does My Anxiety Look Like in Friendships?

Your friends constantly tell you to mellow out, and you rely on them to keep you calm. Eventually, you will begin to stress them out, too. You cancel fun events at the last minute and don't hang out with them very often, because you are too stressed out. When you finally make time for them, you take up most of the evening talking about your stress and worry.

What Does It Look Like at Work?

You stress so much about doing a good job that you stay up late and frequently work nights and weekends. You are driven by worry that if you don't get something done perfectly, you will be viewed as a substandard employee. Initially, your anxiety about work might actually result in getting a lot of affirmation from bosses for doing such great work. Eventually, however, your stress will catch up with you as you become overextended and unable to maintain the pace you have set for yourself. You will become exhausted, and the quality of your work will begin to decline, making your fear come true.

What Will It Look Like in Marriage?

You will have a tough time letting go enough to relax and enjoy your husband's company. He'll probably feel neglected or unimportant due to your obsessive preoccupation with perfection and the fact that no matter how much he tries to reassure you, you can't shake the worrying! If you allow the pattern of worry to take hold now, once you have children, that worrier mentality will worsen. Worrying moms create another generation of fearful, worrying children, and so the cycle continues.

How Can I Keep My Anxiety in Check?

Worry can actually be beneficial if it motivates you to prepare for the future. It's not helpful to spend your energy obsessing over worries about the future, however. Instead, channel your worry into action. After seeing several news stories about fires in people's homes, Jan began to worry that her own apartment would catch fire. She often lay awake in bed worrying that the old wiring would ignite. Her fears didn't let up until she finally decided to take action. Jan installed a new smoke detector, put a fire extinguisher in her kitchen, placed all her important documents and photos in a fireproof box, and made an evacuation plan. Jan's anxiety was averted and her restful nights returned. If you are stuck in a rut of worry, ask yourself these questions:

Worthless or Worthy Worry?

What's the absolute worst that can happen?
Is this a logical fear?
What can I accomplish by worrying?
Will this still cause me to worry a year from now? Five years from now?
Is there anything I can do about the situation, or is it out of my control?

After you ask yourself those questions, figure out which of four categories your problem falls into:

Is this problem Significant or Insignificant? Will it have a major impact on the course of my life or not?

Is this problem Controllable or Uncontrollable? Can I take reasonable steps to change it or not?

SIGNIFICANT

UNCONTROLLABLE	CONTROLLABLE
Already turned in graduate school application. *"I did my best, nothing to do now but wait."*	Big interview coming up *"I can take time to prepare well."*
I have a gnarly zit on my chin. *"Guess I just have to wait this one out."*	I don't have shoes to match my dress and can't afford to buy new ones. *"I can borrow some from my roommate."*

INSIGNIFICANT

Write down some of your own worries. Which category does each one belong in? Now write your thought-out, worry-free response to each.

If your worry is **Insignificant and Controllable**: Sure, you can spend hours online searching for the perfect mango salsa to complement your jerk chicken, but is it really worth it? Make sure that the insignificant problem warrants the time you put into it.

If your worry is **Insignificant and Uncontrollable**: Your time and energy are way too valuable. Learn to let these things go.

If your worry is **Significant and Controllable**: It makes

sense that you would be concerned about the things in this category. The good news is that your action steps can have an impact on the outcome. Make a solid plan of attack so that you can feel confident in your ability to handle this important problem. List at least three steps you can take to avert your anxiety.

1. ______________________________________.
2. ______________________________________.
3. ______________________________________.

If your worry is **Significant and Uncontrollable**: First, make sure that the problem actually fits in this category. You almost always have some control over the outcome of a problem. There's a difference between convincing yourself that your efforts won't make a difference and a situation that is truly out of your control. If the problem does belong in this box, worry is a poor use of your time and energy. Try an Anxiety Buster instead.

Surefire Anxiety Busters

Sing. It's hard to worry or feel stressed out when you are belting out "I'm bringing sexy back!" at the top of your lungs. You might want to be sure that you are the only one in the apartment or car with the windows rolled up so you don't *worry* about anybody else judging your ability to carry a tune.

Pet a dog. Many people report that their stress melts away when stroking the soft fur of a pet. Note: This tip will backfire if you have pet allergies.

Get a massage. Like you need an excuse! Everyone knows that massage literally rubs the tension from your body, but too often we don't partake, because we get too stressed out about spending money, or taking time for ourselves. Hey, this is what turned you into this stressed-out mess in the first place. Get to a masseuse guilt-free! Note: If you are concerned about the cost, check out chiropractors in your area who offer therapeutic massage—it's often covered under health insurance plans.

Change your perspective. Literally. Lie down on the floor and look up at the ceiling. Lie on the grass and gaze up at the clouds or stars. Concentrate on breathing and appreciating your senses. What do you see? Smell? Hear? Feel?

Hug it out. Hug yourself. You heard us. Hug yourself. Don't feel silly about it, either. Hugs are physiologically soothing and reduce your stress levels measurably. Hugs from people you know are good, too, but not if it stresses you out to ask for one.

Do some gardening. Or another mindless but enjoyable chore. Even folding clothes or washing dishes by hand can regulate your breathing and allow your busy mind to flow freely.

Take a warm bath. There is something so calming about being immersed in warm water. It can also provide you with a great chance to clear your thoughts and gain some perspective. As author Edmund Wilson said, "I have had more uplifting thoughts soaking in comfortable baths than I have ever had in any cathedral."

Do I Need Therapy?

If you are experiencing anxiety that is distressing to you and negatively impacting your work, relationships, or general ability to function, you may be suffering from generalized anxiety disorder. The symptoms of GAD are excessive anxiety or worry on most days for the past six months with at least three of the following:

- Restlessness or feeling "on edge"
- Fatigue
- Difficulty concentrating or mind going blank
- Irritability

- Muscle tension
- Sleep disturbance (difficulty falling or staying asleep, or restless unsatisfying sleep)

A licensed therapist will diagnose the disorder and help you learn to manage it with therapy and possibly medication. You should also seek therapy if you have panic attacks or specific phobias (irrational fears about anything from spiders to going outside to crossing bridges).

Emotional Pitfall #3 Insecurity (*aka* clinginess, dependence, neediness, suspicion)

The task we must set for ourselves is not to feel secure, but to be able to tolerate insecurity.

—*Erich Fromm*

T F I don't like to be alone.
T F If I feel sad, I call someone right away to take my mind off it.
T F I have been called clingy, needy, or insecure.
T F I frequently rely on others to make me feel happy or better about myself.
T F When I have a boyfriend, I want to spend most of my time with him.

GIA

"My parents weren't exactly the nurturing type. They were both high-level researchers and worked long hours at the university. I was an only child, so I was alone a lot. I hated being by myself and would try anything I could think of to get them to come home to be with me. I would fake being sick or make up a story about something upsetting that had happened at school. Eventually, I started staying over at different friends' houses to keep from feeling lonely. I joined a sorority as soon as I got to college so I would never be alone. I met Ron my second year, and we got married soon after graduation. We spent all of our time together and I even got a job at his work so I could be near him during the day. It was great for a while, but when he started wanting to hang out with his college friends for Guys Night Out once a week, I kinda lost it. I felt rejected. Why would he rather be with a bunch of guys than with me, whom he's supposed to love? We fight about it all the time and I always end up in tears. He keeps calling me clingy and insists that he needs his 'space.' Space? If he would rather not be around me, I wish he would just come out and say that he wants a divorce. He probably just wants his 'space' so he can look for someone better."

How Will I Recognize My Insecurity?

Insecurity is the emotion that tells you that you crave more emotional support than you are getting. We all feel needy and insecure at times, but when we become *overly* dependent on others to provide our sense of self, or to make us feel okay, our neediness is out of control.

When your insecurity remains unchecked, you never feel satisfied with the amount of attention, affection, admiration, appreciation, or approval you receive from people close to you. This intense desire for more emotional support drives you to cling to people and become uneasy when their attention is turned away from you.

While it is healthy and normal to depend on the people we love, clinginess can quickly destroy a relationship. Couples should lean on each other for support and companionship, not cling to each other out of fear of falling apart without the partner's support. Dependency can easily turn into a vicious cycle:

You don't feel good enough on your own, so you depend on someone else to make you feel worthy. → You demand more of the person's time and emotional connection. → They feel suffocated and begin to pull away, causing you to feel more needy and insecure, thus making you cling more tightly.

Your insecurity becomes a self-fulfilling prophecy. Your feelings of unworthiness are confirmed. This cycle is a recipe for a disaster in any relationship, whether friendship or marriage. You will inevitably be let down and the other person will end up resenting you, feeling smothered, and wanting to run far, far away from you.

So what is the right balance of dependence and self-sufficiency in a relationship? As Robert Bornstein, a psychology professor at Adelphi University, says: "Healthy dependency is the ability to ask for help without feeling helpless." There are three levels of dependence in relationships:

Total Dependence: When you are a baby, you are completely dependent on your parents for survival. If they don't feed you, you will starve. If they don't hug you, you won't feel secure. Childhood is the *only* time in your life when complete dependence is healthy.

Independence: When you grow into young adulthood, you should become more independent from your parents. You reach a point where you can provide for yourself and make your own decisions. You're able to take care of yourself and choose to do it all on your own.

Interdependence: This is the ideal level of dependence for healthy relationships. You are capable of meeting your own needs, but you *choose* to let someone else meet some of them. This allows the people you care about to be involved in your life and communicates to them that you trust them enough to count on them.

What Does My Insecurity Tell Me about Myself?

You doubt that you're worthy of getting your needs met and you fear abandonment. You may have been raised with emotionally distant parents who never seemed to have enough time for you. Or, maybe your parents were physically present, but emotionally unexpressive and checked out. It may also be that you didn't receive enough affirmation from your parents and now tend to look to other people to fill the emotional void that was created when you were younger. Perhaps you grew up in a chaotic household. Maybe your parents fought a lot or divorced; maybe one of them was an alcoholic, or they struggled with financial instability. As a result of the chaos, you never got your emotional needs for stability met and never felt like you had solid emotional footing. It follows that as you get older, you carry within you a sense of instability and search for something or someone to make you feel secure.

What Does My Insecurity Look Like in Friendships?

You often wonder if your friend is closer to someone else than you. You are jealous of her other friends. You're more focused on what you get out of the relationship than what you give. You feel like she never spends enough time with you. You constantly compare yourself with others and usually feel like you come up short. You're often jealous of what others have and what they've accomplished.

What Does It Look Like at Work?

You are always seeking affirmation from your boss and coworkers. You are jealous of others and easily threatened by their successes. You seek credit for an accomplishment even though someone else deserves it. You're petty about who's doing what; always insisting upon equal distribution of tasks. Out of your insecurity, you *demand* respect rather than trusting yourself enough to earn it. You are readily threatened by alliances—if you see a coworker going to lunch with the boss, it sends you into a tailspin, obsessing about why your boss didn't invite you instead.

What Will It Look Like in Marriage?

You are needy, jealous, and suspicious. You need your poor husband's constant approval of your beauty, intelligence, personality, thighs, and so on. But no matter how much he affirms you, you still don't believe him. If he wants to watch the game, you assume it's because he doesn't find you interesting anymore. Eventually, he will begin to feel stifled and suffocated by your overwhelming need to be close to him. You text and call him frequently throughout the day and take it personally when he doesn't take your calls during an important meeting. You worry a lot that he will cheat on you. Your suspicions might culminate in you snooping through his things and checking up on him when he is away.

How Can I Keep My Insecurity in Check?

Study those you envy. Insecurity breeds envy. If you find yourself envious of others, look closely at what you envy, because it will give you a window into your desires for yourself. Learn from the people you envy. If you envy your friend's ability to put together a rockin' outfit, rather than feeling bad about your own sense of style, ask her to take you shopping.

Put away your score card. Take note of how often you compare yourself unfavorably with others. Stop yourself midthought and replace the comparison with an affirmation. Instead of, *She is so much smarter than me,* remind yourself, *I am proud that I did a great job on my presentation at work.*

Be alone. Make a list of activities you would ordinarily never consider doing by yourself. Go to a movie. Make yourself a nice dinner. Grab a book and go to a coffee shop. Choose one and try it this week. You'll see that you are capable of being alone and that it won't kill you. You may surprise yourself and find that you actually enjoy some out-and-about alone time.

Abandon all-or-nothing thinking. Insecurity causes us to think in extremes. For example: *If my boyfriend wants to spend time with the guys, it means he doesn't love me anymore.* Challenge that thought like this: *Where is the evidence that he doesn't love me? Am I catastrophizing* (jumping to the worst possible conclusion)? Then restructure the thought into a more reasonable, realistic statement, like this: *I can't possibly provide everything he needs, so it's healthy for him to be with the boys for a while.*

Do I Need Therapy?

If your neediness feels out of control and you have no idea where the bottomless pit of your emotional hunger originated, you should seek professional help. Your clinginess and fear of abandonment will strangle your future marriage and scare away any healthy man you try to cling to. You'll also miss out on having quality friendships. If you are the child of an alcoholic, you should definitely seek help from a therapist or Al-Anon group (a 12-step program for family members of addicts).

Emotional Pitfall #4: Depression (*aka* sadness, gloom, pessimism, hopelessness, the blues, melancholy)

> *It is a time when one's spirit is subdued and sad, one knows not why; when the past seems a storm-swept desolation, life a vanity and a burden, and the future but a way to death.*
>
> —*Mark Twain*

T F I often feel sad.

T F When I feel down, I pretty much just want to do nothing.

T F I'm disappointed with some major aspects of my life.

T F When things go badly for me, I have a tough time getting myself out of a funk.

T F I am a cynical, negative, or melancholy person.

DEBRA

"I was thrilled when I started dating Rob because he always made me feel so happy. When I felt down, he'd make me laugh, and before I knew it I was actually having fun. I felt like a different person with him. I smiled a lot more and was open to new experiences. I couldn't picture living without him, because he made everything better. Life felt perfect for the first year of our marriage; but after that, I began to slowly slip into my old habits of negativity. Rob complained that I should stop expecting *him* to be responsible for making me happy. I felt let down, and he felt like I wasn't the woman he had married. At the end of our divorce, I started to realize that I had been unfair to Rob—that my happiness is my *own* responsibility. It's such a shame that we couldn't have figured this out earlier. I knew I had these tendencies toward depression before we got married, but I think I believed that Rob was sort of my 'human Prozac.'"

How Will I Recognize My Depression?

Everybody experiences sadness at different times in their lives. Life is full of disappointments, letdowns, and unmet expectations. Our natural reaction to these life events is sadness. Some events call for fleeting frowns (no parking spaces close to the grocery store), others bring tears (you can't afford to come home for Thanksgiving this year), and still others bring longer-lasting sorrow (your favorite uncle dies).

Sadness is an uncomfortable emotion but a necessary part of our humanness. Our sadness illustrates our vulnerability and touches the very core of our beings. Many of us try to mask our sorrow and refuse to cry in front of others. But think of a time when tears (yours or someone else's) brought you closer to a friend. Sadness is such a raw emotion that when someone shares their tears with you, it bonds you with them in a unique way.

While sadness is a normal reaction to a painful event, depression is a more serious negative experience of the world. You lose interest in the things that once were important to you and withdraw from your relationships. When you shut down emotionally, you can't deal with the painful situation that caused you to pull into your protective shell in the first place. The irony here is that in order to leave depression behind, you must face the pain. It can be tempting to just lie in bed and pull the covers over your head, but the pain will still be there when you come out.

What Does My Depression Tell Me about Myself?

The things that make you sad illuminate your vulnerabilities. What kinds of movies or stories make you the saddest? Loss? Abandonment? Scenes depicting reconciliation between mother and daughter? Maybe you miss your mom or missed out on an ideal childhood and you're grieving that loss now.

What does *your* sadness tell you? What makes you sad? Have you allowed yourself the time to cry, to grieve, and to feel the pain? Sadness, like other emotions, will sneak out in other areas if you don't allow yourself to feel it. You might think you are in control of your emotions by holding your tears at bay, but the reality is that your sadness will manifest itself in other ways. For instance, you might begin to have trouble sleeping, difficulty concentrating, or lose your appetite. If you have shoved the sadness down, you might not even be aware of the connection between the physical symptoms and the original event that caused your sorrow.

The way you manage your sadness also gives insight to how you were raised. Some parents simply won't tolerate angry outbursts from their children, but will accept tears and melancholy as normal, giving their tearful children extra attention. Some women grew up in homes with depressed mothers or fathers and learned that life is inevitably depressing. Others, who grew up with mothers and fathers who never let the children see

Personal Insight from Shannon

The other day, I was in a restaurant and looked up to see a mom and her young daughter engaged in conversation over lunch. I heard the little girl giggle with her mom and was surprised to find myself tearing up. When I started thinking about my reaction, I realized that I am still grieving the loss of my mother's health and harboring uncried tears for her ordeal. Let me explain.

My mother was diagnosed with breast cancer in March of last year, had a double mastectomy in May, and began intensive chemotherapy treatments in June. It all happened so fast that I didn't really get a chance to deal with my feelings about the illness. My mom is by far the strongest, healthiest, most capable person I know. When she got sick, it rocked my perception of the whole world. If my mother could get cancer, anything could happen.

I drove to be with her during many of her various doctor appointments, stayed with her before and after the surgery, and sat with her while the chemo trickled into her veins. I shopped with her and helped her pick out the perfect wig in preparation for the inevitable day that chemo made her lose all her hair. I focused on doing things with her and for her to keep my mind off my fear of losing her.

I am delighted to report that she is now cancer-free and returned to teaching shortly after completing her chemotherapy. My mom's a survivor (she'll probably even outlive me), and yet I am crying as I write this. Sadness doesn't just disappear when a situation gets better.

them cry, now equate tears with weakness. Maybe you heard your parents say things like, "Cheer up! There's nothing to be sad about," so now you don't trust your own assessment of what is worthy of sadness.

Take some time right now to figure out what your sadness tells you about yourself and the messages you received as you were growing up.

My Depression Inventory

How did your mother show sadness? Did you ever see her cry?
How did your father show sadness? Did you ever see him cry?
How did your parents respond to you when you cried?
How do you feel when you see someone cry?
How often do you cry?
Do you cry at the drop of a hat?
Are you keeping emotions stuffed inside for fear of letting them out?
What is your biggest fear in letting your sadness show?
Do you wish you could express your sadness more often, or do you wish you could rein it in?
Do you lose sleep or sleep too much when you are sad?
Do you lose your appetite or eat to make yourself feel better?

Now that you have some insight into your sadness, let's examine how depression can affect your life if you don't keep it in check.

What Does My Depression Look Like in Friendships?

Depression is debilitating in friendship. Having a depressed friend can be emotionally draining. You're basically a downer. You don't want to go out because nothing sounds like fun. You rely on your friends to boost your mood. They will soon come to resent having to do a song and dance to cheer you up. On the other hand, if you are depressed but fail to let your sadness show, you're not being honest enough to connect with friends in an authentic way.

What Does It Look Like at Work?

Depression can easily hinder your work performance because it prevents you from feeling passionate about anything. You might be chronically late for work because you just don't feel like getting out of bed in the morning. Your lack of interest and energy translates into shoddy work, and your sense of worthlessness makes effort pointless. Bosses tend to have little patience for unchecked depression when it takes a toll on your productivity. Losing your job only serves to further the depression.

What Will It Look Like in Marriage?

If you don't get a handle on your depression, you run the risk of choosing a husband because he's really good at cheering you up. Your husband will likely take your depression personally, especially early in the marriage when he feels like it's his responsibility to make his bride happy. When you both realize that this is an impossible task, you will wind up resenting each other. As with your friends, you won't have the energy to go out and enjoy life. Because depression lowers your libido, sex is not high on your list of priorities, which will create even more problems in the marriage.

How Can I Keep My Depression in Check?

Take action. Depression begets depression. When you wallow in sadness, you feel more tired and sluggish, and your brain slows down production of dopamine, the "feel-good hormone." The fastest way to counteract this depression cycle is to get moving. Even if you don't feel like getting out of bed, let alone getting dressed and going for a walk, that's exactly what will help you feel better. It will get the blood pumping, clear your head, and enable your body to produce the hormones needed to get you out of your funk.

See your doctor. Thyroid disorders, iron deficiencies, and hormone imbalances are often at the root of depression. Get to your doctor for a complete blood workup. Tell her all your symptoms, especially related to sleep, eating, and lack of energy.

Steer clear of drugs and alcohol. Depressed people are at extremely high risk for abusing substances because they are tempted to self-medicate—that is, to use a substance (or food, or sex, or gambling) to make themselves feel better and avoid dealing with the underlying cause of their emotional difficulty.

Talk it out. Even if your medical doctor prescribes an antidepressant, you may need to seek therapy to deal with the underlying causes of the depression. The medication treats the symptom, but the problem will continue to bubble up in other ways, especially in relationships. Cognitive-behavioral therapy has been proven to help people conquer their battle with sadness or depression.

Do I Need Therapy?

The difference between normal blues and clinical depression is the intensity and duration of the feelings. Clinical depression must be treated by a mental health professional and is defined as persistent sad mood along with at least three of the following symptoms for at least two consecutive weeks:

- Feelings of hopelessness and/or pessimism.
- Feelings of guilt, helplessness, and/or worthlessness.
- Loss of interest or pleasure in activities that you used to enjoy.
- Decreased energy, fatigue.

- Difficulty concentrating, remembering, or making decisions.
- Difficulty sleeping, or sleeping more than normal.
- Significant increase or decrease in appetite.
- Thoughts of death or suicide; suicide attempts.
- Restlessness and/or irritability.
- Physical symptoms such as headaches, digestive disorders, and chronic pain that aren't explained by medical disorders and don't respond to treatment.

If you suspect that you suffer from depression, or if your feelings have been impairing your daily functioning and relationships, you need to seek professional help. Even if you don't have the symptoms of clinical depression, therapy can still be a great way to gain a deeper understanding of your sadness, and can provide invaluable tools to help you feel better.

If your depression is so bad that you have contemplated suicide, it is imperative that you get help immediately. Take the first step by calling 1-800 SUICIDE, or visit suicidehotlines.com for local hotlines in your area.

Emotional Pitfall #5 Fear of Failure (*aka*: control-freakishness, perfectionism, manipulation, obsessiveness, compulsiveness)

> *Confidence comes not from always being right but from not fearing to be wrong.*
>
> —*Peter T. McIntyre*

T F I like to be in control of what's happening around me.

T F I'm usually able to get others to go along with what I want.

T F I sometimes pout or give someone the silent treatment when I don't get my way.

T F I hate to make mistakes.
T F I like things to be done a certain way.

PAMELA

"I've been married for six years now, and things have been pretty tough the whole time. I admit that I've always been a bit of a control freak. My friends used to joke about it, but it never seemed to cause any serious problems until I married Jim. Looking back, it bugged me to no end when my roommate left dirty dishes in the sink, but I just cleaned them along with the rest of the apartment. People at work called me Perfect Pam because my office was always immaculate, I often redid my assistant's work to my liking, and I had a bad habit of correcting my coworkers' grammar.

"I got pregnant right after Jim and I got married, and wound up on bedrest for the last five months of my pregnancy. Honestly, it was complete hell for both of us. Having to lie there in bed while the laundry was piling up and the dust gathered on the windowsills literally drove me crazy. It's not that Jim wasn't helpful. I mean, he *tried* to be. He would try to grocery shop, cook, and deal with the household stuff, but he just never got it right. He complained that I didn't appreciate all of his effort and called me a nag. I felt bad, but I like things done a certain way.

"Things didn't get much better after the baby was born. I didn't like to let Jim take care of her, because he didn't change her diapers right. No matter how many times I showed him how to feed her, she would end up covered in food. We fought about leaving the baby home with a babysitter—he wanted to go out, but I couldn't trust anyone else enough to take care of her. Our relationship has definitely suffered and now here we are in counseling. He says he doesn't know how much more of my 'controlling' and 'nagging' he can take. I love him to death; I just can't seem to give up the reins."

How Will I Recognize My Fear of Failure?

Fear of failure drives people to try to control their world. These tortured souls are often referred to as control freaks or perfectionists. You might find it difficult to trust people, so you do everything for yourself. You make a to-do list for everything in your life and berate yourself when you don't finish it even though it was unrealistic for anyone but Wonder Woman to complete. You tend to be a perfectionist with yourself and with others. Because you believe that you are usually right, you feel justified telling others what to do and how to do it. You see your constant intervention in others' lives as beneficial or even necessary; this can be caused by feelings of superiority, believing that others are incapable of handling matters properly, or the fear that things will go wrong if you don't attend to every detail. Or you may simply enjoy the feeling of power so much that you automatically try to gain control of everything around you.

Control freaks can also be motivated by feelings of insecurity, trying to manipulate everything and everyone around them in an effort not to be "found out" for the inferior people they believe themselves to be. Common tactics of manipulators include sulking, name-calling, threatening, blaming, crying, leaving, or giving someone the silent treatment.

What Does My Fear of Failure Tell Me about Myself?

People usually develop an inflated need for control when something in their life feels out of control. Here are a few possible scenarios that might explain where your controlling tendencies originated:

- You had controlling parents who always told you what to do. → Now that they are not in charge of you, you can and will finally have control over everything.
- Your mother was in charge of the family, and she didn't

respect your father because he let her rule the roost. → Now you respect *yourself* only when you are in control and you lose respect for others when they let you walk all over them.

- One or both of your parents was an alcoholic or addict and you had to be responsible for their well-being from an early age. If you hadn't taken control, the family would have fallen apart. → Now you feel like everything will fall apart if you aren't in control.
- You grew up in a chaotic home in which you felt insecure and unstable. → Now you order everything in your outside world to belie the chaos you feel inside.
- Your parents gave you attention only when you succeeded. → Now you don't want to let them down by failing.

Answer these questions to find out more about your desire for control:

Clues About My Need for Control

Did your parents have rigid rules or did you have to fend for yourself?

Are you afraid of what will happen if you don't do something exactly the right way?

Which one of your parents was most in control of the family?

How did you perceive the parent who wasn't in control? Weak? Not worthy of respect?

What appeals to you about being in control?

What do you do when you don't get your way?

How do you feel about yourself when you react that way?

How do you feel about yourself when you succeed in convincing someone to do it your way?

Reflect on your answers. How do you feel right now? What did you learn about your need for control?

What Does My Fear of Failure Look Like in Friendships?

As a perfectionist, you make life tense for roommates, as you hold them to your exacting standards of housekeeping, decor, and everything else, for that matter. You offer unsolicited advice and get annoyed if they don't take it. Your friends may begin to feel like they don't measure up or that you're secretly (or not so secretly), judging their imperfections. When you go out with your friends, *you* decide where you go and what you do. You are the ringleader, and your friends usually fall in line. If they're honest, though, they'd probably admit feeling resentful at times, even if they are too afraid of your reaction to tell you. Down the line, you might find that they are increasingly unavailable for your "one-woman show" nights on the town.

What Does It Look Like at Work?

You take control of projects even if they weren't assigned to you. You don't work well on group assignments, because you don't like to give up your own ideas in favor of others'. You probably perform better when given independent tasks because you are used to relying on yourself. You might seek out entrepreneurial opportunities because you don't like to have anyone telling you what to do. It will be difficult to succeed in business, however, if you don't take the advice of others who have more experience. You will be doomed to repeat mistakes if you don't learn from others and trust only yourself.

What Will It Look Like in Marriage?

You'll have established ways of doing everything around the house, from how to load the dishwasher to how to discipline the kids. Your husband will feel unneeded and unable to live up to your standards. You'll nag your husband incessantly and won't hesitate to tell him when you think he's screwed up. You will punish him by sulking, crying, or withholding sex when he doesn't give in and let you have your way. This is not a partnership; it's a monarchy. And you are the queen.

How Can I Keep My Fear of Failure in Check?

- ***Look on the bright side.*** You are very adept at noticing mistakes that you and others make. This will be a difficult habit to break, but start by forcing yourself to take note of the positive things about something you or someone else has done. Instead of thinking, *That report Dawn wrote was subpar, definitely not what I was hoping for.* Think, *She worked really hard on that. Her writing skills are improving.*
- ***Set realistic goals.*** Perfectionists tend to have unreasonable expectations of themselves and others. Having lofty goals can create big problems because they set you up for failure. You don't have to sacrifice the end result you are looking for; just break it down into smaller, achievable tasks and don't forget to reward yourself when you accomplish each one.
- ***Don't sweat the small stuff.*** Controlling every aspect of your life is not only overwhelming, it's impossible. Make an effort to figure out what is truly important, and let the other stuff go. If you always clean every pot and pan immediately after cooking, you could try sitting down for dinner with dishes in the sink. When you see that the world doesn't end, it will free you up to let go of control in other areas as well.
- ***Keep your mouth shut.*** It's not your job and definitely not your place to always correct others. Remind yourself to stay quiet if you see someone making a different choice than you would have made. Unless they ask for

your opinion or advice, don't offer it! There are many ways to approach a problem, and your way is not the *only* right way. Steer clear of the "my way or the highway" attitude.

Do I Need Therapy?

If your fear of failure and need for control are negatively impacting your work, relationships, or personal life, you could really benefit from talking to a professional. A therapist can help you pinpoint the issues and offer individualized techniques to overcome them.

Our Fight Against Feelings

"The Five Emotional Pitfalls" is by no means an exhaustive list of emotions that can wreak havoc in your relationships. Any emotion can be destructive if not managed in a healthy way. We often try to soothe our emotions away with alcohol, drugs, shopping, gambling, sex, and—most commonly for women—food. So, how do *you* deal with the ups and downs of life? Do you turn to food when you're feeling angry, anxious, insecure, depressed, or inadequate? Take this quiz to see if you're using food to soothe your emotions.

Are You an Emotional Eater?

1. You screwed up royally at work and it looks like you might lose a big client. You're terrified that when your boss finds out, you'll get sacked. What do you do?
   a. Pour yourself a drink (or two).
   b. Talk to someone close to you who is objective and supportive.
   c. Hit the drive-through and tell them to supersize Combo #3.

2. You just had a nasty argument with one of your best friends. She said some really hurtful things. You feel like crying. What do you do?
   a. Anything to distract yourself from thinking about it—you surf the Internet, do the dishes, realphabetize your sock drawer.
   b. Take a long walk or go for a run. You need to burn off some steam.
   c. Whip up a batch of brownies and then polish most of them off. You'll feel better after you've had a little treat.
3. It's Saturday night and your roommates are out of town for the weekend. Because they didn't bother to invite you, you're alone in your apartment without any plans. What do you do?
   a. To you *alone* and *lonely* are synonymous, so you call anyone who will talk to you, including your bad-boy ex (the one your roommates made you swear you'd *never* contact again).
   b. Take advantage of the time on your own to enjoy your favorite hobby or activity.
   c. Stock up on DVDs, ice cream, and snacks for a night in on the couch.
4. You're up against the deadline to finish a PowerPoint presentation for work, but you can't get it exactly the way you want it. What do you do?
   a. Procrastinate by logging on to PerezHilton.com to see what Lindsay and Britney are up to.
   b. Clear your desk and focus on the task at hand.
   c. Go out to get a Frappuccino and a doughnut. Eating will calm your nerves so you can really focus.
5. Your roommate is with her new boyfriend practically 24/7, so you've been stuck with all the household chores—cleaning the bathroom, emptying the trash, washing her dishes, and keeping the apartment clean.

When she *is* around, she doesn't even seem to notice all your extra efforts. What do you do?

a. Ever the martyr, you continue slaving away in silence. When you're finished, you shop online to treat yourself to some expensive boots that you can't afford.
b. Send your roommate an e-mail telling her that you feel unappreciated and that you need to come up with a fair division of chores.
c. Go to your room, close the door behind you and dig into your secret stash of Cheez Doodles.

Scoring:

If you answered mostly ***a***, you're probably not an emotional eater, but you use other things to avoid dealing with your feelings. Figure out which feelings you are trying to deny and learn to face them head-on. If you think you might be addicted to any of these substances or behaviors or if you just find it difficult to break these patterns, get help from a qualified therapist.

If you chose mostly ***b***, you are not afraid to experience your emotions and express them in a healthy way. Good for you and your waistline.

If you chose mostly *c*, you are an emotional eater. You use food to soothe your uncomfortable emotions. The good news is that once you begin to recognize this tendency in yourself, you can begin to change it. Read on to learn more about where this destructive pattern came from and what you can do to keep it under control.

Family Patterns: It Started Long Ago. . . .

Your attitude toward food was powerfully shaped by your upbringing. Maybe you were rewarded with food as a child. Maybe you were given treats when you accomplished something, or to comfort you when you were hurt, physically or emotionally. If so, you were taught to associate food with comfort.

DANIELLE

Danielle grew up in a home where physical affection was rare. She has few memories of being hugged or kissed or even held when she was hurt or in distress, but she does remember that there was always a lot of fighting and angry silence in her home. No one ever talked about being angry or sad. It seemed to Danielle that the only positive interactions they had centered on food—what they were going to make for dinner or what new restaurant they should try. The food brought them together and filled the emotional void left by such an emotionally distant family. When Danielle left for college, her anxiety about classes, making new friends, and getting along with roommates increased, and so did her late-night binges. She would starve herself during the day when she was out in the world, and then when she was alone with her anxiety at night, she would soothe her feelings with loads of cookies, pizza, and fat-free potato chips. As a child, Danielle was taught that food=comfort, food=love. Whenever she was confronted with a new negative emotion, the only way Danielle knew how to cope was to feed it.

If you find that you try to soothe an emotion by eating, you must take steps toward conquering it instead of running and hiding inside a carton of your favorite Ben & Jerry's ice cream. The next time you think you're hungry and you're heading for the refrigerator, stop. Ask yourself if you are truly hungry or if an uncomfortable emotion is driving your desire to eat. Identify the emotion and its source. More often than not, you'll discover that the culprit is one the Five Emotional Pitfalls.

You Are Worthy of Esteem

Regardless of how you deal with your emotions, it stands that the most important step you can take to manage the Five Emotional Pitfalls is to improve your self-esteem. If you value yourself, you will not feel insecure because you will know you are worthy; you will not be easily angered because you will no longer have to demand respect; you will not feel overly anxious because you will know you can handle whatever comes your way; you will not be overwhelmed by depression because you will be content with yourself; you will not be governed by a fear of failure because you will value yourself regardless of what you accomplish.

As with all your beliefs, your beliefs about yourself were highly influenced by how you were raised. If you were not made to feel unconditionally loved, significant, wanted, valued, trusted, and worthy of your parents' approval, you will likely have difficulty believing that you deserve this kind of acceptance. As a twentysomething woman, it's now up to you to decide for yourself that you are valuable. As Jane Eldershaw says in *The Little Book of Moods,* "Self-esteem is the decision to treat yourself as a beloved, worthy friend. That means respecting yourself, taking care of yourself, nurturing yourself." Notice she calls self-esteem a *decision,* not a *feeling* that's out of your control. You can *decide* to value yourself regardless of how you *feel* about yourself.

Negative self-talk is the enemy of self-esteem. Imagine if someone followed you around all day haranguing you with put-downs about your every action. How annoying! You'd quickly get fed up and tell her to get lost. And yet many of us willingly carry around a negative voice in our heads that judges us constantly. It's time to kick that voice to the curb! But how? The first step to getting rid of this negative voice is to recognize it.

Recognizing Your Inner Critic

It's hard to fight an enemy who has outposts in your head.
—Sally Kempton

In his book *Taming Your Gremlin,* Rick Carson describes the negative, judging inner voice as your personal gremlin that taunts and teases you throughout the day. Carson recommends first that you simply notice the gremlin's voice. It sounds strange to personalize that voice as a monster, but it really does help you get an objective look at how harsh you are to yourself. Once you identify the critic, make some notes below about what it says. Whose voice does it sound like? What does it say?

Examples:

"That was a stupid thing to say."

"You look terrible today. That guy must be an idiot for checking you out."

"That person let your call go to voice mail because they didn't want to talk to you."

"You'll never get control of your eating. You might as well give up your diet and get as big as a whale."

List as many as you hear, and use a separate notebook if your inner critic is particularly vocal.

Now that you have identified the enemy and her verbal attacks against your self-esteem, you can strategize ways to defend yourself. Come up with statements that are opposite to the negative ones you listed. When your inner critic taunts you with one of her negatives, you return fire with your positive statement. Another helpful tool in your arsenal is to have a sense of humor about the whole concept. Imagining your negative critic as a cartoon image in your head who is trying to defeat your self-image can help you gain confidence in your ability to defeat her. Try this defensive exercise:

Battling My Inner Critic

The Critic says: *You'll never amount to anything.*

I say: *I am lovable and capable.*

The Critic says: ______________________________.

I say: ______________________________.

The Critic says: ______________________________.

I say: ______________________________.

Jot down the positive messages you use to counteract your inner critic. Put the notes around the house where you can see them. Find favorite positive quotes and commit them to memory. Here's one of our favorites by Oprah Winfrey: "You can either waltz boldly onto the floor of life . . . or you can sit quietly by the wall and recede in the shadows of fear and self-doubt."

Now try these suggestions to build your self-worth:

Be a friend to yourself. Resolve to talk to yourself the way you would talk to a good friend. Be encouraging and patient. Remember that it took you years to develop the bad habit of negative self-talk. Give yourself the grace to leave that behind and grow in your new feelings of self-worth.

Dwell on the good. Notice all the positive things you do today. Everything you do that's good, no matter how small—driving safely, getting to work on time, remembering your aunt's birthday, holding the elevator for someone. Give yourself some credit and a pat on the back. Actually, several pats on the back.

Gimme five. Studies show that for relationships to succeed there must be a ratio of five positive interactions to every negative one. The same goes for your relationship with yourself. In order for you to have a healthy self-image, your positive self assessments must outnumber your negative put-downs 5 to 1. When you catch yourself putting yourself down, quickly affirm yourself for five things you did well. Yes, five!

No apologies! People with low self-esteem constantly say "I'm sorry" for everything. When you always apologize for your opinions, you send the message that your needs aren't important and you don't value yourself as much as others. Stay true to your feelings and opinions and state them with certainty.

No more put-downs. Take notice of when you put yourself down or belittle yourself: "You probably don't remember me, but . . ." "This might not be relevant. . . ." "I'm not very good at this. . . ." Whenever you qualify what you say, you give the power to decide your value to the other person. Don't allow anyone to have control over your own self-image.

Impress yourself. If you really want to have self-esteem, the best, most foolproof way of all is to do things to make yourself proud. Run a 5K, become a Big Sister, master a new hobby, anything you thought you could never do. When you earn self-esteem through hard work and tenacity, no one can take it away from you. You will be proud of yourself, knowing that you have worked hard and overcome obstacles to achieve your goals. Impressive!

By the way, what happened to the self-esteem you had when you were younger? You used to be so sure of yourself, unapologetic about your feelings and opinions. Studies show that girls experience a dramatic internal shift in early adolescence that persists well into adulthood. They lose their optimism, becoming less assertive and more concerned with pleasing others than themselves. They sense the pressure to be something they're not. In a quest to be, do, and say what others want them to, they lose their authentic selves. You can't have a positive self-image if you don't hold on to your true self.

Empty Chair Exercise

Sit across from an empty chair. Think about the ten-year-old you in fifth grade. Now imagine her sitting in that empty chair. Don't feel self-conscious. If you commit to it, this can be an extremely revealing and emotional exercise. Ask the ten-year-old you these questions:

What is your favorite thing to do?
What is your favorite food?
What do your friends like about you?
What is your favorite subject in school and why?
What do you want to be when you grow up?
What are you good at?
What are your favorite things about yourself?

Write down your reactions to this exercise. What did you learn about yourself? Which qualities would you like to recapture in your adult life? Honor that young version of yourself by resurrecting her high self-esteem.

As a woman who has learned how to keep her emotions in check, you will be able to speak your mind when you aren't being respected, hold your tongue when your partner needs understanding, deal with loneliness without falling apart, be vulnerable with your sadness, accept your flaws and those of your husband and children, and adapt readily when plans fall through or when life doesn't turn out exactly as you had hoped. Free from fear of out-of-control emotions, you can now enjoy life to the fullest with a solid sense of your worth and your ability to handle the challenges that come your way.

Chapter 8

Key #6: Get a Self-Accepting Life

Appreciate Your Body

This is Your Body, Your Greatest Gift.
—Walt Whitman

When you were young, you viewed your body as a means of interacting with the world. You loved your body because it could do a cartwheel and because it could jump rope. Your arms could swing you quickly from rung to rung on the monkey bars. Your legs could carry you down the soccer field and propel you off the diving board. When you were tired, you rested. You didn't judge your body; you enjoyed it.

When did we stop appreciating our bodies for the amazing creations they are? When did we begin viewing our bodies as our enemies, as something to be changed? Your twenties and early thirties is the time to right this adversarial relationship with your body. You can't love yourself and hate your body. And you can't have fulfilling and lasting relationships until you learn to love yourself. Now is the time to begin to honor your body, before a poor body image sabotages the most important aspects of your life.

Body Image Defined

So what is body image? It's a combination of how we perceive our bodies and how we *imagine* that others perceive our bodies. Body image is what's triggered in our minds when we look in the mirror: how we *feel* about our bodies.

A negative body image can cause a distorted perception of size or shape, as well as feelings of awkwardness, shame, and anxiety. A woman with a negative body image tends to see her physical imperfections as a sign of personal failure. She obsesses about her appearance, holds herself to unrealistic standards of beauty, and assumes that others focus on her flaws with the same level of scrutiny. She can rattle off a list of her physical imperfections at the drop of a hat, but struggles to come up with three things she loves about her body. She's deflects compliments about her physical appearance, refusing to believe them. Studies show that women who suffer from poor body image are likely to experience low self-esteem, anxiety, depression, sexual dysfunction, obsessive dieting, and even life-threatening eating disorders.

You have a positive body image when you can appreciate and enjoy your body, flaws and all. A woman with a positive body image understands that healthy, attractive bodies come in many shapes and sizes, and that physical appearance says very little about her character or value as a person. Because her perception of her body doesn't determine her self-esteem, she isn't driven to spend inordinate amounts of time and energy dwelling on her physical appearance. She fuels her body with nutritious food, but isn't obsessed with calorie-counting. She strives to maintain a healthy body weight, but isn't ruled by the numbers on the scale. She cares for her body by exercising, but limits her workouts to a reasonable intensity.

Is your relationship with your body one of disdain and dissatisfaction or one of peace and acceptance? Take this short quiz to find out.

Are You a Body Hater?

1. Are you constantly trying to lose weight, even if others think you're at the right weight for your frame?
2. When people compliment you, especially on your appearance, do you respond with a criticism of yourself?
3. Do you avoid situations that make you feel self-conscious about your body, such as going to the beach?
4. Do you constantly compare yourself with the other women in a room? Do you always notice who's thinner or more attractive than you?
5. Do you avoid looking in mirrors? Do you always find something to critique when you look in a mirror or see yourself in photos?
6. Is your self-talk filled with critical comments about your appearance?
7. Do you find yourself thinking that if you could just lose a few pounds, you'd feel content and secure?
8. Does your negative body image affect your relationships? For example, do you avoid physical intimacy because you're ashamed of your body?
9. If you were asked to list ten things you really like about your appearance, would it be difficult for you?
10. If you were asked to list ten things you dislike about your appearance, would it be easy for you?

If you answered YES to any one of these questions, you are in a battle with your body. The good news is that you can decide that now's the time to call a truce. The first step to doing so is to understand when and why this battle began in the first place.

The Moment the Battle Began

Many of us can pinpoint the exact moment when our carefree attitude toward our body took a turn for the worse. In her classic *Reviving Ophelia,* Mary Pipher describes this period as the time "when your wholeness is shattered by the chaos of adolescence." The body-image battle begins when girls stop thinking *Who am I and what do I want?* and start thinking *What must I do and how must I look to please others?* Throughout childhood and adolescence, this body image battle is waged on three fronts: with your parents, your friends, and the opposite sex.

Your Parents

Our parents hold much sway over how we view our bodies. As children, we define ourselves according to how they describe us. If you frequently overhear your parents describe you as shy, you will believe that about yourself; chances are you will forever regard yourself as shy, even if your personality belies that perception. So it is with body image. If your parents refer to you as big-boned or tall for your age, you carry that image with you. Even the smallest negative comment from a parent can ignite the body image battle. Here's how Hannah's battle began:

HANNAH

Hannah is now twenty-seven and still remembers with clarity the exact moment when her battle began. She was in the dressing room of a department store with her mom, shopping for back-to-school clothes. She was ten. The pair of pants she was trying on was too tight and a little too short. "Mom," said Hannah, "I need a bigger size." Her well-meaning but weight-obsessed mom replied, "Well, Hannah, you know, if you lost a few pounds, those pants would fit you perfectly. They're so cute—why don't we buy them and you can work on that?" And that was the beginning for Hannah—the moment she first began to see her body as deficient, as something that needed to be changed, to look somehow different, better.

Your Friends

Once you move into adolescence, you begin to look to your peers to define you. You start looking around, comparing yourself with sisters, relatives, friends, and the girls in the locker room after gym class. If you're still barely filling out your training bra, you long to be like the girl with the curves. If you're the girl who developed early, you are embarrassed by your big chest. As you watch your friend brushing her smooth, straight hair, you begin to loathe your ringlet curls. If you're the tall girl at your junior high school dance, you slouch, trying to hide the fact that you tower over your dance partner. For many women, these comparisons begin a lifetime of evaluating their appearance against others'.

JENNIFER

Jennifer's battle began the summer after her eleventh birthday. Twenty-five-year-old Jennifer still recalls the first day of the family reunion like it was yesterday. Lunch was just ending and the whole gang was getting ready to go for a swim in the ocean. As Jennifer peeled off her T-shirt, she caught a glimpse of her thirteen-year-old bikini-clad cousins running toward the water. She stared at their slim legs and tiny waists; then Jennifer looked down at her own soft, fleshy tummy with new eyes. Embarrassed at the stark difference between her body and those of her skinny cousins, Jennifer quickly put her T-shirt back on and sat down.

The Opposite Sex

Women all want to be desirable to the opposite sex. In fact, when you were a teenager, having a boyfriend was the universally accepted sign of being desired. It makes sense, then, that your body image is also significantly impacted by how men respond to you and what they communicate about how you stack up to other women.

KATHLEEN

Kathleen's defining moment came when she was fifteen. She was at lunch sitting in the cafeteria with her boyfriend and a couple of his buddies. An ultra-skinny girl walked by, wearing the same pink pants Kathleen was wearing. "Hey," remarked Kathleen, "she's wearing the exact same pants as me." "Yeah," said Kat's boyfriend, "but you don't look like *that* in them." And so it began for Kathleen. Right there and then, she decided that she *would* look like *that*. No matter what the cost. Thus began Kathleen's ten-year battle with bulemia.

Can you remember a similar moment or a series of messages you received growing up that caused you to see your body as less than ideal or in need of change? Take time to journal about your experiences. Reflect on how those experiences have affected your body image over the past decade or so.

How the Media Intensifies the Battle

As women, we are trained from childhood to believe that appearance is extremely important and that we must invest considerable time, effort, and expense into being beautiful if we want to be happy and successful. But who decides what is beautiful? Are standards of beauty measured by the real women on college campuses, in conference rooms, and around kitchen tables across the globe? Not quite.

Magazines, TV, and movies single-handedly determine the unrealistic standards of beauty that relentlessly bombard us. It has been estimated that young women now see more images of extraordinarily beautiful women *in one day* than our mothers saw throughout their entire adolescence. These so-called standards of beauty being pushed by the media make anything short of perfection seem abnormal and even ugly. Seriously, did your girlfriends back in high school at all resemble the leading ladies of *Beverly Hills 90210*?

The current media ideal for a woman's body size is achievable by less than 5 percent of the female population. Less than 5 percent! So where does that leave the other 95 percent of women? Perpetually focused on their less-than-perfect appearance. And what does this obsession breed? Further dissatisfaction. No wonder three-quarters of the normal-weight females we surveyed said they thought about their weight or appearance "all the time."

PAM

Pam, a woman in her mid-thirties, told us, "My twenties were spent in a perpetual quest for thinness. More than anything else, I wanted to look like Keira Knightley. People used to tell me that I looked like her, and I was determined to make my body like hers as well. Each time I read about a celebrity diet secret, I would embark on a new regimen. Believe me, I've tried them all—Britney's no-carb diet, Jennifer Aniston's Zone Diet, and Katherine Heigl's diet of cigarettes and sushi. I finally found success when I tried Beyoncé's Master Cleanse, but unfortunately I gained back all the weight I lost. I wanted so badly to be skinny and hated my body for not cooperating with my mission. I loathed it. All I cared about was that it wouldn't fit into a pair of size 2 jeans. Never mind that I was doing really well at work or that I had a lot of friends and a family who loved me. Never mind that I had a healthy body that could hike for hours in the mountains or run along the beach at sunset. Is it any coincidence then that my twenties were also a time of perpetual depression and feeling bad about myself? At the time, it didn't dawn on me that there could be a connection between my unhappiness and how much I hated my body. I'm now thirty-three and I can finally see that my desire to look like a super-skinny celebrity was a big, giant waste of my twenties. I'll never get that time back."

How many of us have flipped through magazines, enviously gazing at the airbrushed photos in the ads or at the skeletal celebrities strutting down the red carpet? The more we look, the more we accept these images as the ideal and inevitably begin to compare ourselves. The more we compare, the worse and worse we feel about our bodies. But wait a second. In the first place, these doctored images are not *real*. Not even close. So from the start, we are comparing ourselves to perfection that doesn't exist. Second, what we don't see when we look into the smoky eyes of these svelte creatures is the desperation and the self-abuse that's often going on when the cameras are gone. Yes, they're rail-thin, but at what price? Read the celebrity quotes on the next page to catch a glimpse of what's really going on.

She Said *What*?!

Can you match the quote with the starving celebrity? Marcia Cross, Gwen Stefani, Sara Ramirez, Charlize Theron, Elizabeth Hurley, Liv Tyler, Anne Hathaway.

A. "I've been on a diet, ever since I was in the sixth grade. It's an ongoing battle, and it's a complete nightmare."

B: "I basically starved myself [when trying to break into television], living on a stick of celery, some peanut butter and two protein shakes a day, working out like a fiend. Sure enough, I lost twenty-five pounds and booked a TV pilot—scary, because it was almost like a reward for treating myself in an unhealthy way."

C: "I have often felt there was a lot of pressure on me to look good. . . . It's like they pay me not to eat. It's a living hell."

D: "I diet every day of my life. It's part of my discipline. I basically stuck with fruit, vegetables and fish to slim down for my last movie. I wouldn't recommend that. My co-star and I would clutch at each other and cry because we were so hungry."

E: "I've been working out since I was fourteen. Being pregnant was the first time in my life that I wasn't on a diet and didn't have that kind of pressure. I had time to not be obsessed about myself and what I was eating, and enjoy my family."

F: "Getting pregnant doesn't excite me, but having kids does. . . . I don't really want to look like a whale, you know?"

Answers: A. Gwen Stefani; B. Sara Ramirez; C. Marcia Cross; D. Anne Hathaway; E. Liv Tyler; F. Charlize Theron

Life was a "nightmare"? "Living hell"? "Scary"? So why do we want to be like them, again?

Body Image and Relationships

Between the messages we receive in childhood from family and peers, and the barrage of media depictions of beauty, most women can't help but struggle with their body image. Not only does this struggle lead to depression and feelings of unworthiness, but it also profoundly impacts your most important relationships.

Poor Body Image=Poor Friendships

If you have a poor body image, it will be tough for you to develop close relationships with women. Your insecurity will undermine your friendships and prevent them from being rooted in authenticity and honesty. Friendships are supposed to be the safe haven within which you give and receive encouragement and affirmation. But if you're riddled with self-doubt and feelings of inferiority, you're unable to receive any sort of affirmation from a well-meaning friend. When your friend tells how you great you look, your immediate reaction is to start in about how you have a big zit on your forehead or that you had to wear your fat jeans today.

When you have a poor body image, you are self-focused. Instead of concentrating on the good things you have to offer your friends, you are focused on yourself and your inadequacies—how do *you* measure up physically, how do *you* compare with them? Is your friend prettier than you? There's no way you're going to go out with her because she's going to get hit on more than you. Is your friend skinnier than you? There's no way you're going to go shopping with her, because you know she'll look great in everything she tries on. By constantly playing the comparison game, you rob yourself of truly mutual friendship.

Not only does negative body image limit the friendships you have now, but it also prevents you from making friends with new people who trigger your body-image issues. Do you intentionally avoid talking to the beautiful woman at a party, simply because you know you would feel ugly and awkward? Do you automatically categorize women as the "Beauty Queen," "Skinny Bitch," or the "Barbie Doll" and immediately write them off as potential friends? If so, you are letting your insecurities dictate with whom you connect and are probably missing out on a lot of great friendships.

Poor Body Image=Poor Romantic Relationships

In a recent study of two thousand women, 80 percent of them reported that their negative body image was ruining their sex lives. It's true: Poor body image overwhelmingly translates into bad sex. Sadly, 67 percent of the men surveyed reported that their wives' poor body image was a significant source of frustration for them and had a negative impact on the happiness of their relationship. If you a have poor body image, you may avoid sex altogether because you don't want to be seen naked. When you do end up having sex, you're so consumed with the way your body *looks* that you're not focused on how your body *feels*. Of course this preoccupation inhibits a woman's enjoyment of sex. As Dr. Thomas Cash, a researcher into the link between body image and sex, found, women who like the way they look reach orgasm twice as frequently as those preoccupied with their "physical defects."

Women often worry that unless they have the perfect body, they won't be attractive to the opposite sex, but the reports from men consistently contradict this fear. There's no denying that men like to look at the perfect ten in a magazine or on the big screen, but as one man told us, "The biggest turn-on for a man isn't having a woman with the perfect body; the biggest turn-on is having a woman who is confident, passionate, and responsive."

MOLLY

"Ever since I was in college, I've had a hard time accepting my body or feeling comfortable in my own skin. I've never been super-overweight, but always wished I could lose fifteen or twenty pounds. When my husband and I first started being intimate, he constantly reassured me about my appearance and told me how beautiful and sexy he thought I was. We've been married for two years now, and during that time I've put on a little more weight. I assumed that being married would make me feel more secure about my body, but I'm really struggling. I usually turn him down when he initiates sex; I just can't stand the thought of him seeing my naked body. It's gotten to the point where we have sex maybe once a month, if that. Even then, I make sure the lights are off, and to be honest, I can't wait until it's over. The whole time, I'm just worrying about how gross my body must feel to his touch. I guess the body-image demons from my twenties never really went away; they just got pushed aside for a while. I feel bad for my husband, because I'm not much fun in bed, or out of bed, for that matter. I just can't get past how ugly I feel."

Your negative body image doesn't just impact you. Your husband is affected as well.

TODD

"When Michelle and I first started dating, she seemed super-confident, which was a pleasant change from many of the other women I'd dated in the past. But just before we got married, I started noticing how critical she was about her appearance. She was obsessed with begin skinny for the wedding, which I figured was pretty normal. Over the past seven years, I've come to understand that Michelle truly thinks of herself as fat, ugly, and unworthy—which is so far from the truth that it's just plain ridiculous. I've tried everything from complimenting her, to encouraging her to get counseling, to explaining to her in detail how irrational she's being. I have to be very careful about what I say and how I say it because she twists my words and takes everything I say as a criticism. It's like walking on eggshells and I'm sick of it. I'm starting to lose respect for her as a mature adult. She's acting like a teenager, always worried about how she looks—her hair, her body, her skin—always feeling insecure. I don't know what to do anymore. I'm at my wit's end."

Molly and Michelle's ongoing struggle with their body

image is damaging their romantic relationships. Sadly, these are the very relationships that are supposed to bring them the greatest feelings of security. What a shame to be in a loving, committed relationship with an adoring man and not be able to accept his love.

Poor Body Image=Poor Family Relationships

If you allow your body-image issues to remain unchecked in your single life, you will subconsciously pass them along to your children. When you're a mom, your children will watch you intently and, like little sponges, will soak it all in, and then file it away.

Your child will base her own body image on her observations of the way you treat your body and talk about your flaws. Your positive words about her body will have far less impact than your negative reactions to your own body. If you're always complaining about your weight or your body shape, your child will learn very quickly that these are important concerns. If you are attracted to new "miracle" diets, she will learn that restrictive dieting is better than making healthy food choices. If your daughter sees you lamenting your size as you try on clothes in the dressing room, she will begin to critically examine her own body.

In one recent U.S. survey, more than 80 percent of ten-year-old girls reported having been on a diet at least once. Ten years old? Where did this epidemic come from? You guessed it: Mom. A 2005 study published by researchers at Harvard Medical School found that frequent dieting by mothers was associated with frequent dieting by their adolescent daughters. "If their mothers diet, it's a marker of how important weight is in the household," said Alison Field, lead author of the study. "Even small cues—such as making self-deprecating remarks about bulging thighs or squealing in delight over a few lost pounds—can send the message that thinness is to be prized above all else."

Take some time now to think about how your body-image struggles may affect your future children. Imagine if you had a five-year-old girl trailing you today. What would she learn about her body from the way you view yours? That it's something to be appreciated, or that it's a source of unhappiness and dissatisfaction?

Personal Insight from Celeste

As I look at my three precious daughters, I am filled with excited anticipation for all the opportunities that await them but also with dread at the inevitable difficulties they will face as they navigate the world's unrealistic standards of beauty. Like most women, I've struggled with body-image issues myself and sometimes feel less than equipped to guide them through their own journey. I am painfully aware of how, as their role model, my attitude toward my body will shape their own body images.

They are watching as I survey myself in the mirror. They are watching when I check out how my butt looks in a new pair of jeans. And just when I think they're not listening, they overhear me complain to my husband, "I think I've gained a pound or two." They notice the food I eat, and don't eat. They see me returning, sweaty and tired, from an early-morning run.

Even though my oldest daughter is only seven, I've already begun to think about how I can best help her and her sisters develop a healthy perspective about their bodies. We talk a lot about the importance of inward beauty and discourage prolonged lingering in front of the bathroom mirror. We talk about food as fuel and about all the amazing things our body can do if we take care of it. My fervent hope for all three of these little girls is that they grow into young women who, instead of being obsessively distracted by the pursuit of elusive perfection, are women who love and accept their bodies and who choose to devote their energy to becoming agents of compassion and change in their world.

As women, we have a huge responsibility to pass along positive attitudes about the female body to the next generation. If body image is an issue for you, now is the time to start dealing with it, head-on. This issue won't magically disappear with age or because you get married or have children. Working through the exercises in the following section will help you begin to combat your negative body image.

Proven Strategies to Win the Body-Image Battle

You've seen how your perception of your body affects everything from how you feel about yourself to how you participate in your relationships. Fortunately, it is within your power to change the relationship with your body into a positive one. Begin this important process by learning about the three most common ways your thoughts and actions contribute to your negative body image and how to combat them.

Enemy Tactic #1: You Compare Yourself with Others.

Women have a nasty habit of comparing themselves with other women. And when we do, it usually seems that we come up short. The inevitable result of such comparisons is unhappiness and dissatisfaction with our own bodies.

Battle Plan

- **Go on a fast.** No, not one of those silly grapefruit-and-water fasts. We're talking about a magazine fast. Cancel your subscriptions or stop buying those insipid publications crammed full of photos of impossibly skinny women. Instead, start focusing on appreciating the real but imperfect women in your life.
- **Define yourself.** When you compare yourself to others, you are defining yourself in relation to them. Take out a pen and paper and start describing your body. Not in relation to anyone else, or with any judgment, just objectively. For example, "I am five-two (*not* "I am shorter than my friend"); "I weigh 125" (*not* "I'm fatter than my roommate"); "My hair is straight" (*not* "My hair is more stringy than hers"); "My arms are thin" (*not* "I'm less toned than my coworker"). The purpose of this exercise is to get you to start thinking of yourself in objective terms, rather than the way you stack up when compared with others. If you can see your physical attributes for what they are, independent from others, you will begin to appreciate the unique beauty you possess.

Enemy Tactic #2: You Live in the Future.

It's easy to fall into the trap of always thinking about your body in terms of the future. "Someday when I lose some weight, I'll buy that cute outfit. Then I'll look good." "Someday, when I get a tan, I'll feel comfortable wearing a sundress. Then I'll look feminine." "Someday, when I get breast implants, men will notice me. Then I'll be sexy." *Someday.* One of the most annoying celebrity quotes we've heard came from former Bachelorette Trista Sutter: "I'm definitely not pleased when I look in the mirror," admitted the five-foot-two star, who at the time weighed 116 pounds but was longing to get down to 106. "When I fit into my size 2 Hudson jeans, *then* I'll be happy." As if her doting husband and healthy new baby girl weren't enough to make her happy *right now*!

Battle Plan

- **Update your wardrobe.** Get rid of clothes that don't fit you. Buy clothes that fit the *real* you, *right now.* Don't shop for the "fantasy you," who is ten pounds lighter, and don't wait until you lose those ten pounds to buy a nice swimsuit or a pretty dress. Wear comfortable clothes you feel good in. Just don't go the muumuu route. Laura, a twenty-five-year-old woman Shannon counseled a few years ago, had always been a healthy weight until a stressful job, long hours, and too much takeout caused her to gain twenty pounds. None of her clothes fit anymore, but she didn't want to give in and buy "fat clothes." Because Laura didn't have anything to wear, she stopped going out with friends or to work events and usually just wore baggy clothes or sweats. Shannon encouraged her to buy some new clothes that fit her at her current size. When Laura showed up at her next counseling session wearing a fashionable, fitted dress, she looked like a new woman! She realized that she had been afraid that buying clothes in her larger size would signal defeat and she would stay that size forever. But when she saw how good she looked in her new "right size, right now" clothes, she felt better about herself and even more motivated to get back to her healthy weight.

- **Determine to be happy now.** If you place your hopes for happiness on that elusive day when you achieve your particular ideal of perfection, you'll be waiting until the day you die. And in the meantime, you'll be miserable and ungrateful. As Wendy Shanker, author of *The Fat Girl's Guide to Life,* observed upon returning from her nationwide book tour, "The best lesson I learned touring is that every woman, no matter how heavy or how skinny, feels fat. When you're thin, you're never thin enough." Decide that your happiness starts today. Let go of perfection. Grab on to gratitude.

Enemy Tactic #3: You Belittle Your Body.

You're constantly telling yourself, *My butt is too big, my thighs are too fat, my feet are ugly, my skin is dry, my eyelashes are short, and my nose is too big.* And on and on it goes. This nonsense becomes the Muzak soundtrack of your life, always playing on a loop in your head. You disregard the positives about your body, and you're practically unable to receive a compliment because it contradicts your deeply ingrained negative perspective.

Battle Plan

- **Talk to yourself.** Really! Try this. Talk to yourself in the encouraging and nurturing way you would a child. It's time to replace your internal soundtrack with words of affirmation and approval. Instead of berating yourself—*Get your fat butt off the couch and go for a walk, you lazy pig*—try being kind: *I know you're tired, but you can do it, girl. Think of how much better you'll feel after a little exercise.*
- **Be kind to your bod.** Instead of focusing on how your body looks, try shifting your focus to what makes it feel alive. Feed your senses. Pick five things you can do to enjoy your body this week. Turn on some music and

dance. Go for a walk after work. Watch the sunset. Take a bubble bath with the most expensive aromatherapy bath oil you can afford. Drink a glass of wine or sparkling water while you luxuriate. Schedule a massage or a manicure. Figure out what makes your body feel good, and make time for those things.

Don't Hate Me Because I Want to Be Beautiful

We've talked a lot about the importance of accepting and appreciating your body, but does that mean that you shouldn't make strides to maximize your assets (and minimize your ass)? Some people preach the message that you should stop striving for beauty and focus only on the significant parts of your life such as career, accomplishments, cures for cancer, and world peace ("How can you be so worried about whether you're having a good hair day when polar bears are being driven to extinction by global warming?") Here's the rub: While we don't want to be so focused on our outward appearance that we end up like one of the "Stupid Girls" from Pink's music video—girls obsessed with their big boobies and "itsy bitsy doggies," *we do want to be pretty.* Every woman wants to be attractive. And there's nothing wrong with that. Denying that desire in the name of "female empowerment" makes women feel unnecessarily guilty for their natural desire for beauty. The key to solving this dilemma is to find a balance between accepting your eternally flawed self, loving yourself as you are, and making reasonable changes where you can. The ideal balance allows you to care about your appearance without going overboard, but to do so within the context of love, appreciation, and respect for your body.

In order to reach this important balance, you first need to determine whether the issues you have with your body are major or minor, changeable or unchangeable. The following chart will help you figure it out.

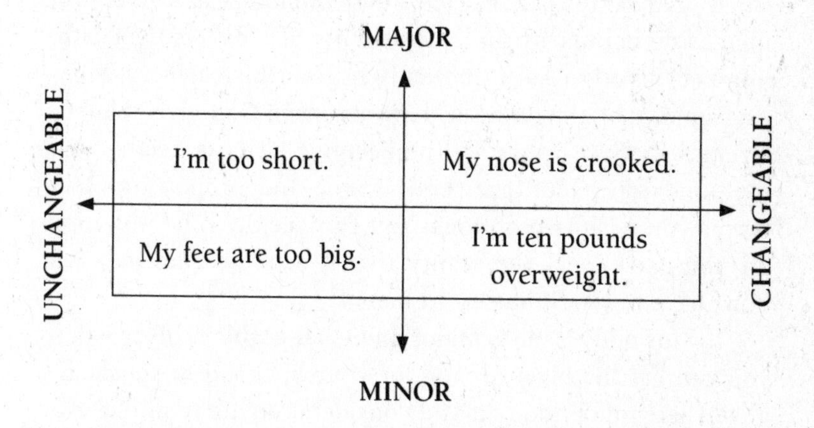

Make a chart of your own and write down some of the things about your body you wish you could change. Which box does each one belong in? We know it's hard, but try your best to be objective about your perceived flaws and in which category they fit. Be real: Frizzy hair is *not* major.

If your body issue is **Minor and Changeable:** What are you waiting for? If you can improve the way you feel about your appearance with a small amount of time and effort, go for it. But remember, you have to first ask yourself if it's worth it—worth the time, the money, the risk, and the pain. If your unibrow is the cause of your body-image grief, down an Advil or two and head to the aesthetician without delay. But if you hate your porcelain skin and long for a savage tan, visits to the tanning booth may not be worth the risk of melanoma.

If your body issue is **Minor and Unchangeable:** Spending your time worrying about things in this category is pointless. The reality is that you are probably the only one who even notices this so-called flaw. Your friends tease you, not about the object of your dissatisfaction, but about the fact that it even bothers you. So stop with the whining about how your big toe is shorter than the one next to it. If this is one of your most distressing "flaws," you should be rejoicing.

If your body issue is **Major and Unchangeable:** With the increasing popularity and accessibility of plastic surgery, the number of body issues that truly fit into this category is getting smaller by the day. But there are some God-given characteristics that are yours for the keeping, such as height, skin tone and type, foot size, body frame and proportion. That leaves you with two options: You can decide to be unhappy. Or you can accept the reality that it can't be changed. You don't have to love it; just don't hate it.

If your body issue is **Major and Changeable:** This is where you can get the biggest bang for your buck, so to speak. It's also where much thought and consideration are required. Not everything in this category is an easy fix. Some changes, like losing weight or getting fit, will take a great deal of time, effort, planning, and discipline and will happen over the long term. Other things in this category, like breast reduction or getting rid of acne scars, can be changed more quickly, but are expensive. If you decide your best solution for your body-image issue involves any form of plastic surgery, you'll find some important questions on our website that you need to answer before you go under the knife.

Putting It All Together

As you complete the following exercise, consider all you've read about your body image—where it comes from, what contributes to it, how it impacts your relationships, and what it means to find a healthy balance. Get ready: Although it may seem silly at first, this exercise is powerful and will offer a great deal of insight into your relationship with your body, for better or for worse.

Take out a piece of paper and write a letter to your body.

Tell your body whatever you think about it, good or bad. Be specific. No one will see it, so be honest. Here's an example:

Dear Body,

Why are you always so tired? And why do you seem to hang on to fat like it's your best friend? I try to stay away from carbs, but you're never satisfied until you get them. Thanks for the way you keep going when I have to work late and for perking up when I give you caffeine. I do like the way you feel when you dance. Sorry I don't let you do it more often. I like your eyes, but I wish you were sexier. I also wish your hair was a little thicker. I like that you can run, but why does it take only a few minutes before you get winded? I hate your big butt and the cellulite on the outside of your thighs. I don't mean to be harsh, but I guess I really don't like you that much.

Sincerely,
Serena

How do you feel? What did you learn about the way you relate to your body? What was the overall tone of your letter? Was the letter a tirade or a lovefest? A bit of both?

Don't stop here. Now it's your body's turn. Turn your paper over and write a letter from your body to you, in response.

Dear Serena,

I had a chance to read your letter and I'm sorry to hear that you're so unhappy with me. I have a few questions of my own. For starters, how do you expect me to have energy when you never give me enough sleep? And if you wouldn't go for hours on end without feeding me, maybe I wouldn't think I'm being starved and may even let go of "my best friend," fat. Of course I like carbs—I'm human, after all. Not sexy? If you'd slow down once in a while, you might be surprised to find out how sensual I really am. How about a bubble bath or some nice lingerie for a change? Regarding the exercise, you're really going to have to give me a chance on that one. I mean, you can't just move me like that every couple of weeks and expect me to be able to keep up. A little consistency would go a long way. You'll have to take up the complaints about your cellulite and hair with your mom. Don't blame me, that's just your genes at work. You should just be thankful you didn't get your uncle Harry's nose.

Yours truly,
Body
P.S. I promise you'd like me better if you took me dancing more often!

Life in your twenties and early thirties can be an insecure time. It can be tempting to base your self-worth on how you measure up to what society says is beautiful. If you're engaged in a battle with negative body image, your confidence will be undermined at the time in your life when you need it most. You don't need to wave the white flag in surrender to a life of dissatisfaction and constant striving. Make peace with your body, and take hold of the wonderful opportunity you have to be the healthy woman, daughter, friend, girlfriend, wife, and mother you were meant to be.

Chapter 9

Key #7: Get an Independent Life

Establish Yourself Apart from Your Parents

Independence is happiness.
—*Susan B. Anthony*

The decade of your twenties is known among developmental psychologists as the launching stage—the time when you are launched like a rocket into the orbit of your life as an independent woman. While that may sound pretty exciting, let's think about the process of launching a rocket for a moment. Much preparation goes into building this intricate machine. Years and years of research, money, and energy. Finally, the day of the launch arrives. People gather to witness this momentous event and watch in awe as the countdown begins. 10 . . . 9 . . . 8 . . . The astronauts wait in anticipation, filled with a mixture of excitement and dread . . . 7 . . . 6 . . . They know that it takes an enormous amount of energy to leave the earth's gravitational pull . . . 5 . . . 4 . . . Fears of failure race through their minds. "What if something goes wrong?" . . . 3 . . . "What if we're not quite ready?" . . . 2 . . . "What if we just don't have what it takes to get off the ground?" . . . 1 . . . The countdown is complete and now is the time to go. *Blastoff!* The amazed spectators watch as the rocket blasts into the air. Houston, we have liftoff! Then, suddenly, a piece of the rocket breaks off and plummets to the ground! What's happening? No, nothing has gone wrong; that is just the engine separating from the cockpit. The rocket must release the excess weight if it is ever to successfully reach orbit.

Launching as a developmental stage in your life is similar. During this time, it's normal for you to experience feelings of excitement, fear, nervousness, curiosity, and doubt, sometimes all at once.

Just as the rocket releases the engine when it is no longer needed, you are going to need to let go of some things. Think about it. If the rocket held on to its now-unneeded engine, it would never make it into orbit. Similarly, separating from your family of origin is a crucial step in your personal development. It is nearly impossible to embrace this new phase of life if you remain childlike in your family relationships. Rising to the challenge of breaking free from reliance on your parents will transform you into a woman who thinks for herself, stands by her decisions, maintains her own address, and pays her own way. In short, a woman to be respected and admired.

Launching is a time of emotional distancing, becoming physically and financially independent, and transforming your parent–child relationship from an adult–child dynamic to an adult–adult one. Your parents will always be your parents, but your relationship must change as you begin to relate to one another more as adults. In this critical phase, you transition from a child in your parents' home under their control and care to a young woman with her own opinions and ability to care for herself.

The Triad of Independence

If you live with your parents and do not contribute to the household expenses or cook your meals, you remain a child who depends on Mommy and Daddy to take care of you. You must attain **physical independence** from your parents! If you continue to rely on your parents to bail you out and pay to have your cell phone turned back on, you remain a child who cannot function in the world apart from Mommy and Daddy. You must declare **financial independence** from your parents! If you continue to be depressed by your inability to please your hypercritical mother or father, you remain a child whose emotions are determined by whether or not you have Mommy and Daddy's approval. You must gain **emotional independence** from your parents!

Physical Independence— It's Time to Leave the Nest

The proverb warns that, "You should not bite the hand that feeds you." But maybe you should, if it prevents you from feeding yourself.

—Thomas Szasz

The women we've spoken to who moved straight from living with their parents to living with their husbands overwhelmingly expressed regret that they missed out on the opportunity to prove to themselves that they could make it on their own. The first important aspect to becoming an independent woman is physical independence. Take this revealing quiz to find out how physically independent you are.

Are You Soaring or Stagnant?

1. You have no clean underwear left. You
   a. Yell downstairs to Mom and ask her to bring up the clean load of laundry she just washed and folded.
   b. Pack up your car with three weeks of dirty clothes and head to the Laundromat armed with rolls of quarters and a good book.
   c. I always have clean underwear—I wash my own clothes every weekend.
   d. Go commando to the store to buy a new pair of undies.
2. Hooray! It's payday! You take your check and
   a. Cash it as fast as you can to buy those Louboutins you've been coveting.
   b. First pay your rent, car payment, and insurance, then treat yourself to a movie.
   c. Pay every bill before it is due, then put the rest in your 401(k). After all, you plan on retiring in just forty short years!
   d. Throw a wicked party for all your friends and their friends.
3. You are tired and hungry after a long day at work. You
   a. Kick it awhile in front of the TV, ask Mom what's for dinner, and then sit down to a home-cooked meal, complete with cloth napkins.
   b. Fix yourself a small salad from the bag in the fridge and pop a Lean Cuisine into the microwave.
   c. Whip up a bowl of ramen and a refreshing glass of tap water—a meal for less than fifty cents, now that's dee-lish!
   d. Call the Ivy for takeout. Delivery is twenty bucks extra, but you are really beat!

4. There is a mound of dirty dishes in the sink. You
   a. Go up to your room. If Mom doesn't ask you to help out, you never do.
   b. Wash them, but make a mental note to have a roommate meeting about the importance of cleaning up after oneself.
   c. *What* dirty dishes?
   d. Eww! Gross! Throw them away and buy new ones.
5. You have a hot date with a guy you've been crushing on for months. When he arrives to pick you up, you
   a. Try to get to the door before your dad so the poor guy doesn't have to answer the inevitable, "What are your intentions toward my daughter?"
   b. Invite him into your apartment to meet your awesome roommates, thereby impressing him with your great taste in friends while simultaneously showing him off.
   c. Meet him at the restaurant so your cats don't get too attached to someone with whom you might not have an enduring love connection.
   d. Meet him at the door with a bottle of bubbly . . . naked.

If you answered mostly ***a:*** It is time to get out of your parents' house. Yesterday! You are too reliant on your parents to provide the things you should be learning to handle on your own. Follow the steps outlined in this chapter to make your escape plan. *Now!*

If you answered mostly ***b:*** Well done, grown-up! You are out on your own, living your own life. Sure it can be tough to make ends meet some months and you don't always get to buy the things you want, but you are independent! Feel free to move on to the next section.

If you answered mostly ***c:*** Whoa, sister! You need to dial it back a notch. Yes, your twenties are a time to become independent and prepare for your future, but this is also the time to have fun! Live a little! Budget in some indulgences for yourself. You need to find some balance or you will be old before your time.

If you answered mostly *d:* Okay, Paris, we're glad to see you're enjoying our book. Really, we are.

Remember the movie *Failure to Launch* starring Matthew McConaughey and Sarah Jessica Parker? McConaughey's character, Tripp, is a full-grown adult who still lives with his parents. He insists on remaining in an adult–child relationship with them—even though he's well over thirty. Mommy cooks delicious meals, washes his dirty boxers, and cleans up his childhood room. Let's consider how his failure to launch in his twenties will inevitably affect his ability to function as an equal partner in a marriage. He has no motivation to exit his parents' house, but continues to live as an emotionally stunted boy who will likely try to marry someone with all the characteristics of his doting mother. He will have to find someone to replace his mother's role, or worse yet, a woman who will take a backseat to his relationship with dear ol' Mom.

Most of you can see the problem inherent in a *man* living like a *boy* in his parents' house (although most of us would jump at the chance to marry McConaughey even if he lived in a cage and his mommy fed him from a bottle!), but what harm is there in your staying in your parents' house for a few more years? After all, it's tough to find a good roommate, especially one who cleans up after you. And do you have any idea what a one-bedroom apartment in a safe neighborhood is going for these days? We understand that today's job market is incredibly tough and that the cost of living—especially in major cities, where coincidentally the best jobs are—can be exorbitant. Despite these challenges, it is imperative that you take whatever steps are necessary to establish your own address. If that means forgoing the spacious condo abounding in character in favor of a standard motel-style apartment with several roommates, then downgrade already! What it will probably mean is that you will have to cut out extras such as eating out, trips to the mall, cab rides, and cutting-edge technology. Even without these things, you'll survive. The pain of the cutbacks will be lessened by the pride you'll feel, knowing that you are making it on your own and providing the basics for yourself. Oh, and by the way, no fair taking your laundry back to Mommy every Sunday afternoon. You're on your own now!

Personal Insight from Celeste

I'll never forget the moment that old what's-his-face handed me the keys to my very first apartment. Well, it wasn't exactly all my own, but I did have a one-third right to the lease, along with my two roommates. The apartment may have been on a busy street and may not have had those gleaming hardwood floors we were after, but it did have nice, clean apartment-grade carpet. The carpet actually turned out to be a real positive, since it was quite some time before we could afford furniture to sit on.

I spent half my first paycheck on new pots and pans, towels, spices, and a set of cement blocks, also known as My New Bookcase. My roommates and I cooked in *our* kitchen, lazed around in *our* living room and took out *our* trash. I can't say we never waited for the pink Disconnect Notice to arrive before paying *our* electric bill, but it was *our* electric bill (and *our* reconnection fee . . .). It was this experience of living on my own that taught me about the practical aspects of life such as cleaning up after myself, grocery shopping, bill-paying, laundry, and the importance of keeping the ice trays filled. It's not that I was raised in a barn—far from it. (Hi, Mom.) In fact, I had more than a vague sense of all-things-domestic before moving out on my own, but it was much different when I didn't have Mommy and Daddy around to fill in the gaps.

Living on my own with roommates was stressful at times, especially on days when rent was due, or when there were disagreements about whose breakfast dishes were in the sink or why someone's favorite ice cream had disappeared without her permission. In the end, signing that very first lease and the several more that followed taught me to become self-sufficient and was worth every challenge along the way.

Dorothy Was Right: There Really Is No Place Like Home

This just in . . . "2009 College Grads Flock Back Home—Four Out of Five College Grads Move Back in with Their Parents!" According to a July 2009 poll conducted by CollegeGrad.com, 80 percent of college grads reported moving back home with their parents after graduation. This is up from 67 percent in 2006. What's going on? Some career experts cite a troubled economy and an increasingly high cost of living as the culprit; others attribute the trend to Gen Y's especially close relationships with their parents; and still others claim that it's easier to move back home now because doing so carries fewer stigmas than in previous generations. While all these factors may contribute to the growing trend, we're not convinced that any of them fully account for it. Family support and closeness are one thing, but delaying the leap into adulthood by remaining financially and emotionally dependent on your family is another. We suspect that twentysomethings are moving home in droves because of their unrealistic expectations of post-college life and their unwillingness to adjust to a lower standard of living than they enjoy at Mom and Dad's. Our suspicions led us to conduct our own poll on the issue. Here's what we found. . . .

When asked to list their *basic necessities,* 83 percent of those polled listed such things as cell phones, biweekly manicures, TiVo, gym memberships, and bottled water; 71 percent thought it was reasonable to expect that they should be able to go out to dinner and a movie (or drinks) with friends at least once per weekend and 44 percent reported spending more than $250 on a purse in the past six months. Most alarmingly, the percentage of those who had at least four thousand dollars in credit card debt was 66 percent. When their entry-level incomes can't support their inflated lifestyle expectations, these disillusioned twentysomethings flock home. Ladies, it's time for a reality check.

Most of the women we polled expected to be able to duplicate their parents' standard of living within two years of graduating from college. Did these women just forget that their parents' lifestyle was the result of years of sacrifice and hard work? Do you think that you can't move out on your own until you land a job that affords you the comforts with which you were raised? Do you expect that you should be able to move directly from your college dorm to a nice apartment, full of nice furniture, in a nice neighborhood, on your nice entry-level salary? If you expect that your lifestyle should be as it was growing up, or even as it was in college when everything was heavily subsidized, you need to rethink your expectations. The goal is to be on your own, living like the grown-up that you are, even if that means living frugally for a while. Sure you may miss the home-cooked meals served on your mom's mahogany dining room table, but we know from experience that even Top Ramen can be pretty tasty when you're eating it in your own apartment, on your own Formica kitchen table that you got for a steal on Craigslist.

Back in the Old Hood: A Temporary Solution

If after taking an honest look at what you *actually* need versus what you *think* you need, you still decide that living at home is your best option, make a promise to yourself that it will be *temporary*. There are only a few situations in which moving home should be an option: You are unemployed with no real prospects in sight, you've just graduated and don't have a specific plan in place yet, or you've just moved back into town after traveling abroad and haven't found an apartment or roommates yet. While moving back home can certainly ease the initial financial strain, it is not a permanent solution. If moving back home is the only or the best option, it should be entered into with a very specific time line in mind. If you don't set a time limit on how long you remain living at home, it will be very easy to lose your motivation to establish your own address. After all, it's pretty comfy there.

How long should you stay? Six months is ideal. You need just enough time to find a job and save enough money to cover your initial expenses, including first and last months' rent. *One year* should be the absolute max, unless, of course, you are dealing with some extraordinary circumstance, such as illness or family emergency. And while you're back at the old stomping grounds, we challenge you to set up a few of your own house rules. Here are some suggestions:

House Rule #1: Work. Even if you are working diligently at finding a full-time job, you should pick up a part-time job during your search. This could mean working at your local Starbucks or department store or selling stuff on eBay. Now is not the time for pride. It's important for you to maintain a sense of productivity, save up, and contribute at least something to Mom and Dad's household expenses during this interim period.

House Rule #2: Pay rent. Even if it's as little as a hundred bucks per month. Your contribution will help you feel more like the independent woman you *almost* are and less like the freeloader you don't want to be. Tip: If your parents don't need the cash, you may want to work out an arrangement with them where they set aside the money you pay them for rent and put it toward a deposit for your own pad.

House Rule #3: Help out. Make it a point to clean up, grocery-shop, cook, garden, and do laundry (yes, even your little brother's) without being asked. Think of how pleasantly surprised and proud your parents will be! And what great practice for your upcoming role as Domestic Goddess.

If you want to make the most of this time at home and get to your launching pad as quickly as possible, there are several practical things you can be doing in addition to your job search. This temporary layover at your parents' house is the perfect time to figure out exactly what you will need to make your launch a reality.

Four Steps to Fleeing the Nest

Step 1: Check your credit score—FICO surprises aren't happy surprises. One of the smartest things you can do in anticipation of moving into your own place is to check your credit report to make sure it's accurate. A low credit score could disqualify you from being able to rent an apartment. If there is a mistake on any one of the three credit reports (Equifax, Experian, and TransUnion), you will need to contact the credit bureau and challenge the item. This process usually takes a few months to complete, so don't wait to begin. If your report is accurate, but your credit score is really low (below 600), you will probably need a cosigner to rent an apartment.

Step 2: Locate the perfect digs—home sweet rental. It's not too soon to start researching potential apartments. Getting a feel for what the rents are in various areas will help you focus your search. Can you afford to move to your first-choice area, or do you need to look at a less expensive, nearby neighborhood? Will you be able to afford to live on your own, or is it better to start with a roommate or two? A good rule of thumb is to limit your rental expense to no more than 30 percent of your *net* monthly income. Are utilities included? How much will be required for a deposit, and can you pay this over a few months or is it all due up front?

Before you decide on an apartment, you should definitely spend some time in the neighborhood to get a feel for neighbors, merchants, and safety of the area. Be sure to visit the apartment prior to moving in, and don't hesitate to bring a parent or wise (older) friend with you to ask questions, check the plumbing, and evaluate the neighborhood.

Step 3: Find great roommates—psychos and/or freeloaders need not apply. Sharing an apartment or house with roommates is often the ideal way to go when moving out for the first time. The obvious benefit of roommates is shared rent and utilities, but there are other perks as well. They'll help keep the place clean, your DVD collection will instantly expand, and if you choose well, you may even find that you enjoy their company and gain some new friends along the way. Another important benefit of living with roommates is that you're getting great practice for marriage. You are learning what it's like to live with a non-family member, in a real-world (read: non-college) situation. You are learning to divide labor, be thoughtful, and peacefully coexist with someone—all things that will ease your eventual transition into marriage.

The best way to find good roommates is through personal

networking. Fellow school alums, friends, friends of friends, and coworkers are all good possibilities. If those are all dead ends, there are plenty of other available resources. Gyms, cafés, churches, synagogues, and local newspapers often have listings of people looking for roommates. There are also several established online resources worth looking at such as EasyRoommate.com, RoommateNation.com, Roommates.com, and Craigslist.org.

Make sure that these potential roommates have the proven ability to hold down a job, reasonably decent standards for cleanliness, and respect for others' belongings. Check and double-check references. Doing your homework will ensure that you don't come home from work one day to find your roommate and six of her pot buddies sprawled out naked on your new couch, finishing up the Chinese food leftovers you were looking forward to having for dinner and washing it down with the bottle of vintage champagne your favorite uncle gave you for graduation.

Step 4: Gather the basics—building your nest. Check out our website for a list of the basic household items you will need to set up shop at your new pad. If you start rounding these things up now, it won't seem like such an effort or expense in the end. You should have enough to help you survive your first months on your own, without having to run back home to raid your parents' kitchen cupboards or order out every night. Acquiring these things can require a serious chunk of change, so you can always make the plea to family and friends for old furniture and dishes. They're usually happy to help.

For more helpful tips, pick up a copy of, *Out on My Own, Now What?: Tips and Insights So You're Not Left Hanging in the Real World*, by Joe Kahler.

Getting the key to your apartment is exhilarating, but be forewarned: That feeling of pride in your independence may wane upon the arrival of your first set of bills. Even if you are stalwart in your decision to remain physically independent, you can easily be lured back into the trap of financial dependence on your parents. This next section will bolster your resolve.

Financial Independence: It's Time to Cut the Purse Strings

It is easy to be independent when you've got money. But to be independent when you haven't got a thing—that's the Lord's test.

—Mahalia Jackson, gospel singer

If you are serious about this independence thing, you have to be willing to let it hit you where it counts . . . in the Prada wallet you probably can't afford. Unless you are a full-time student, it's officially time to stop accepting money from Mom and Dad. Yes, even if "they really get a lot of joy from helping" or "they can afford it" or "they could really use the tax break." Yes, even if you won't be able to afford your _____ (fill in the blank—apartment, car payment, gourmet cheese habit, summer house in the Hamptons) without their assistance.

AUDREY

Audrey moved out on her own six months ago. Now, whenever she meets her parents for dinner, she makes a point of telling them how she is taking control of her life, making responsible choices, and really "coming into her own." Yet as the first of each month rolls around, Audrey finds herself on the phone with Daddy asking for his help with rent. Does she really believe her own claims of independence? By allowing Daddy to subsidize her "independent" life, she's just playing grown-up and cheating herself out of the self-respect that results from bona fide self-reliance.

The cold hard truth is that until you meet the challenge of being truly financially autonomous, you will miss out on the confidence that comes from knowing, for the first time in your life, that you are no longer dependent on someone else to take care of you. How empowering it will be when you don't have to use your parents' financial help as a crutch, knowing that you can stand on your own self-pedicured feet.

She Who Controls the Purse Controls the Person

Gaining financial independence clears the way for you to develop a more adult relationship with your parents. Now you can actually call Mom or Dad for the sole purpose of saying *hey* rather than always concluding the conversation with a request for cash. Standing on your own two feet financially frees you up to talk to your parents about your purchases and plans in a way that you never could when it was *their* money you were spending. At last, you will be free to admit to Mom that, yes, your sweater *is* new—without that sheepish look on your face.

As Melody Serafino wrote in her recent *Newsweek* article, "Subsidized in the City,"

> At 25, I'm still questioning what it means to be an adult. But I know that part of it means having the financial independence to never have to rely on my parents for my decision-making. This is indicative of a sort of social independence as well. If I want to plan a vacation halfway around the world, I do—and no one can tell me otherwise, because I am depending on my own means to get there. I can live wherever I want because I am paying my own rent. Financial independence has allowed for absolute control over my own life—an undeniably liberating feeling.

Beware: Strings Attached

For some of you, the process of becoming fiscally free from your parents may be fraught with some unexpected obstacles. In many families, parents express their love for their children by showering them with money or big-ticket gifts. The ugly underbelly of magnanimous parents is that they may be using gift-giving as a way of exerting control over their adult children. This may be the case in your family and might even be a long-standing family tradition, going all the way back to that collection of two-hundred-plus Beanie Babies you owned by the time you were six. That tradition may also be in full force today as evidenced by your twentysomething apartment furnished, compliments of Mom and Dad, with multiple plasma-screen TVs and top-of-the-line cookware. To find out whether these gifts are string-free or not, you need to ask yourself a couple of tough questions. Your answers will help clarify whether the money or gifts you accept from your parents are creating an obstacle to your independence.

Am I able to make it each month without my parents' help? Answering this question requires you to distinguish between necessities and luxuries. Are you able to cover the basic necessities of your life, such as rent, food, insurance, transportation, and so on with *your* paycheck, or do you rely on a supplemental check from Bank of Daddy-O? It is imperative that you are able to provide for yourself when it comes to the basics. It's different when you're talking about luxuries. If your parents get a kick out of showing up on your doorstep with bags and boxes filled with extras that you wouldn't be able to swing on your entry-level salary, we're not suggesting that you refuse to accept them in the name of financial independence. By all means, take that new digital camera, panini press, or cashmere anything. Just don't forget to send a thank-you note.

Am I giving my parents too much control over my decisions

by accepting their money? If the answer is yes, you are robbing yourself of the self-assuredness that will only result from making your *own* decisions and trusting your *own* judgment.

SERENA

Serena moved back home after graduation. Her plan was to save up some money over the summer and then move to a cool new up-and-coming neighborhood in Chicago, where several of her college friends were already living. Money would be tight, but she thought she would be able to get by. When Serena shared her plans with her parents, they were less than thrilled and full of protests about her choice of neighborhood, ranging from the cost of rent to the lack of nearby el train stops. After listening to their string of complaints, Serena was convinced that the *real* reason they didn't want her to move to that area was because it was racially mixed. Her parents' racist streak had always been a source of tension between them, and Serena was determined not to let their narrow-minded values influence her decision. A few days after Serena's conversation with her parents, she received an e-mail from her dad that read, "Sweetie, your mom and I have decided to buy you a two-bedroom condo as a graduation present. We love you!" Serena was, of course, ecstatic. But there was one catch: If she wanted the condo, she would have to give up her hopes of moving to the city and instead stay put in the suburbs near them. Serena was furious, but eventually caved when she saw that the condo was nicer than anything she could afford on her own. She's been mad at her parents ever since for trying to control her life. But she's the one who sold them the reins for the price of the condo.

When you take the money and gifts your parents offer, you are accepting the strings that may come with them. Some parents will expect that they have bought some measure of control over your life as well. By taking money or sizable gifts from your parents in exchange for allowing them an inappropriate foothold in your life, you're making it impossible for your parents to view you as a mature adult and to respect your well-reasoned decisions. So don't get mad at Mom and Dad if they continue to treat you like a dependent child. You're acting like one.

Dangerous Curves Ahead

Carrying on this dicey financial dance with your parents can also have disastrous results on your future marriage. Don't fool yourself into thinking that once you get married this pattern will miraculously change. If you don't bite the bullet now and start learning how to live within your means, you are setting yourself up for some tough times in the future.

COURTNEY

Courtney and her mom enjoyed spending time together and always had plenty to talk about, but there was one thing they bonded over like nothing else—their love of shopping. Courtney had blissful childhood memories of days spent at the mall with Mom, pouring out of department stores with heaps of bags swinging on their arms. Those were the days. Courtney's shopping habit mellowed a bit through college, only to return with a vengeance after graduation.

To her roommates, it looked like Courtney was doing just fine. She had a good job and paid her part of the rent, a hefty car payment, and other bills on time each month. Incredibly, Courtney also seemed to have enough cash left over each month to treat herself to the latest designer jeans and dinners at the hip new restaurants in town. No one knew that Courtney and her mommy had a little secret . . . a joint credit card account. Courtney shopped to her heart's content and never saw the bill. It went straight to Mommy and Daddy, who promptly paid it off each month.

Courtney failed to share her secret with her boyfriend, Ryan, even after they were engaged. Courtney convinced herself that Ryan really didn't need to know and that it was between her and her mom, anyway. About six months after Courtney and Ryan were married, Ryan finally started taking notice of Courtney's seemingly endless purchases. He knew what their combined income was and knew that after paying the bills they couldn't possibly afford to pay for the things Courtney was buying. When Courtney tearfully admitted that her parents were subsidizing her spending habits, Ryan was understandably hurt and angry. "So your parents don't think we can make it on our own? Do you have any idea how that makes me feel? Is our lifestyle not enough for you?" Courtney reluctantly agreed to stop taking money from her parents and returned the credit card.

Needless to say, the transition was a hard one for Courtney. For the first time in her life, she was forced to be realistic about money, live within her means, and actually save up if she wanted to buy something extra, instead of just whipping out Mommy's Amex. After several years and countless fights with Ryan over money, Courtney has finally gotten to a place where she is financially responsible. As she told us, "I wish I'd never allowed myself to take that kind of help from my parents. Not only did it cause a lot of trouble in my marriage, but I also failed to learn the discipline of budgeting and delaying gratification in my twenties: two things that would have made my early years of marriage a lot less rocky."

When you continue to take money from your parents, you are hindering your own ability to become independent and are setting yourself up for problems down the road. As challenging as it can be to maintain financial independence, you can't be in charge of your own life as long as you rely on anyone else to pay your way. Once you've cut the parental purse strings and are experiencing the pride of fiscal freedom, you might become aware of the emotional entanglements preventing you from declaring complete independence. . . .

Emotional Independence: It's Time to Say No

Be who you are and say what you feel because those who mind don't matter and those who matter don't mind.

—*Dr. Seuss*

Having a close relationship with your parents is one of the greatest joys of life. We both adore our parents, value their wisdom and advice, and see them regularly. Never would we recommend that you separate from the love and emotional support of your parents. At this point in your life, the challenge is to monitor the emotional control your parents continue to wield over you. Take this quiz to help determine whether you have a healthy emotional connection with your parents:

Emotional Independence Inventory

T F I chose a major or job because my parents wanted me to.

T F I live where my parents want me to live.

T F I would never date a guy my parents wouldn't approve of.

T F I attend family events because my parents would be disappointed if I didn't.

T F I talk to my parents at least once a day.

T F I don't express opinions about religion or politics that differ from my parents', because it would devastate them.

T F I don't tell my parents about important life decisions that conflict with their values because I feel guilty.

If you answered TRUE to two or more of these questions, you need to get your emotional relationship with your parents in check. There is a good chance that your relationship is being harmed by an interpersonal dynamic called enmeshment.

The term *enmeshment* refers to a relationship in which the lives and identities of the members are so tightly intertwined that it is difficult for any of them to function independently. Enmeshed families can be difficult to identify because they are usually the ones that seem the closest and most nurturing. The problem is that these enmeshed families discourage any form of independence. Any separation from the family's emotional center is felt as abandonment and is resisted at all cost. If your parents are dependent on you for their happiness and sense of wholeness, they will oppose your efforts to separate and create an independent life. Sometimes your parents will express their opposition loudly and clearly; other times they communicate more subtly through emotional manipulation by making you feel guilty, as if your actions have let them down or you have disappointed them. Here are a few real-life examples of enmeshment.

"I don't want to disappoint my parents."

Kara wrote to us: "The hardest thing about becoming independent? I would definitely have to say that I have had a really tough time coming to the realization that I can trust my own judgment to make good decisions without worrying what my parents will think. I've learned that emotionally healthy grown-ups do things because they want to, or because it is the right thing to do, not because they want to please their parents or fear disappointing them. I hate to feel like I'm letting my parents down, but their vision for my life is so different than my own. I want to live in Boston and work in a design firm—maybe even start my own firm someday. My parents will only be happy if I stay in my hometown and become an architect like my mom. I don't want to make them unhappy, but I don't want to trade my dreams for theirs either. I guess that breaking away from their expectations of me is bound to cause them some pain, but I have to remind myself that it's part of growing up."

"I can't seem to stand up to my parents."

Warning: If you continue to let your parents govern your decisions now, you'll be hard-pressed to break the pattern once you are married, and will end up with a husband who resents you for putting your desire to please your parents before him.

Kelly and Brian were on the brink of divorce. For years, Brian had been frustrated by Kelly's pattern of bending over backwards to please her unreasonable and temperamental mother, no matter what the cost. At Kelly's insistence, holidays were always spent with her parents. Brian would sometimes put up a fight, but in the end, he always acquiesced, quietly making excuses to his own family. During their engagement, Kelly and Brian talked often about their future family and agreed that they would like to have at least three or four children. After their second child was born, Kelly's mom very loudly stated her opinion that "given the state of the world," it was irresponsible of anyone to have more than one or, at most, two children. For Kelly, that was the end of that. Despite Brian's trying to convince her otherwise, she had her tubes tied.

The most recent battle between them started when his long-term employer told Brian that he was going to be promoted to a position at the company's headquarters in a neighboring state. As expected, Kelly's mom reacted very negatively to the news, and Kelly was now refusing to move away with Brian, suggesting that he instead quit his job and work for her father in town.

"I make choices in order to gain my parents' approval."

All of us yearn to feel the glowing satisfaction of making our parents proud. You can still remember how good you felt when you brought home the soccer trophy and your dad said, "Good job!" or overhearing your mom at the salon bragging about your SAT scores. Of course it feels good when your parents approve of your accomplishments, but making decisions in order to gain their approval is giving them too much control over your life.

Take Annie, for example: No matter what Annie did, she could never gain her dad's approval—her grades were never good enough, her performance on the softball field was never up to par, and none of the guys she brought home could ever meet Dad's standards. Until Alex. Annie's dad more than approved of Alex—he adored him. For the first time in Annie's life, she felt like she had done something to gain her father's approval.

Annie was dating Alex for about a year when she discovered that he had been cheating on her the entire time he was away at college. She promptly broke up with him. Annie couldn't tell who was more devastated, her or her dad. Despite knowing the reason for the breakup, Annie's dad constantly encouraged her to reconcile with Alex. For Annie, the worst part of the breakup was not the loss of the relationship, but the loss of her father's approval.

A few years later, when Annie came home for Thanksgiving dinner, she was greeted at the door to her parents' house by none other than her old boyfriend, Alex! "Welcome home! Your dad invited me over for dinner—isn't that great?" She was initially annoyed at her dad's meddling, but sitting around the Thanksgiving table, seeing that look of pride in her dad's eyes that she had missed so much, felt really good. In response to her dad's persuasion and against her better judgment, Annie got back together with Alex and they eventually married. Not surprisingly, Alex cheated on Annie less than three years into their marriage. Annie told us after the divorce, "Looking back now, I can see clearly that I let my intense desire for Dad's approval cloud what I knew was right for me."

"I feel guilty when I do something my parents don't like."

Jenn grew up going to Mass every Sunday morning with her family and attending Catholic school. Both her parents were devout in their faith and made every attempt to instill their religious beliefs in their children. As a child, Jenn enjoyed going to church and attending catechism classes with her friends. She fondly remembers her confirmation as a day she was surrounded by loving friends and family who gathered to celebrate her commitment to the faith. But when Jenn left home for college, she began to question her faith and struggled to figure out what she believed, apart from her parents. By the time she reached her junior year, Jenn had stopped going to Mass altogether and began inquiring about several different religions. When Jenn turned twenty-seven and started graduate school, she had openly renounced Catholicism.

When it came to her parents, however, Jenn's renouncement was more of a whisper. Jenn just couldn't bear the thought of telling them that she was no longer a practicing Catholic, let alone that she wasn't even sure she believed in God! When her parents would come to visit for the weekend, Jenn continued her charade by taking them to Sunday Mass at a local church, playing along as though she were a regular. Jenn was always furious with herself afterwards for not having the guts to just sit down with her parents, adult-to-adult, and be honest about her decision to leave the Catholic Church. Why couldn't she just be true to herself? It's not like she had come to the decision rashly and couldn't defend it. It was just that she felt so guilty about going against something she knew was incredibly important to both of them.

If you can identify with any of these women, you may be allowing your parents to dictate your decisions or actions to your own detriment. It might seem more comfortable to avoid the pain of emotional separation by doing what your parents want you to do right now, but it's *your* life. You are the one who will have to live with the consequences of your decisions.

Complete this exercise to see how you'll feel in the future if you choose to give up something you truly want, in favor of making Mom and Dad happy now.

It's My Life

Are your parents trying to control a certain aspect of your life? Are you allowing their feelings to determine their choices? Are you considering an upcoming choice between what you want to do and what will please your parents? Remember, in order to make grown-up decisions on your own, you have to think like a mature adult. Have you considered the practical aspects of your decision? Do you have the money? Is it safe? Is it consistent with your long-term goals? Assuming you have thought through the logistics of your decision, let's think through your feelings about your decision.

Decision I'm facing: Example: My parents think I should go back to graduate school in the fall, but I want to take a year or two off to learn Chinese in Beijing.

How will I feel if I do what my parents *want me to do?* Like a good kid. Burned out and burdened by the thought of more studying. Good because I made them happy. Relieved that I won't have to deal with their disappointment in me. Mad at myself that I caved in to their pressure.

How will I feel if I do what I *want to do?* Free! Like a grown-up who can make my own decisions. Guilty for going against what my parents want for me. Excited to have a new cultural experience. Worried that I'll have a tough time transitioning back to grad school. Smart to beef up my résumé with Chinese fluency. Refreshed when I return ready to jump back into school.

How will I feel in twenty years if I don't *do what I want to do?* I will regret it. I'll probably have a husband and children and won't have as much freedom to pick up and go. I'll feel like I wasted a great opportunity. I'll wonder what career opportunities I will have missed.

Will my parents' reaction last twenty years? No, I'm sure that they will get over it if I make my own choice. And besides, even if I do go along with their wishes, their happiness will last only so long. At some point in the next twenty years, it's inevitable that I will make a decision that conflicts with their desires. So no matter what I do now, they will eventually be disappointed with my choices.

My decision: China, 我来! (Here I come!)

Brace yourself for the inevitable fallout when your parents discover that you are making your own decisions. You and your parents have established quite a groove. From the moment you were born, you have relied on them to guide you and help you make decisions that were best for you. Throughout your twenties and early thirties, as the balance of authority over your life tips in your direction, both you and your parents will naturally feel some degree of upset and awkwardness. It's okay to express your discomfort and uncertainty to your parents; they are going through their own difficult transition. Remember, you're not getting rid of the relationship, just rearranging it a bit to allow room for important growth in your life.

Making the Break Without Breaking the Relationship

After all these years, your parents still know how to push your buttons and resurrect old doubts. They're your biggest fans and harshest critics. No matter how mature, evolved, independent, or successful you become as an adult, you will continue to desire their approval. The good news is that if you're aware of this fact, you'll be able to give your parents' opinions their proper place and will begin to transform your parent–child dynamic into more of a peer relationship.

Establishing yourself as an emotionally independent woman doesn't mean that your relationship with Mom and Dad has to become distant or nonexistent, but it will require some adjustments (and maybe a little therapy on the side). Here are some guidelines to help you make the transition.

Draw Clear Boundaries

Growing up, your parents' nurturing, support, and involvement in your life were crucial to your healthy development. But as an adult, if you don't work to establish your separateness from Mom and Dad in your day-to-day life, that nurture can easily start to feel more smothering than supportive. In order to keep their involvement within appropriate limits, you'll need to establish and communicate clear boundaries around your physical and emotional space.

SASHA

Sasha's mom invaded her physical space by rearranging her furniture each time she came to visit. Instead of telling her mom that it offended her, Sasha would fume silently and wait until her mom left to put the furniture back where it was. At our suggestion, Sasha greeted her mother at the door one day with a hot cup of tea and said, "Mom, I love when you come to visit, so let's go sit on the couch *right where it is* and use the short time we have together to catch up instead of redecorating." While there was no magic in the words we gave her, approaching her mom in this mature, nonreactionary way enabled Sasha to draw a clear physical boundary.

Parents are even more likely to cross emotional boundaries than to violate physical boundaries. You don't need to keep your parents abreast, in real-time, of your day-to-day life. Even if they ask, it's all right to answer their questions with limited information. When Mom wants the details of your hot date or your pay raise, it's okay—it's really okay—to respectfully refuse to divulge. The tough part is being clear with them when you don't feel comfortable about what they're asking. While skirting the issue or changing the subject are both viable options, the Mature, Emotionally Independent Adult response is to tell them, lovingly and calmly, that you don't want to discuss that particular subject with them. When in doubt, humor is always a good option. Here's an example of how a typical conversation might go. You'll be playing the part of the Mature, Emotionally Independent Adult ("MEIA").

MOM: *So, how was last night?*

MEIA: *It was fun! Rob's a really nice guy.*

MOM: *Did you stay out late?*

MEIA: *Not too late—I was pretty tired after working all day.*

MOM: *Well, did he come back to your apartment after dinner?*

MEIA (STARTING TO GET UNCOMFORTABLE): *Yeah, for a bit.*

MOM: *And? I want details! . . .*

MEIA: *Well, you're* not *going to get any, primarily because it's none of your business. But if you just can't stand the suspense, I'll be happy to send you a copy of the nanny-cam video.*

Nicely done! Notice how you balanced clear boundaries with easy breezy humor? See how you avoided whiny protests about how your mom is too nosy, controlling, and doesn't respect your privacy? Now, doesn't that feel good?

Address Hurts as Quickly as Possible

Small rebuffs such as an insensitive comment about your new haircut or choice of paint color for your living room can be hurtful, but can be overcome. Don't overreact by allowing a small comment to send you hurtling backwards into pouty-child mode. If a friend said something that hurt your feelings, you would tell her so because you know keeping it inside will hurt the friendship. The same should now be the case for your parents. When they do something to offend you, find the right time to explain to them how it upset you. Ask them to do the same with you. That way, you're treating your relationship with the same respect and hopes for longevity as you would with any friendship that is important to you.

Stay Connected

All parents want to feel appreciated and acknowledged as having an important place in their adult children's lives. An easy way to satisfy this need is to stay in touch with them. Even if your parents don't appear to need you to take the initiative in the relationship, they probably do. Remember, the world moves pretty fast these days, and your parents may think you are too busy with your full life to bother keeping in regular contact with them. This concept of taking the initiative may be a new one for you to consider since, as a young adult, you have usually been on the receiving end of the communication with your parents. Even your small efforts to stay connected can be very meaningful for your parents. Calling to say hi and update them on your life can go a long way toward making them feel important, especially during this time when you are separating from them in your quest for independence.

Find Common Interests

When you start viewing your parents more as friends and less as authority figures, you will have a great opportunity to enjoy them in new ways. One of the best things you and your parents can do is to pursue common interests together. These interests could include everything from charitable causes to sports, politics, and gardening.

Catherine, twenty-six, and her dad recently spent the day together planting tomatoes, kitchen herbs, and dahlias in the window boxes of her new apartment. "Our relationship has changed dramatically over the past few years," said Catherine. "Things were a little rocky between us during college and right after, but we're finally starting to make a transition. After years of not trusting my judgment, he is starting to view me more as an adult and I'm able to take his advice without feeling so defensive. Spending time together working in my makeshift garden was really nice. We truly enjoyed each other's company."

There are many ways to enjoy your parents as adult friends. Here are a few:

- Introduce your parents to your friends. Include them in social gatherings when appropriate.

- Eat out together. Experience a cuisine none of you have tried before.
- Tell your parents about your favorite author or musician. Send them a copy of a book or CD you enjoyed.
- If you are close in proximity to them, join a book club or sign up for a 5K together.
- Take your parents to a concert or local theater. Wanna really show off your independence? Foot the bill!

Gaining physical, financial, and emotional independence is a challenging but critical undertaking. But take heart: This triad of independence is not something that must be accomplished by the time you finish reading this chapter, or even by the time you finish reading the book. If approached properly, it will take you throughout your twenties and into your early thirties to completely gain independence. Still, that doesn't give you license to snuggle up in your childhood room in front of your new Apple 2.5GHz Quad-Core PowerPC G5 your parents just bought you while they hover around, helping you sift through profiles on Match.com. Now is the time to gain independence from your parents and begin to live your life on your own terms. If you rise to the challenge, you'll find in the end that you've become a woman who trusts her own judgment and can take care of herself. You'll be free to choose marriage out of a desire to share your life with somebody, not because you can't make it on your own. We are officially pushing you out of the nest. Stretch your wings and fly like the wind!

Chapter 10

Key #8: Get a Spiritual Life

Clarify Your Beliefs

Just as a candle cannot burn without fire, men cannot live without a spiritual life.

—*Buddha*

Spirituality is simply the way of answering the big questions we all ask: *What is my purpose in life? Why am I here? How should I live? What's life all about?* Finding the answers to those questions is, of course, a very personal journey. While no one should dictate your personal faith, we do encourage you to clarify what you believe, *before* you get married. Here's why: We've worked with hundreds of women who didn't take the time to clarify their spiritual beliefs before marriage and who ended up marrying men whose faith differed from their own, resulting in serious marital problems, and even divorce down the road.

(Note: For the purposes of this chapter, we will often use the term *God*. This is not a reference to any particular reli-

gion's deity; it is simply the most common title for "higher power" and more concise than writing "Higher Power, YHWH, Buddha, Allah, Krishna, and the many Hindu gods.")

Some women make the mistake of marrying a man they clearly know has different beliefs than they do, but reason that it is really no big deal. Like Carrie . . .

CARRIE

"I grew up Jewish but wasn't practicing my faith when I met David. He was Mormon and went to church every weekend. I respected his beliefs, even though they were a lot different than mine, and knew he was going to be a good family man. We never really talked much about religion before we got married because it wasn't as important to me then as it was to him. But when our first son Joshua was born, I assumed we would have a bris. My husband absolutely refused. Something inside me snapped. While religion hadn't been very important to me, I just couldn't bear the thought of not circumcising my son according to Jewish tradition. When I told David how I felt, he just stared at me with a confused look on his face and said, 'Then why didn't you marry a Jew?' It was a fair question. I guess I reasoned that his religion was *his* business, but now that I had a child, I wanted desperately for him to view God as I did.

"This issue of religion has caused many fights between us over the years. With the help of a good therapist, we finally agreed that we would teach Joshua about each of our religious beliefs and let him decide which religion, if any, he wants to follow. That sounds like a decent solution, but sometimes it feels like we are both trying to get Josh to pick one of us over the other."

Other women encounter spiritual problems in their marriages because they didn't take the time to define their own beliefs before they got married. Like Julia . . .

JULIA

"I didn't grow up in a religious home. My dad grew up Southern Baptist and hated the rules and restrictions. My mom died when I was young and my dad didn't really talk to me about religion, so I don't know what she believed. I met Finn on a trip abroad my junior year of college and we got married shortly after graduation. Finn was a very spiritual person, but he hated organized religion almost as much as my dad, which felt familiar to me. One day, I answered the door to our apartment and ended up talking to a missionary for forty-five minutes. She seemed so peaceful and talked about God like he was an authentic part of her life. I had never heard anyone talk about God like that. For her, it was a lot more than just rules and restrictions.

"Meeting that woman was the first step of my own religious journey. After that, I started searching. I read books about all the different religions; I visited a Catholic priest, a Buddhist monk, a Methodist pastor, and a Jewish rabbi. I asked questions, journaled, and prayed. Once I figured out what I believed, I discovered a deep satisfaction and peace. The particular religion that resonated with me is irrelevant, but I will tell you that it had a dramatic impact on my relationship with my husband. And not in a good way. He felt betrayed that I chose to believe in something he was so vehemently against. I wanted to discuss my newfound faith but he refused, accusing me of trying to convert him. I always thought we could weather any storm, but we've separated for now and we're going to counseling to see if we can work it out or not."

Marriage and Faith

One of the most rewarding aspects of a marital relationship is shared spiritual beliefs, which can create a strong bond, a solid foundation, and a common purpose for a family. Studies show that marriages between people of the same faith have a greater survival rate than those between couples with differing religious beliefs. Many reports reveal that religiously mixed marriages are less satisfying than single-faith marriages. As Esther Perel, an interfaith marital therapist wrote about the difficulties of Christian and Jewish interfaith marriages in *New York* magazine, "The difference isn't just between Moses and Christ. You're dealing with issues of money, sex, education, child-rearing practices, food, family relationships, styles of emotional expressiveness, issues of autonomy—all of these are culturally embedded."

Sometimes women argue that spirituality simply doesn't matter to them. Other times, one or the other person in a couple agrees to convert to their partner's religion. Unfortunately, this doesn't necessarily solve the problem. As Egon Mayer points out in *USA Today*, "When you bury something that is really important to you, all you're doing is building up a kind of pressure within the family relationship, which becomes a source of tension, which ultimately becomes a time bomb. If there's any reason why inter-faith marriages break up, it's because of that time bomb."

Studies show that commitment to religion is at its lowest point among eighteen- to thirty-nine-year-olds, the very years when you are deciding whom you will marry! Most people experience a resurgence in their spirituality later in life. Although spirituality might seem like a less-than-crucial issue at the time you are dating someone and contemplating marriage, it's common for your spiritual beliefs to reveal themselves later when it comes time to educate your children about religion.

Many women report that they put aside their relationships with God and the church during their twenties, but that once they had children, they experienced a recommitment to the religion of their childhood. Why is that? Your spirituality is an important part of who you are, whether you focus on it or not. Having children brings out your true beliefs and desires when it comes to God. You know deep down that your beliefs provide a solid foundation for your life, and you want nothing less for your children. It may seem that you won't need to visit those issues for years to come, but now is actually the time to decide what you will teach those children about God and the world we live in. Is God involved in everyday life? Do miracles happen? Do you thank God when good things happen? Does God get the blame when bad things happen? What happens when you die? Is God a personal, loving God or harsh and punishing? How does God communicate with you, if at all?

Disagreements on how to raise children are a major cause of interfaith marriage breakups. If you plan to raise your children with your spiritual values, you must give them a father who shares those values or you are bound to struggle throughout your marriage. Do you want your child to be baptized? Circumcised? Go to private religious school? Celebrate your religious holidays? It might seem like it's way too soon to be thinking about what you want for your children, but now is actually the perfect time to determine what you believe so you can make the most compatible choice in a spouse. Your twenties and early thirties are a time to examine the beliefs your family raised you with and decide which are truly your own.

Faith of Your Family

Your beliefs are indelibly impacted by your parents' beliefs and how you were raised. We're not saying your beliefs were *determined* by your parents, just *influenced*. Here are some of the most common ways our clients report having been influenced by their parents' beliefs:

The Do-as-I-Say, Not-as-I-Do Parents

Sophie's parents made sure the whole family went to church each Sunday. They prayed before meals and at bedtime. They thanked God for good weather, parking spaces at the mall, and flourishing flowers in the garden. Sophie's parents were well known in the church and community as model Lutherans. But Sophie saw a different side. She knew that her father had been having an affair with a fellow churchgoer and that her mother drank too much and cussed like a sailor at Sophie and her brother. Because Sophie identified religion so strongly with her parents, she concluded that religion was for hypocrites. If the most pious of believers in the pews every Sunday were such blatant sinners at home, she didn't want any part of it. As soon as she got out of the house to go to college, Sophie swore off religion and vowed never to set foot in a church again.

You might have come from a similar situation in which your parents put up a façade of sainthood but were far from holy. Maybe they went to church but had a raging porn addiction, or abused you physically or emotionally. Understandably, you might have thrown the religious baby out with the hypocritical bathwater.

The Choose-Your-Own-Religion Parents

Regan's parents insisted that religion was a personal decision and sought to let her choose her own spiritual path. Regan's friends always thought she was so lucky to have parents who let her do what she wanted and didn't make her go to church or synagogue. She told herself that she should feel thankful for the freedom to make her own choices, but she actually just felt confused. If faith was really that important, why didn't her parents have an opinion on the subject? And if it was such a significant, life-defining decision, why wouldn't her parents help her think it through? She went to religious services with her friends but ended up more confused than ever. She studied world religions in college but never looked beyond the intellectual aspect to develop her true spiritual life. Regan could answer any question about what each religion professed, but never had a personal experience of God. She told us, "I feel spiritually empty even though I know more about religion than most people. I wish that my parents had at least taught me about the importance of my soul. I'm envious of people who talk about God with confidence in what they believe."

If your parents left it up to you to decide which religion you would follow, they might have communicated to you, by example, that spirituality is not important. They shared with you their views about politics and social issues, why not their religious views? Because they were not passionate enough about their own spiritual beliefs to share them with you, they demonstrated that faith was simply not significant. By taking a hands-off approach to faith, they actually sent you a subtle but clear message that your soul didn't warrant their attention or guidance.

The Hellfire-and-Damnation Parents

Nina grew up believing that if she didn't go to church and keep the Ten Commandments, she would burn in hell. Her parents painted a picture of a God who created her to do good deeds and to obey his rules without question. Whenever Nina asked questions about the faith or Scriptures, her parents shamed her and made her feel sinful for daring to question the Truth. Her parents had very strict rules and justified them by telling her that "God wanted to tame her sinful ways." When Nina went to college, she turned her back on her parents, their religion, and God. She partied hard and slept around, rebelling against every rule her parents had ever imposed on her in the name of religion. Needless to say, church was no longer part of her Sunday-morning routine.

If you can relate to Nina's upbringing, you might still feel the sting of guilt and shame whenever you break the rules or "sin." Because your parents taught you to view God as harsh, it makes sense that you wouldn't want to have anything to do with their judgmental, condemning God. Or you might fall on the other end of the spectrum and hold tight to your parents' beliefs because they were drilled into your head and you weren't ever allowed to question your faith. But if something is really the truth, it will always stand up to questioning. Examine the faith for yourself and decide to believe something because it is *true,* rather than because your parents *told* you to believe it. Whether they guided you with a heavy hand or took a hands-off approach, your parents' attitudes about spirituality left an imprint on yours.

The Bitter-at-God Parents

Bella grew up in a home where God was a sore subject. Her parents were both raised in very religious households, but after her mom died of stomach cancer when Bella was three, her dad completely turned his back on his faith. When Bella asked if she could go to church with a friend from junior high school, her dad went ballistic and said, "Sure you can go, but when you're there, why don't you ask God why he took your mother away from us?" Though Bella was curious about God and spiritual things, she never pursued faith because to her, it would have felt like a betrayal of her father. Bella shared with us, "I felt like praying was the equivalent of hanging out with my dad's sworn enemy. Out of loyalty to my dad, I just couldn't bring myself to seek out God. I often think I'm missing out on an important part of my life, but I have some of my own bitterness toward God as well. Besides, my dad would be pretty unhappy if he thought I was interested in religion."

Maybe you or your parents experienced a great loss that seemed like a betrayal from God. Your parents' bitterness toward God became your only knowledge of spirituality. You might have experienced something terrible yourself and never found a way to reconcile the tragedy with a loving or fair God. Either way, your view of God is colored by your experience. This rejection of spirituality is a reaction to a specific set of circumstances. Don't let bitterness determine your beliefs. Ask questions about God until you are satisfied with the answers.

We are all influenced by our parents' messages about God, whether by listening to what they said or watching the way they lived. As you look back on those experiences, it's important to remember that your parents are flawed and not a perfect representative of any religion. Basing your personal beliefs on your parents' hypocrisy, bitterness, legalism, indifference, or moral failings is a childish approach to faith. As an adult, your faith must instead be formed by objectively considering the six essential elements of spirituality.

Six Essential Elements of Spirituality

1. **Conviction.** What do I believe?
2. **Character.** Who am I really?
3. **Change.** What will I do to better myself?
4. **Community/Culture.** Who knows me?
5. **Contribution/Charity.** What will I give?
6. **Commitment.** Where will I place my faith?

Conviction: What Do I Believe?

Faith is not belief. Belief is passive. Faith is active.

—Edith Hamilton

Now is the time to take out your beliefs, dust them off, and examine them. Do you claim to believe something that you've never even completely thought through? Are your spiritual beliefs your own, or were they just inherited from your family? How would your faith stand up to questioning? Let's find out.

What Is My Personal Faith Statement?

1. What is your name for God?
2. List as many characteristics as you can of God.
3. Where do I practice my faith—church, synagogue, home, the mountains, the ocean?
4. Which religion, if any, do I belong to or agree with?
5. Is God active or inactive in my life?
6. How do I demonstrate my faith?
7. How do I feel about God—ambivalent, loving, grateful, doubtful, angry, unsure, peaceful?
8. How does God feel about me?
9. What would I like to learn about God?

Now plug the answers from the questions above into the faith statement below.

My Current Statement of Faith:
I believe in (1)________________________ who is (2)________________________. I worship (1)__________ at (3)________________________. I consider myself to be (4)________________________. My God is (5)______________in my life. I show God I am faithful by (6)________________________________.
I feel (7) ________________ about God. I think God feels (8) ________________ about me. If I could ask God one question, it would be (9) ________________________?

If you had difficulty completing this exercise, it means you have some work to do to figure out what your convictions about God are. The best ways to determine your convictions are through education and experience.

Education

Spirituality is about much more than religion, but if you don't know exactly what you believe, investigating various religions is a great place to start. For an overview of the five main world religions, go to LastOneDownTheAisleWins.com and look at the Spirituality section. You might want to check out religionfacts.com or beliefnet.com. You can also get a deeper understanding of any religion by reading its sacred texts and talking to someone of that particular faith.

Experience

Attend a worship service. When you attend a service, pay close attention to how you feel inside, in your soul. You might find that the traditional service of the Orthodox Temple feels like your spiritual home, or perhaps you will feel most comfortable in a nondenominational Christian church with a modern, upbeat band, or maybe the reverential Catholic Mass with its admiration and awe of God will be the place you most feel God's presence. Newspapers list the service times of various houses of worship in the Saturday paper, or you can always check online for services in your area.

Pray. Prayer is simply communicating with God. As Gandhi said, "In prayer it is better to have a heart without words than words without a heart." It is not necessary to even have a specific name for the God to whom you are praying. You can just pray a simple prayer like this: "Reveal yourself to me. I want to know you." Talk about whatever is on your mind. If you are confused, question God. If you are angry, yell at God. If you feel lonely, cry out to God. If you feel ashamed, confess to God.

Coming to God in prayer is a key part of any spiritual practice because it keeps us honest with ourselves and with our God. It's impossible to keep our hearts hidden during sincere prayer. The simple act of praying reveals our hearts to ourselves and to God, clearing the way for deeper spiritual communion.

Be silent. We don't get a lot of silence in our lives these days with cell phones, constant texting, and iPods blasting music, from the moment we open our eyes in the morning until we plug them in at night while we try to recharge our *own* batteries. But the voice of the soul is quiet, and it best communes with God when we are silent. We realize that this is a tall order for some. Silence makes many of us anxious and antsy. We are so used to being busy that we don't know what to do with ourselves once we intentionally quiet the noisy din of life and sit in silence. As you try the following exercises, you might discover that your constant busyness has been a means of avoiding dealing with some painful soul issues. Silence reveals what is brewing under the surface, so listen to your heart and let it draw you into the stillness of your soul.

Meditation. Sit in a quiet place with your eyes closed. Take deep breaths. Let your thoughts flow in and out of your mind without judging them. Try a "breath prayer" in which you think a word like *peace* with every inward breath and *grace* with every outward breath.

Prayer journal. For this journal exercise, begin with five to ten minutes of silence or listen to music without words, to help your mind ease away from daily distractions. Make this a letter to God. Write whatever comes to mind. Don't censor your writing or worry about punctuation. Ask God a question, pray about the things that are weighing on your mind, thank God for all the good things in your life. . . .

Character: Who Am I When Nobody's Looking?

Reputation is what men and women think of us; character is what God and the angels know of us.

—*Thomas Paine*

Spirituality determines who we are at a basic, soul level. Are you authentic? Do you live your life with integrity? Do you respect yourself and do others respect you? Take the following true-or-false quiz to see how you stack up.

Character Quiz

Integrity: Do I do what I say and say what I do?

T F I always keep my promises.
T F I tell the truth even when it makes me look bad.
T F I am known as a woman of my word.
T F I don't talk behind people's backs.
T F I don't make commitments until I'm sure I can follow through.

Morality: Do I live my life by upright standards?

T F I don't betray a friend's trust by disclosing her secrets.
T F I value my body and don't do anything with it I regret the next day.
T F I don't fudge the truth to get myself out of a bind.
T F I don't lie on my taxes.
T F I don't cheat on my boyfriends.

Authenticity: Do I live what I believe?

T F I don't try to pretend to be something I'm not.
T F I don't try to impress people with clothes or things.

T F I'm not overly concerned about appearances.
T F I admit it when I don't know the answer to someone's question.
T F I don't fake interest in people.

Generosity: Do I treat others as I want to be treated?
T F I stick up for people who are being treated unfairly.
T F I give of my time and money to others less fortunate.
T F I show compassion toward people who are suffering or in emotional turmoil.
T F I am available for my friends when they need me even if it's inconvenient.
T F I give others the credit they deserve.

Tally up your TRUE responses in each category. If you have three or fewer in a category, you need to focus on building your character in that area. Make yourself a promise right now that you will strive to become a woman of integrity, morality, authenticity, and generosity. List three small steps you will take this week to build your character. For example: *I will go to Mark's birthday party like I promised, even though Jill invited me to a concert that I'm dying to go to.*

1. ______________________________.

2. ______________________________.

3. ______________________________.

Change: What Will I Do to Become My Best Self?

I believe each human being has the potential to change, to transform one's own attitude, no matter how difficult the situation.

—Dalai Lama

Think of someone you regard as a spiritual person. What are the characteristics that make him or her spiritual, in your opinion? We asked women what they noticed about those who professed spirituality, and this is what they told us:

"A spiritual person has a happy spirit. You can just sense it."

"They are loving. They're willing to go out of their way to help out."

"They seem to be able to handle the challenges life brings them."

"Spiritual people are kind to others regardless of what they stand to gain from them."

"They don't get upset easily. They tend to take things in stride."

"They seem to be more at peace with themselves and the world."

At the heart of most religions is the axiom that we should always be striving to be "good people." What does it mean to be a good person? While everyone has their own definition of the spiritual ideal, the following spiritual characteristics seem to be universal:

Love. You embody love when you do something for others simply out of concern for their best interests and not your own. When you respect others, offer them encouragement, and refrain from judging them, you are loving. Loving people tolerate different opinions, cultures, and worldviews.

Joy. You embody joy when you experience happiness that can't be simply attributed to outward circumstances. It usually goes hand in hand with gratitude. Not the kind of gratitude that compels you to send Grandma a thank-you note for the scarf she gave you, but an appreciation for life, love, and nature.

Peace. You embody peace when you maintain a deep contentment that isn't easily shaken by life's challenges. This has been described as "the peace that passes understanding," because feeling peaceful is not a natural reaction to life's stress and pressure. Peace stems from being secure in your spirituality and knowing who you are in relation to God and the universe.

Patience. You embody patience when you allow for others' imperfections. We all get rattled now and then, but patience is a critical aspect of showing respect to ourselves, to others, and even to God. When you are patient, you allow yourself the space to fail without unnecessary self-criticism. You create an atmosphere of acceptance in your relationships, and you understand that God's timetable may be different than your own.

Faithfulness. You embody faithfulness when you are loyal, trustworthy, and true to your word. You honor your commitments and refuse to jump ship at the first sign of trouble. As we all know, your ability to remain faithful is key to a successful marriage.

Kindness. You embody kindness when you treat people the way you want to be treated. Many people find it easier to be kind to strangers than to their own family and spouses, but it is especially important to treat those close to you with kindness. And don't forget to extend that thoughtfulness to yourself—your soul craves it.

Gentleness. You embody gentleness when you choose not to be harsh or angry in a way that harms others. A gentle person considers the impact of her words and chooses them accordingly. She is not unassertive, indecisive, or wimpy. She stands up for herself and people who need protection, but she does not use violence, threats, or manipulation. Treating your spouse with gentleness eases tension in marriage and defuses conflict.

Self-control. You embody self-control when you rein in your inclination to do things that are destructive and instead make decisions that are life affirming. A woman who possesses self-control keeps her words in check when she is angry. She resists her impulses when she is tempted to give in to emotional spending. She controls her sexual urges when she is propositioned by a hot guy at work. She is not inhibited; rather, she is disciplined.

What do you need to change in your life to develop these spiritual qualities? Which qualities do you already embody? Which ones do you need to work on? Change takes place gradually, but without effort, your bad characteristics will stay the same, so start with small steps today. List three of the qualities you want to work on and one small step you will take toward becoming your best self. For example: *I will strive to be more patient with Jeannie at work when she asks about things I've already explained.*

1. ____.

2. ____.

3. ____.

Community and Culture—Where Do I Belong?

The religious community is essential, for alone our vision is too narrow to see all that must be seen. Together, our vision widens and strength is renewed.

—Mark Morrison-Reed

Our souls flourish when we participate in a faith community. One of the ways we experience God is through connecting with other people. "Often, people who are finding a faith are finding a family," says Rabbi David Wolpe of Sinai Temple in Los Angeles. "When you join a faith and a community that reinforces it, this can be more powerful and lasting than purely an intellectual conversion. You have entrée to a world of lived belief as opposed to theoretical belief." Many people who choose faiths differing from those of their families find that they create a new community with other believers. Still, nothing will replace the culture in which you were raised.

A big part of your spiritual journey involves the traditions, practices, and culture of the group of people you identify with most. For instance, you may not be a firm believer in all the teachings of Judaism, but you love the traditions of Friday-night Shabbat and Chanukah celebrations. You strongly identify with the culture and the community, but this doesn't have to define your faith. You can be a practicing Buddhist who attends seder feast with your family. Or an agnostic who wouldn't think of skipping the sweat lodge ceremony of your Native American ancestors. You don't have to sacrifice your culture altogether simply because your beliefs might have changed.

ANYA

"I was raised in the Catholic Church and always loved the strong traditions we celebrated growing up. I became Seventh-Day Adventist a few years ago, but I still participate in some of the most meaningful Catholic traditions like going to confession and atonement Mass. Although my beliefs have changed, I still feel a strong connection to Catholicism and even find myself slipping into the cathedral down the street from my office when I need to think and pray. It just feels like part of me belongs there."

Cultural Clarification

What is important to you about your community and culture?
Which religious traditions are most meaningful to you?
Would you still be able to participate in these traditions if you converted to a different religion?
Are you holding on to your religion because you fear losing the community or because you truly believe in its teachings?
How can you celebrate and embrace your culture while keeping true to your beliefs?

Contribution—What Will I Do to Help the World?

Be the change that you want to see in the world.

—Gandhi

Sacrifice is an important part of spirituality. Giving is a natural expression of gratitude for all we have been given. Unfortunately, we are selfish creatures by nature and can find it difficult to make sacrifices. When we get too caught up in the daily grind of making a buck, we find that we don't have time or emotional resources left over to give of ourselves. But here's the deal: We will never be truly fulfilled spiritually if we don't sacrifice once in a while to contribute to someone else.

The classic folk song from the '70s that says, "They will know we are Christians by our love . . ." tells it like it *should* be. Regardless of your specific spirituality, others should be able to recognize it by the way you live. All the major religions teach that helping others is a true sign of faith. If you profess faith, do you give of your time and energy to help those less fortunate? An interesting thing happens when we give: We actually feel better about ourselves, God, and the world. Giving of our time and talents makes us more appreciative of what we have, and helps us hold less tightly to possessions. We've talked to a lot of young women after they've returned from trips to third-world countries to teach, feed, provide medical supplies, build houses . . . and each one of them came home with a renewed sense of spirituality and purpose in life. Through their experiences of helping the poor, their own sense of faith and gratitude were strengthened.

RILEY

"I first learned about Operation Smile through my boyfriend, who was in dental school at the time. I loved that they were helping so many children all over the world. I started by sending money. I couldn't afford much, about fifty dollars per month. A couple of years later, I had the chance to go to Bolivia with my boyfriend and several other dentists to assist in a week-long Operation Smile clinic. During that week, we operated on more than a hundred children to correct their severe facial deformities. Seeing the look in the eyes of those kids when they saw their new smiles for the first time changed my view of how spiritual service fits in my life. For me, giving money isn't enough anymore. I need to get involved, to get my hands dirty."

ADRIENNE

"When I was working for the county, each office was required to participate in a community service of its choice. When my office chose the Special Olympics, I wasn't too thrilled. I didn't have any experience with the special-needs population, and to be honest, I didn't think I would like it very much. When the day of the event arrived, I thought about calling in sick, but wound up going anyway. I was assigned the prominent job of 'hugger,' which is pretty self-explanatory. I just waited for the runners to cross the finish line and before I knew it, a pigtailed girl was hugging me as if her life depended on it. At first I tried to remain aloof, but despite my best efforts, I soon found myself tearing up as I watched these special athletes compete their hearts out. They didn't care what they looked like or who won, they just ran for the love of running. I came away from that day with a renewed sense of compassion for people who've struggled to overcome challenges. That compassion has gone a long way in helping me be more patient and less self-centered."

VICTORIA

"I wanted to volunteer somewhere, but none of the typical opportunities seemed right for me. I had a friend who volunteered in a hospital, but the smell sent me running for the elevator. I tried serving in an inner-city soup kitchen with my church one Thanksgiving, but the neighborhood sort of freaked me out. My sister used to sing at the local nursing home, but besides the fact that I had no musical talent whatsoever, I didn't feel comfortable there either. I kept looking for a place where I could help. I was in a coffee shop one day and saw a lady with a Seeing Eye dog struggling with a hot drink and the door, so I jumped up to help her. I ended up walking with her and she told me about the Center for the Sight Impaired and how they were always looking for people to read books to the students. I thought, *That's it!* And it was. It's been six months now, and I've been volunteering at the center for a couple of hours each weekend. I've made some new friends and always feel energized when I leave. I would encourage everyone to keep looking for somewhere to contribute until they find a good fit."

Opportunities to give are everywhere. You are probably already familiar with traditional places to give time or money: homeless shelters, World Vision, Big Brothers/Big Sisters of America, Habitat for Humanity, Susan G. Komen Race for the Cure. But if none of these are a good fit for you, don't give up on giving. Think outside the box and use your talents and resources to make giving part of your everyday life.

- Good with your hands? Make balloon animals for sick kids at your local hospital.
- Love babies? Volunteer to be a baby cuddler and hold hospitalized infants.
- Got a car? Offer to run errands for a homebound or elderly neighbor.
- Like to cook? Prepare Thanksgiving dinner for your friends and coworkers who can't make it home for the holidays.
- Like kids? Teach Sunday school at your church.
- Got a little extra time? Reach out to a sleep-deprived new mom and give her a break.

As you can see, giving doesn't have to involve a significant amount of money, time, or expertise. Contributing to others changes your perspective in a way that nothing else can. Giving cultivates gratitude not only in the people you give to, but, more important, in yourself. Maintaining a grateful attitude keeps you in tune with the spiritual nature of the world.

Take a minute to brainstorm some ways you can begin to contribute to others today. Get out a sheet of paper and write down anything that comes to mind. Then commit to try one this week.

Commitment—What Will I Commit to Believe?

The difference between "involvement" and "commitment" is like an eggs-and-ham breakfast: The chicken was "involved"; the pig was "committed."

—*Author unknown*

If it is really important to you to take care of your soul and be dedicated to your spiritual journey, you must make a true commitment. You can't wait and choose what you believe based on what your future husband believes. Your faith commitment is between you and your God. You make your *own* commitment because it is your *own* soul. You can't blame your lack of faith on someone else; it's all on you. Faith is one of the most *personal* commitments you will ever make, yet it will have serious impact on your relationships with your future spouse, children, and your family. Your faith will grow and evolve over your lifetime, but *now* is the time for you to decide what you believe and why.

Chapter 11

Key #9: Get a Sexy Life

Honor Your Sexuality

> *Sex: the thing that takes up the least amount of time and causes the most amount of trouble.*
>
> *—John Barrymore*

Sex is everywhere, from *Good Housekeeping* to *Glamour,* from *The Tyra Show* to *Gossip Girls.* What could we possibly tell you about sex that you don't already know? You've read *Cosmo*'s "10 Sexy Moves Your Guy Wishes You'd Try Tonight," watched endless hours of *Sex and the City,* and own a dog-eared copy of the Kama Sutra. The problem is not that we talk about sex, but *how* we talk about it. Most of our dialogue about sex centers around techniques, turn-ons, and titillation. But sex is so much more than the media and modern society would have us believe. Sex can reaffirm a commitment, create a powerful bond, and provide soulful communication between partners.

But when it is misused, sex can be the source of tremendous emotional pain, disappointment, and damaged self-worth for many women.

As we've listened to countless women talk about their sex lives, a common theme of regret has emerged. "I feel used." "I'm mad at myself." "I resent it when a guy doesn't call me after I slept with him." "Men hold all the power in a relationship. If they decide they want to sleep with other women, there's nothing I can do about it." "I wish I wouldn't have had sex so early in the relationship." Many of these women are in crisis and are confused about the role sex should play in their lives. Others are honest about their negative feelings and experiences with sex, but have come to accept them as simply "the way it is." A woman's sexual experiences in the midst of this confusion create a rocky foundation for her future sex life in marriage. An alarming 43 percent of married women report having sexual problems. In fact, sex is one of the top three causes of unhappiness in marriage. (It's right up there with money and kids.) If you want to avoid many of the difficulties that sex causes in marriage, you need take the time to clear up your own confusion about sex while you're still single. You can do this by understanding how your childhood experiences impacted your sexuality, identifying potentially damaging patterns, and defining the values that govern your sexuality.

Your Parents Made Your Marital Bed

Your parents raised you with specific beliefs about sex, whether they spoke about it or not. Along with your early sexual experiences, you will carry these beliefs into your marriage.

GRETA

"My parents never talked to me about sex. Never. I learned it all from my friends and by watching movies. *American Pie* was particularly informative. By the time I hit thirteen, pretty much everyone was hooking up. If you wanted the attention of the most popular guys, you had to put out. But that wasn't enough, because if you wanted to *keep* their attention, you also had to be really good at it. I remember watching a porno when I was fourteen with two of my girlfriends so we could learn how to give the perfect blow job. Apparently, we learned well, because our services were in high demand. I had full-on sex for the first time when I was fifteen, with a guy I knew from my geometry class. I was the last virgin in my group of friends and just figured it was time to do it. That first experience was the beginning of a string of hookups with lots of different guys over the next few years. It's not that I loved sex, but I did love the feeling that guys wanted me and wanted to be with me. It's not like I was ever in some big lovefest with these guys; it was just sex.

"I married Luke two and a half years ago, and now we are having a lot of sexual problems, which frankly has taken me by surprise because I've always been good in bed. I'm really creative and always game, but Luke is still full of complaints. He explains it by saying that he can't 'feel' me during sex, like my body is just going through the motions. He says he wants to make love not just 'screw' and that I act like sex is about some sort of performance instead of us connecting on a deeper level. He says he's sick of the role-playing and the games and just wants to know that my heart's in it. I don't know how to give him what he wants."

You Should Know . . . Sex is about more than getting off. It's a soul connection. One of the purposes of sex in a marriage is to help husbands and wives reconnect emotionally and to deepen the bond they have with each other. When you've viewed sex primarily as a physical act, you prevent it from serving that purpose. You may describe yourself as being sexually "uninhibited and free," but the reality is that you are *emotionally* inhibited when it comes to connecting during sex. Sex should be person-oriented, enabling two people to connect intimately in the same way they would if one were talking about something very personal. Imagine if you were telling your boyfriend about something that made you very sad, and you were crying and pouring your heart out to him. But when you looked into his eyes, you realized that he was just going through the motions of listening—nodding, saying, "Oh, poor thing," but not really there. He's wasn't "feeling" you. What should have been an emotionally bonding moment between the two of you was just about you meeting your need to vent. Totally unsatisfying! So it is with sex. You both must be able to connect in an emotionally vulnerable way, or sex will become virtually meaningless as a way of bonding.

Don't Let This Happen to You. Don't get caught up in performance-oriented sex. If sex is all about your skill in the bedroom, you'll never be able to experience the powerful emotional bonding that person-oriented sex can offer.

COREEN

"I was always taught that sex was bad. According to my parents, the Bible teaches that sex is only for procreating, not for pleasure. And by watching their relationship, it was clear they believed that. I can't remember ever seeing my parents touch, let alone hug or kiss. I'm pretty sure they've had sex exactly three times—just enough to conceive me and my brothers, then never again. My mom wore flannel pajamas to bed and seemed to disdain anything remotely sexy. Because of how I was raised to view sex, I felt guilty for even making out with my boyfriend in high school. I didn't date much in college. I'm sure I gave off the uptight-prude vibe, but I was relieved not to have to deal with guys' expectations about sex.

"In grad school, I met a great guy who understood my hesitance to have sex. We eventually slept together even though I always thought I'd wait until marriage. The sex wasn't great, because I felt so guilty every time. I couldn't allow myself to enjoy it until I was married, but even now that we are married, I still feel the same way. Even though it's not 'sinful' anymore, I still don't like it. I can't let go and have an orgasm unless I've had several glasses of wine. In a weird way, I still think of sex as bad and shameful. My mom used to always joke that sex is only enjoyable for men. I guess she was right."

You Should Know . . . Many parents tell their daughters that sex is not pleasurable in order to scare them away from premarital sex. Unfortunately, this discouraging message about sex forms the foundation for your beliefs and expectations about sex. Sure, the Bible has a lot to say about the proper context for sex in marriage, but it *never* says that sex itself is bad. God wouldn't have designed women's bodies with the ability to climax if sexual pleasure wasn't one of the goals of sex! If you believe that sex is good only for a man, you will disregard your own sexual pleasure and will disengage from your sexual desires, numbing yourself to your body's natural response. By disconnecting from her sexuality, a woman also robs her husband of the pleasure of satisfying his wife. Married men overwhelmingly say that pleasing their wives is the most satisfying aspect of sex.

Don't Let This Happen to You. Explore your beliefs about sex and where those beliefs originated. Do you think sex is dirty? Shameful? Sinful? Something only men enjoy? If so, it is crucial that you reframe your views about sex. Unless you have a positive view of sex and your own sexuality, your marriage will suffer. Heads up: This usually requires the help of a therapist.

JESSICA

"This is not something I like to talk about unless I have to, but maybe my story can help other women. My stepdad molested me when I was nine. He said all the things that I now understand to be typical of abusers: It was my fault for being so sexy, it was too shameful to tell my mom, it was what I deserved/wanted, et cetera, et cetera. When my mom found out, she went to the police and divorced him right away, but the damage was already done. I have always felt ashamed of what happened and since then I haven't felt like I fit in with other girls my age. I slept around a lot in my early twenties, but never had a serious relationship.

"Carlos and I dated for a year or so before we got married. He's good to me and very different from most of the guys I've known. I really do love him and feel bad that we are now having a lot of problems with our sex life. When we have sex, I just basically check out. Sex brings up all of my childhood crap, and I feel like damaged goods. Carlos deserves someone better, someone whole. I know I should tell him about the abuse, but I don't want him to think less of me."

You Should Know . . . Sexual abuse always carries repercussions, even if the abuse is not clearly remembered. As a result of the abuse, sex becomes associated with guilt, fear, and pain. It's typical of an abused child to become promiscuous in early adulthood, but to shut down sexually once she's married. She's willing to engage in casual sex because being *used* for sex feels familiar to her. But she's unable to receive loving sex from her husband, because she doesn't feel worthy. *Note:* If an adult woman suffers a rape, her sexuality will also be severely impacted in similar ways.

How to Keep This from Ruining Your Sex Life: If you are a victim of sexual abuse or rape, you will need therapy in order to work through the trauma that you've suffered. A therapist will help you disconnect the shame, guilt, and trauma from your current sexual experiences, which will help you clear the way for a healthy sex life. Because sexual abuse is so isolating, you may also find that joining a sexual abuse survivors' group will help you find support and realize that you are not alone.

Sex for the Wrong Reasons

Keep your knickers on, change your life.

—Wendy Keller

If you want to be empowered by your sexuality, rather than a victim of it, you need to respect sex. You misuse sex when you do it for the wrong reasons. It's time to be honest with yourself about why you decide to be sexually involved with someone in the first place. What are the motivations that drive your sexual behavior and relationships? Are your choices in line with your values, or are you engaging in sex in a way that conflicts with what you really want? Can you relate to any of the following wrong reasons women have sex?

"I have sex to feel sexy."

Here's how you think: *He's hot, he wants to do me, I must be hot, too.* If you're having sex to feel pretty, sexy, or desirable, you are misusing sex. We'll let you in on a little secret: When it comes to casual sex, men set the bar fairly low. To quote musician Tori Amos, "Guys would sleep with a bicycle if it had the right color lipstick on." Ray, twenty-six, applauded Tori's insight, saying, "If a woman gets an ego boost just because a guy wants to sleep with her, she clearly doesn't understand guys. I know it's crass, but as my British friend likes to say, 'Every hole's a goal.' If she's not a complete dog and is a willing participant, I'm going to try to have sex with her. But when it comes to having a real relationship with a woman, my standards are much, much higher."

"I have sex to feel loved."

You're fooling yourself if you think that physical intimacy and emotional intimacy are synonymous. You could put down this book, walk down the street, and be having hot and heavy sex with some dude within fifteen minutes. (You'd have to act fast, but you could do it.) But just because you've intertwined your bodies doesn't mean you've made a heart connection. Emotional intimacy is something that is created over time by sharing experiences, revealing your true selves, and building trust. As women, we are wired for intimacy, so it's not surprising that we often lie to ourselves by romanticizing uncommitted sex. We think, *Now that we've had sex, he must have deep feelings for me. This connection we've got is really special.* As Brian, twenty-eight, told us, "Of course I enjoy having sex, but it's not the thing that makes me want to have a relationship with a woman. I honestly hate that dreamy look women get after sex—the one that says, 'now we've *bonded*.'"

Sex *feels* intimate because it is a physically intimate act. But you can't fast-forward past the steps to building emotional intimacy by just pushing the sex button. It doesn't work that way.

"I have sex as a means of introduction."

Having sex too soon in a relationship completely wipes out your ability to see a guy objectively and can make you stay in a bad relationship longer than you should. Because you didn't bother getting to know him before getting naked, you can't know if you are compatible outside the bedroom. Once sex is in the equation, you can forget about trying to find out if he's a keeper through good old dating and conversation. Stay out of the bedroom and spend some time getting to know each other before you allow sex to take center stage.

"I have sex to feel powerful."

Some women think that casual sex puts them in the driver's seat because they are in control of the guy's feelings. If you choose not to call a guy back after a sexual encounter simply to feel the rush of breaking his heart, you are a big meany and are probably trying to get over the fact that someone has done that to you in the past. You justify your cruel behavior by telling yourself *I've been hurt before, and it feels a lot better to be the one with the power.* But contrary to popular belief, men do have feelings, and it won't make your broken heart heal any faster to break someone else's.

"I have sex to keep a guy."

Whether your guy expects sex on the third date, the third month, or the third year, his expectations shouldn't be the driving force behind your decision to sleep with him. Any man who's out the door because you don't want to have sex was never into you; he just wanted to be *in* you. Will, twenty-nine, told us, "If I'm not that interested in a woman, I'll wait a month, max. Then I'm on to the next girl. But if I really like her and she tells me she wants to wait, I'll stick around, no problem."

"I have sex for the perks."

Sex is supposed to be an act of giving and receiving, not taking. When you use sex to get something, whether status or stuff, you're a user. You're turning sex into a commodity by offering something that's supposed to matter in exchange for goods. No matter what *you're* getting, *he's* getting a bargain. You might as well turn tricks on the corner. At least that way, you'd get cold hard cash and wouldn't have to wait around to see what he buys you. Dave told us, "Yes, I guess you could say that I'm using her for sex. Do I see potential for a relationship? No. But I kind of feel like I owe her something for sleeping with me without any sort of a commitment. It's not like I can leave money on the nightstand, but I do take care of her rent every month. That way, she's close for the late-night booty calls."

"I have sex to feel better."

If you use sex to soothe feelings of depression, rejection, anxiety, or loneliness, you are using sex like a drug. When you have sex to self-medicate against uncomfortable feelings, you are on dangerous ground because using sex as a quick fix can easily become addictive. Sharon, twenty-four, told us, "I feel better instantly when I have sex. It's the one time when I can forget about whatever is depressing me and just live in the moment. The high only lasts for a day or two, then I have to get another fix." Having sex increases the feel-good chemicals in your brain, instantly making you feel happier and more loved. It's easier in the short-term to use sex to numb your painful emotions; in the long term, however, avoiding those emotions will only compound your problems, making them worse.

"I have sex to lose weight."

If you're using sex as a form of exercise, you are . . . silly. We're sort of kidding here, but you've all seen those articles in various women's mags that talk about how missionary sex burns hundreds of calories per hour and that if you throw in a little girl-on-top action, your calorie burn skyrockets. The truth is, intercourse burns less than five calories per minute, on average. So if you need to lose a pound, you'll have to have more than twelve hours of nonstop sex. Not exactly the most efficient weight-loss method.

"I have sex for fun."

We love sex. Sex is fun. Sex feels good. But as you already know, recreational sex puts you at a higher risk for some nasty consequences. For starters, there are 19 million new sexually transmitted infections in the United States each year, and studies show that one in two sexually active people will contract an STI by age twenty-five. Can you tell if that guy at the bar is one of them? Let's see . . . what are the telltale signs of a guy with an STI? Facial hair? Taller than five-eight? Shorter than six-two? Blue eyes? Not sure? That's because there are no telltale signs. Even if the infection is staring you right in the face. Yeah, yeah, we know you use a condom "most of the time," but did you know that some STIs can get around condoms (sneaky little buggers)? In fact, condoms are only 60 to 70 percent effective against herpes and HPV. And you can even contract an STI through *oral* sex. We know that's hard to swallow, but it's true. Sex always put you at risk for pregnancy, abortion, cervical cancer, and sterilization. Now, doesn't the reality of these consequences make jumping into the sack with that guy who's checking you out from across the bar seem a little less fun?

If you have sex for any of these wrong reasons, you may have begun to suspect that uncommitted sex is a problem for you. Take this quiz to find out.

Hooked on Hookups?

1. Are you and your roommates all too familiar with your morning-after look—the one where you slink home sporting the wrinkled version of the dress you wore last night, smudged mascara, and that unmistakable look of regret?
2. Do your hookups "happen" to coincide with your drinking a few too many pomegranate martinis?
3. Are you a willing recipient of the Midnight Booty Text? Are you flattered by it?
4. Would you never dream of leaving home, even for a quick trip to the grocery store, without your

Supplies for a Lively Unplanned Tryst (*aka* your SLUT bag)?

5. Do you have sex to show your appreciation when a guy helps you move, takes you out to a nice dinner, or holds the elevator for you?
6. Do you meticulously straddle the toilet in order to protect yourself from a stranger's germs but willingly return to that same bathroom minutes later to straddle a stranger?

If you answered YES to *any* of the above, you do indeed have issues with uncommitted sex that need to be addressed. Now. So do yourself a favor—put off your next raunchy romp long enough to read through to the end of this chapter. You just might emerge with a new perspective.

If you answered NO to all of the above, we congratulate you for having enough sense to steer clear of hookup sex, but you're not quite out of the woods yet. Read on to learn more about the lies you've been told, and may even believe, about uncommitted sex.

Sex, Lies, and the Truth

During the past two decades of working with young women, we have witnessed a dramatic shift in the value women place on sex. Not coincidentally, we have also seen a rise in their levels of depression, anxiety, and feelings of emptiness. Sadly, these women have bought the lies that uncommitted sex is the ideal and that promiscuity is the ultimate expression of female liberation. Here are some of the most common and harmful messages young women are buying:

Lie #1: You Should Have Sex Like a Man

This lie tells you that in order to establish your equality, you must be able to have sex like a man—with no consideration for emotions or commitment. This measure of equality is, by its very nature, sexist. Why should women be pressured to conform to a man's approach to anything, much less sex? You'll never hear a man say, "I need to learn to act more like a woman. I should shave my legs to prove my equality." Why aren't men being forced to accommodate women's needs in sex, first and foremost? Imagine what would happen if every woman felt empowered to demand that sex be on her own terms. What if equality for men meant that they had to be able to have "sex like a woman"? We imagine there'd be a lot more marriages and a lot less meaningless sex.

How can women be told to have "sex like a man" when it's women who necessarily bear the brunt of the consequences of sex? As Amy Herzog, Professor of Media at Queens College puts it, we now live in "a culture in which men win and women lose. While women bear the unwanted pregnancies, abortions and emotional pain wrought by casual sex, men are free to move on to the next bedmate."

According to Shannon's former co-host, the popular sex therapist Dr. Ian Kerner, "You can try to have sex like a man, but just know, the more casual the situation, the less likely you'll achieve satisfaction or indeed any emotional state of happiness." The concept that women are empowered by casual sex is actually undermining women and the power of our feminine sexuality.

Lie #2: Sex Is Only Physical

This lie tells you that you can have sex whenever, and with whomever, and enjoy it as a *purely* physical act; that hookup sex can and should be devoid of emotional entanglements. We're being taught that a woman who has uncommitted sex is "embracing her sexuality," but if she feels bad about it afterwards, she is experiencing undeserved shame, imposed upon her by an oppressive male-dominated society.

Frankly, we're surprised that women are buying this line of reasoning. After all, hasn't feminism taught us that a woman is more than just a sexual object? Throughout history, feminism has worked overtime to decry the objectification of women. Don't we all get offended when a guy can't stop checking out our boobs long enough to look us in the eye? "Hello, my eyes are up here!" Why is this? It's because we know that it is impossible to separate our sexuality from our whole being. This lie that "sex is only physical" is encouraging women to treat their bodies as sexual objects, separate from their hearts and minds.

The truth is that recreational, uncommitted sex will usually leave you feeling empty and wanting more. As women, we are wired to connect emotionally in order to fully connect sexually. You might be vehemently shaking your head no right about now, but be honest with yourself. How do you feel about past random hookups? Really, how did it feel when he didn't call you back after you shared such an intimate part of yourself with him? Deep down, how do you think casual sex has worked out for you? A recent Princeton study revealed that 91 percent of women had regrets after having casual sex. And even the most vocal promoters of sex as a strictly physical act, the authors of *The Hookup Handbook,* Andrea Lavinthal and Jessica Rozler admit that the frequent fallout from a night of "unemotional" hookup sex is the girl waiting in obsessive agony for the "f___ing phone to f___ing ring." Sounds like someone's feeling pretty emotional about sex.

A Little Science

Even if society would have us believe differently, a woman's *body* knows that there is, in fact, an emotional component to sex. When a woman has sex, her body releases a hormone called oxytocin. This hormone is commonly called the "bonding hormone" because it creates intense feelings of emotional connection and bondedness. Oxytocin is released during sex in greater amounts for a woman than a man and is responsible for her feelings of infatuation afterward. See if you can recognize the effects of oxytocin in the following recounting of a series of dates as told to Jasmine by her roommate Jane:

> Date #1: "How could you have set me up with that loser, Mike? Could he have been any more boring? He talked the whole dinner about his muscle car and how he spends every weekend hunting for vintage parts. Did you know that he still lives with his mom? Do womankind a favor and stay out of the matchmaking business."
>
> Date #2: "Ugh. I can't believe I went out with Mike again. On the way to the concert, he made me go to a junkyard with him to look for some special rearview mirror thingamajiggy for his car that they only made in 1969, blah, blah, blah. What a bore. If I didn't love Green Day so much, I never would have agreed to go out with him. The concert was fantastic, but Mike kept embarrassing me with his lame dance moves. He actually tried to kiss me on the way home, but I totally blew him off."
>
> Date #3: "Did I tell you I ran into Mike last night? I went to happy hour with some friends after work and ran into him at the bar. He started buying me drinks, and well, one thing led to another and we ended up back at his house. We spent an amazing night together. The sex was great, seriously amazing. Why did you wait so long to set us up? He's everything I've been looking for in a boyfriend."

Okay, so we may be exaggerating a bit to make our point, but you've just witnessed oxytocin at work. Oxytocin doesn't care what you *think* about sex. It doesn't care if you think sex can come with "no strings attached" or that sex is only physical. Nor does it care if you like the guy, if you *should* like the guy, or if he's way too old to be living with his mother. Oxytocin is an *automatic* response to sex and wields its effect no matter what your clear-headed judgment tells you.

If emotional bonding is a biological response to sex, doesn't the campaign to separate sex from emotions amount to emotional repression of women? Here's how this Cycle of Emotional Repression goes:

You have uncommitted sex.→Your body experiences an emotional connection.→You feel bonded.→You are then told that this feeling is a sign of weakness and you should deny it or "get over it."→ In an effort to "get over it," you have uncommitted sex. And the cycle is repeated. . . .

Why should women be made to feel weaker because of our natural response to sex? Rather than deny those emotions, we should be celebrating them. It is our innate ability to connect on a deeply emotional and even spiritual level during sex that allows women to have such a powerful, whole-person experience of our sexuality. And why would we ever want to repress *that*?

Lie #3: Uncommitted Sex Is Liberating

This lie tells you that uncommitted sex is empowering to women. That if you engage freely in casual sex, you are no longer considered a slut; in fact, you are actually applauded for being "sexually liberated." That embracing your sexual freedom requires that sex be free from emotional entanglements. That in order to throw off the shackles of sexual oppression and get out from under the confines of patriarchal society, you must throw off your clothes and get under the sheets without any type of commitment.

The women we've spoken with who have bought this lie report feeling anything but liberated. In fact, these women overwhelmingly agree that their experiences with uncommitted sex have left them feeling empty, depressed, rejected, and worthless. Dr. Miriam Grossman, a psychiatrist at UCLA's student health services, confirms our own professional observations. In her book *Unprotected,* Grossman recounts story after story of the emotional destructiveness of casual sex. Based on her firsthand experiences with hundreds of young women, Grossman declares hookup sex "hazardous to a woman's mental health."

Angie's story illustrates Dr. Grossman's point perfectly: "My experiences with men over the past five years have taught me that having sex without a commitment isn't all that it's cracked up to be. I hate that it took me this long to figure out that when you offer sex without expecting anything in return, you're just setting yourself up for heartbreak. My reality check came after I was flat-out rejected by my coworker whom I'd been having 'no strings attached' sex with for over a year. One day, out of the blue, he told me he was moving home to marry his college girlfriend. I was surprised at how devastated I was. I cried myself to sleep for months and refused to go out for anything but another pint of Häagen-Dazs. I felt completely and utterly rejected. I mean, he knew me intimately, but clearly didn't value me at all. I used to think that when I slept around, I was exercising my 'right' as a modern woman. But I know now that I'm only truly empowered when I respect my own sexuality by reserving it for someone who is committed to me."

Shocker of all shockers, even *Cosmopolitan* magazine is saying no to casual sex. *Cosmo* editor Lorraine Candy refers to casual sex as "McSex," the fast food version of sex—because it "leaves you feeling empty and slightly nauseous." *Cosmo* admits that this "soulless sex" causes lasting emotional damage. Dr. Terri Apter, a social psychologist at the University of Cambridge agrees with *Cosmo,* stating, "There have been some misguided assumptions linked to the sexual revolution and one is that sex can be both casual and happy. In human beings, sex is usually linked to an emotional bond, and without that it is at best unsatisfactory but at worst humiliating and degrading. In time young people discover they are likely to feel shame, regret, and anger [after uncommitted sex]. It has to be more than entertainment."

When you refuse to believe these lies about sex, you are empowering yourself to make positive choices about your own sexuality. You'll then be able to protect yourself from the harsh consequences of "soulless sex." Now that you understand how casual sex can negatively affect you, how will it affect your marriage? In fact, how does any sex affect your marriage?

Single-Woman Sex Patterns and Marriage

Many women don't realize that the sex you have when you are single, whether it occurs in a committed relationship or with a virtual stranger, affects the sex you have after you get married. Any sex you have in your single life, whether you end up marrying the guy or not, sets patterns of interaction and expectations for sex in your future marriage.

The Pattern of Performance

When you're single, sex tends to be *performance*-oriented, while married sex tends to be more *person*-oriented. When women have sex without a ring on their finger, they are often full of uncertainties and questions about their partner's level of commitment and intentions regarding the future. As Abby told us, "It's not like I want to marry Justin tomorrow or anything, but I do want to know we're on the path to happily ever after. Until we're officially engaged, though, I know I won't feel secure in the relationship and will feel pressure to make sure I hold his attention in the bedroom." Until a man commits to you "for better or for worse," you will always feel pressure to make sure the sex is "for better." Your unmarried pattern might be to prepare, study techniques in magazines, and plan various new sexual positions. While we highly recommend creativity in the bedroom, we know that focusing on performance will rob you of experiencing the intimacy of simply enjoying each other's bodies without fear of judgment or comparison.

In a recent survey of married women, 50 percent of the women complained about sex being a hassle. One of the causes of their sexual dissatisfaction is that these women are stuck in the performance trap. After a day at work and an evening with the kids, the last thing these married women want to do is perform by dressing up in black lace and coming up with some new acrobatic position to impress their man. Because these women established patterns of performance-oriented sex during their single years, they are now missing out on person-oriented sex in their marriages. What these women fail to understand is that marriage can actually free you up to experience sex as a time to simply enjoy the *person* who loves you, body and soul.

The Pattern of Obligation

If you're having sex because you think you should or because you fear that if you don't, your relationship will suffer, you are establishing harmful patterns of viewing sex as an obligation. By agreeing to sex out of a sense of duty, you're relinquishing your power to *choose* whether or not you have sex. You're taking the choice out of your hands and submitting to the so-called duties of the relationship.

When sex takes on this sense of obligation, it becomes drudgery and is robbed of its intended enjoyment. It makes sense that if you feel like you *must* do something, you are more likely to resent it and have an unsatisfying experience. On the other hand, if you feel the freedom to make a choice, you are more likely to be willing and able to enjoy it.

Sure, there will be times in marriage when you have sex with your husband even though you're tired or may rather read a magazine, but even this sex should never be out of a sense of duty. When you don't see sex as merely an obligation, you're free to choose to have sex because you love your husband and love connecting with him.

The Pattern of Poor Communication

In a recent survey of over 2,500 women, 48 percent of married women admitted to faking orgasms with their husbands. Not coincidentally, 44 percent of the women in this same survey admitted using sex toys without their husbands' knowledge. This means that nearly half the women surveyed are lying to their husbands during one of the most intimate acts they can share with him. How wrong. How sad. Each of these women's patterns of dishonest communication about sex likely started well before she became someone's wife. Somewhere along the way, during her dating years, she short-circuited her ability to talk honestly with her partner. This pattern of dishonesty may have begun out of a desire to protect her partner's ego, to hide her embarrassment about her sexual needs, or to bring an end to a less-than-stellar lovemaking session.

These poor communication patterns you establish during sex will be tough to break once you are married. Honesty during sex is critical to a positive, mutually fulfilling sex life. You've got to be comfortable enough with your sexuality to tell your husband what feels good and what doesn't. It's your responsibility to share your thoughts, feelings, and experiences. It's unfair for you to expect that your partner will automatically know what you like, in the bedroom or out, and then to resent him for failing to please you. Commit to communicating honestly in your relationships now, because it won't get any easier once you are married.

The Pattern of Manipulation

Single women often use sex as a tool to get nice things or get their man to do something. When you establish a pattern of using sex to get something from a man you're dating, you're using sex for your own gain. This pattern of exchanging sex for something you want causes you to view sex as a commodity that you possess and dole out strategically, rather than something special to be shared between two equal partners. Your husband shouldn't have to jump through hoops in order to get a "treat" of intimacy with his wife. Would it be acceptable for him to say to you, "I'll listen to how your day was if you do me first"? Of course not! Then why do so many women think it's okay to use sex as a means to an end rather than experiencing it as a true connection? Sex cannot be used as a dangling carrot, or as your favorite bargaining chip. Sex should be a mutually enjoyable means of expressing your love.

The Pattern of Justification

When you justify your partner's bad behaviors while you're dating, you are establishing patterns that can destroy your marriage. The most destructive male behaviors that women are all too willing to justify are pornography and infidelity.

Justifying Porn. Women are convincing themselves in droves that it's no big deal if their man views porn on a regular basis because "boys will be boys." Many women, in an effort to play the role of the "cool girlfriend," even support their boyfriend's habit by buying porn for him or watching it with him as a substitute for foreplay. A supercool girl is one who buys her guy videos of naked strangers for him to fantasize about and masturbate to while she is doing the dishes in the other room? If women really believe this, why then did 47 percent of more than two thousand women surveyed say that their partner's porn use makes them feel uncomfortable and less attractive? Maybe it's because these women know, despite all their justifications, that it undermines the relationship.

Porn teaches you that real bodies aren't good enough. It separates sex from real people and real connection. It is destructive because it creates false expectations and unrealistic sexual ideals. As Naomi Wolf writes, "The onslaught of porn is responsible for deadening the male libido in relation to real women. For the first time in human history, the images' power and allure have supplanted that of real naked women. Today, real naked women are just bad porn." Recently, a young woman lamented to us, "My boyfriend is so obsessed with Internet porn that he won't sleep with me unless I act like a porn star."

If you brush this issue aside in your dating relationships or excuse it as no big deal, you won't consider it to be a deal breaker when choosing a husband. This is a dangerous justification. Porn has been reported as a significant cause of marital unhappiness and divorce. In fact, divorce lawyers are estimating that Internet porn is now a factor in at least one out of three divorces in the United States. In light of these daunting statistics, keep in mind that you don't have to accept porn as a part of your relationship.

Justifying Infidelity. While it should go without saying, if you are willing to excuse a boyfriend's unfaithfulness, you are on the road to being cheated on by your husband. And out of those couples who experience infidelity, only 35 percent of the marriages survive. Loyalty should be the foundation of any relationship, and if you don't respect yourself enough to make fidelity a nonnegotiable in your relationships, no one you choose will respect you enough to give it to you. If you justify being cheated on by telling yourself that "it was my fault for not keeping him satisfied," or "it's okay because he's really very sorry," or "all men are dogs," you're conditioning yourself to accept cheating as the norm. If you don't hold fidelity as an ideal, or believe that it's just too much to expect, chances are high that you will marry a man who doesn't value it either.

The Sacredness of Sex

No one will argue that sex is powerful. It was intended to be so. It can lead to the creation of another human being, it can uniquely bond you to another person, and it can bring you unrivaled pleasure. Sex is sacred; it's the direct line from your body to your soul. It's your responsibility and privilege to harness its power for good and not for harm.

It's okay to want to be loved. It's more than okay to expect love to be an integral part of sex. And it's even more okay to require a long-term love commitment from the man you are having sex with. It makes sense to associate the most intimate physical act, sex, with the most intimate emotion, love. Sex, in its essence, is a profound experience. Deep down, you know there's more to sex; you know you deserve more. You deserve to be cherished. Did you catch that? A man should *cherish* you—yes, you. He should cherish your body and your sexuality. If you're wondering why your experiences with men have left you feeling anything but cherished, don't go the "men are pigs" route just yet. First, you need to ask yourself some important questions: Do you have strongly defined values when it comes to sex, or do you leave it up to the guy? Do you have sex on your own terms, or do you cave in to his expectations? Do you value yourself enough to set high standards for yourself when it comes to sex, or do you let him determine your value?

A man will follow your lead when it comes to respecting your body. If you respect yourself and your sexuality, he will, too. If you don't, how can you expect him to?

Personal Insight from Shannon

I could never understand why many of my girlfriends got so wrapped up in the guys they were dating (and sleeping with). I can't tell you how many times a girl complained to me that a guy treated her badly, wouldn't refer to her as his girlfriend, or cheated on her. I always suggested that she just break up with him. But these women had invested too much in the relationships (their bodies, their hearts, and their hopes), so they put up with the guys' disrespect. They couldn't understand why guys never treated me like that. "Where do you find those guys?" they'd ask. "It's like my mom says, 'Boys will be buoys—they rise or sink to the level of your standards.'" I believed that my sexuality was a prize, so the guys I went out with believed it, too. My friends who readily gave sex away communicated that it wasn't worth more than dinner and drinks, if that, so no wonder the guys they gave it to didn't value it either. I believed that I deserved to be pursued, so guys called me, asked me out, and sent me flowers. I believed I was worth waiting for, so guys waited. I believed I was worthy of respect, so guys opened doors for me, called when they said they would, and didn't cheat on me. I believed sex was sacred. Thankfully, I also had several friends who shared my approach of placing a high value on their sexuality, so we were able to help strengthen each other's resolve.

I had a guy tell me once, "You are the only girl I've ever gone out with who won't sleep with me. Come on, it's no big deal." In addition to his honest astonishment, I know he was trying to make me feel like a prude. But he actually proved my point. Of course it was no big deal to him, because it was no big deal to the many girls he had slept with. I wasn't about to join their ranks. Who wants to be "just another girl" to any guy?

What does it mean to respect your sexuality? Before you can answer that question, you've got to define your own sexual values. If you don't take the time to figure out your values now, the culture, your peers, and the next guy you go out with will define them for you.

Defining My Values

Are you being honest with yourself about the effects of casual sex?
Do you have regrets about your past sexual relationships?
Do you want more from sex?
Do you long for sex to be experienced with someone who cherishes and loves you?
Would you rather have sex in a committed relationship?
Would you rather wait until you've made the ultimate commitment by exchanging vows?
Do you believe that it's possible to have a healthy sex life?

What do you need to change about your current sexual behavior to get a healthy sex life?
What specific sexual parameters have you set for yourself? What do you feel comfortable doing and when?
What do you think a healthy sex life looks like in marriage?
What can you do now to make your married sex life the best it can be?
What do you need to change about your current sexual patterns?

If you steer clear of establishing unhealthy, disrespectful patterns of sex now, you will set yourself up for a better sex life with your husband. In marriage, sex is a powerful means of communicating your love, affection, appreciation, and desire for every aspect of your partner. Keep this goal in mind now, by giving sex its due.

Sexuality doesn't have to be about despair, regret, or losing part of yourself. Healthy sexuality shouldn't require that you deny your emotions to fit into anyone else's ideas about what sex should or shouldn't mean to you. Healthy sexuality never requires you to compromise what you really want in order to conform to someone else's desires. If you treat sex with respect, you won't emerge from your twenties feeling like damaged goods. So honor your sexuality: respecting the amazing gifts of your body, your heart, and your soul.

Chapter 12

Key #10: Get an Exciting Life

Pursue Adventure!

Life is a daring adventure or nothing at all.
—Helen Keller

Do you remember when you were little and the world was full of wonder? Everywhere you looked, there were new things to discover. You could easily spend a whole Saturday "exploring" with your friends, going from house to house, taking in all the sights and sounds along the way. All you needed was your bike, your buddies, and a sack lunch. "Mom, we're going on a butterfly hunt," you'd say as you headed out the door. That little girl who found a sense of wonder in the crunch of the leaves beneath her feet and the challenge of climbing to the highest branch of the oak tree would never have believed that life would ever be anything less than an exciting adventure.

Yet here you are, so immersed in the everyday demands of life that those beloved Saturdays of your youth have been long forgotten. You're consumed by work or school, paying your bills, keeping up with friends, boyfriends, and your endless to-do lists. Now that you're a little older, you're more cautious and you find comfort in the familiarity of your daily routine, no matter how humdrum. It's not that you don't get out once in a while, it's just that now your idea of adventure is trying a new restaurant once a month during your Girls' Night Out. Let's face it, if that pigtailed version of yourself pedaled by your house, she'd stick out her tongue and yell, *"Bo-ring!"*

HELLO! FIRE UP! This is your life! *Your only life.* This is your Fabulous Single Life! This is your time to go, to see, to do. Even if you have a great job and don't want to jeopardize your career path. Even if your parents might think you're being irresponsible. Even if you don't have a lot of money. Even if you would really miss your boyfriend, dog, or favorite barista. Now is not the time for excuses. *Hear this:* If your twenties are full of *excuses* that keep you from your adventures, your thirties, forties, and fifties will be filled with *regrets.* And don't you just hate regrets?

What's So Important about Adventure?; or Do I Really Need to Get off This Couch?

Only those who will risk going too far can possibly find out how far one can go.

—*T. S. Eliot*

If you're cruising along, happy enough with your life as it is, you may be asking, *Why do I need adventure?* For so many reasons! Nothing enhances your life like adventure. Finding your adventurous spirit awakens you to new possibilities that lie undiscovered within you. Adventure inspires you to actively participate in life—to throw back the curtains and fling open the windows, welcoming whatever surprises life brings. Here are some ways adventure will enhance your life:

- **Adventure invigorates you.** Pursuing adventure gets you off the couch and engaged in life. It is the fuel that fires you up and makes you feel more alive. What's more exhilarating than the thrill that comes from stepping out of your daily routine and doing something for the first time? Sure, it may feel awkward or uncomfortable in the moment, but in the end you're glad you took the opportunity to try something new. The more you expand your repertoire of experiences, the more interesting you become, to yourself and to others.
- **Adventure infuses you with confidence and courage.** When you experience new things, whether a new culture or new route for your morning jog, you are stepping outside your comfort zone. When you take a risk and accomplish something new, you are forever changed. You walk away from that experience with a newfound confidence in yourself and in your ability to overcome fear and discomfort. *Warning:* As you continue to flex your "adventure muscle," this confidence will infect all other areas of your life. You just might become unstoppable.
- **Adventure expands your horizons.** When you say, "Yes, please!" to adventure, you begin to experience the world in brand-new ways. Opening yourself up to others' ideas and beliefs about cultural values, politics, and religion causes you to look within your soul to examine your own values. As Americans, we are often criticized for having myopic and narrow worldviews. Travel adventures help us expand that worldview by challenging our beliefs about what is truly important and giving us a deeper understanding of how our

country impacts the rest of the world. Experiencing different cultures also shows us that our way really *isn't* the only way.

- **Adventure teaches you about yourself.** Adventure feeds your curiosity about the world, the people around you, and ultimately yourself. It reveals passions and interests you never knew you had. New experiences give you the chance to discover the things and places that bring you joy and a sense of thrill. As French novelist Andre Gide once said, "It is only in adventure that some people succeed in knowing themselves, in finding themselves."
- **Adventure raises the bar for your future husband.** When you make adventure seeking a way of life, you are naturally going to be drawn to others who have the same zest for life. This will be true for friends, boyfriends, *and* your future husband. You will no longer be able to imagine life with a guy whose idea of an exotic adventure is trying Dijon mustard on his turkey sandwich, no matter how tall, dark, and/or handsome he may be. Instead, you'll be attracted to guys who are curious about the world and willing to try new things. These are also the guys who will be supportive of, not threatened by, your adventurous spirit.
- **Adventure will energize your future marriage.** Having a sense of adventure in your marriage can mean the difference between getting stuck in an inevitable rut or knowing just what to do to pull you both out. When you're used to viewing the routine of daily life through a lens of adventure, you will never find yourself moping around the house, looking to your husband to make your life interesting and exciting. You'll be an expert in your own right at livening things up and bringing a sense of newness to your relationship.
- **Adventure will make you a cool mom.** Your finely

tuned adventure-seeking skills will come in very handy if you decide to take on the Adventure of Motherhood. Imagine how thrilled your children will be when you surprise them at school on a Friday afternoon and whisk them away for a weekend train trip and apple-picking adventure. Or when you tell your kids to grab their raincoats because it's time to go "worm hunting in the rain" or when you institute new family traditions like Saturday outdoor-movie night or caroling at the local nursing home during the holidays. If you take the time to develop your adventurous spirit before you marry, you will encourage your children to try new things and not be fearful of new experiences. You'll teach them to be accepting of people who look different or come from a different background. You'll nurture their natural curiosity about the world. You'll model for them what it means to have an open mind, an open heart, and an open spirit.

- **Adventure is fun.** Need we say more?

Why Now? Can't You See I'm in the Middle of My Quarter-Life Crisis?

There's no better time to pursue new experiences, whether big or small. While you may appreciate the benefits of adventure in theory, you may be wondering why we're insisting that you make space for it in your life right now. Why can't it just wait until later? The truth is, not only are your twenties and early thirties the *best* time for you to seek out challenging and exciting experiences, we believe it would be irresponsible for you *not* to. Your single life is uniquely suited to pursuing adventure. Here's what makes this the best time of your life to develop your adventurous spirit:

- **You're unencumbered.** You probably have a job, an apartment, and friends. You may even have a car, a dog, and a gym membership. While these things may feel like deal breakers, take it from us, they are all relatively easy to disentangle from your life. They're little things. One of the greatest things about being young and single is that you don't yet have to consider the not-so-little things. You have no big fat mortgage looming overhead and no long-term investment in your career to jeopardize. Another plus: You don't have a lot of stuff that will need to be put in storage.
- **You've got friends.** You probably have several friends who would make great adventure companions. They may need a little encouragement, but chances are, once you begin talking about the adventures you're contemplating, your friends will catch your spark of enthusiasm and begin to make plans to join you.
- **You've got what it takes.** It's standard operating procedure for you to dance your heart out until 3 A.M. and then get up the next morning for a game of volleyball or to meet up with friends for pancakes. It's that kind of youthful energy that will propel your jet-lagged butt to the summit of the mountain or the top of the Eiffel Tower.
- **You're (relatively) low maintenance.** Unless you're one of these pampered types who celebrated her thirteenth birthday with Mother and Daddy at the Paris Ritz, you are used to the minimalist lifestyle (*aka*: you're usually broke) and won't be scared off by the first sight of a little dirt on your bunk in the Amsterdam youth hostel. Give yourself ten years or so, and you probably won't be able to stomach the idea of staying somewhere that doesn't offer room service or in-room movie selections.

Personal Insight from Celeste

As I sit at my computer with my daughters playing dress-up around me, I consider my to-do list for the day:

1. Meet with Ava's teacher
2. Call babysitter—date night
3. Talk to gardener about trimming trees
4. Make Halloween costumes (Pippi Longstocking, Supergirl, Cruella De Vil)
5. Disneyland Hotel—make reservation

The tasks that occupy my to-do list today are noticeably different from the following, taken from some of the lists of my twenties:

Buy plane ticket—Africa
Send deposit for apartment in San Francisco
Follow up about internship in Washington, D.C.
Order copies of pictures from Vienna
Plan itinerary for cross-country road trip

If you compare these lists, you might be tempted to think that one is much more adventurous than the other and that the items on the list from my twenties sounds a heck of a lot better than my current one. The truth is that I am thrilled with my life as a busy mom and wife and wouldn't trade my current list for anything. In fact, it is the adventures of my twenties that allow me to enjoy the adventures of family life now.

As I think back on my fabulous single life, it's

clear to me that the sense of fulfillment I feel now is at least partially due to all the amazing adventures I pursued during my twenties. Sure, I'd love to pick up and go to Belize on a moment's notice or go sky-diving without worrying about whether I would live to see my children on the other end, but I don't wish for those things with any shred of regret or resentment. I am thankful that I lived my single life to the fullest and I know I'm a better mom, wife, and woman as a result.

- **You're a free agent.** Outside of your nine-to-five, you're the only one you have to answer to. You've no little people depending on you for their very existence and no legally binding relationships to tend to. You don't have to consider the fact that your husband may prefer mountain climbing while your ideal adventure involves an exotic island.

What's Stopping You? Common Barriers to Adventure

The trouble is, if you don't risk anything, you risk even more.

—Erica Jong

As the responsibilities of life keep piling up, you could easily conclude that it would be irresponsible to invest your resources of time and money into something so seemingly frivolous as adventure. The truth is, there will always be obstacles that threaten to keep you from pursuing new experiences and adventures. Luckily, there are equally as many ways of overcoming those obstacles. We've compiled the most common excuses from young single women reluctant to take the leap into adventure.

"I don't have enough time."

The key to finding time for adventure is planning. A daylong adventure can be accomplished with little or no planning, while a six-month or yearlong adventure will require a seriously detailed plan of action. Trust us, no matter how busy you may feel now, you will look back at these years and wonder what you did with all your free time.

Take a few minutes to make an honest list of the things that occupy your time. Now, which ones could you eliminate, which ones could you put on hold, and which ones could you delegate to others? Cross all of those out. Now, whatever's left on your list, ask yourself: *Can this survive without my attention for a little while?* Remember, saying no to some of the things on your list means saying yes to adventure.

"I can't afford it."

As with time, the key to the money factor is planning. Even with an entry-level income, you can sock away money for a trip as long as you're willing to make sacrifices. Maybe you'll need to get a part-time weekend job in order to save. You may have less time for watching reality show marathons and creating new playlists, but the sacrifices will be worth it when you're trekking through Thailand on the back of an elephant. Working a little on the weekend will have the added benefit of keeping you occupied and less inclined to spend money, which will put you at the starting line of your adventure even sooner.

"I don't have anyone to go with."

While seeking out new experiences with a friend can be fantastic, you shouldn't put off that dream trip just because your friends aren't interested in hopping on board. Going somewhere new or taking on a new challenge on your own could be one of the best experiences of your life. In fact, many guided trips and tours are full of solo travelers. What a great way to meet new friends from all over the world.

"My parents would never approve."

You may be fortunate enough to have parents who value adventure and even encourage you to seek it out. Or you may have parents who regard adventure as frivolous and who won't be particularly supportive when you announce that you're quitting your job at the bank to become a whitewater rafting instructor in Japan. Regardless, we encourage you to stand strong against the naysayers and stick to your guns. In time, when they see your well-thought-out plan become a reality, they will likely applaud your willingness to take risks and try new things. If all else fails, promise to send them a postcard. (Note: Look back at chapter 9, "Get an Independent Life," if you need a refresher on how to gain emotional independence from less-than-unsupportive parents.)

"I can't take time off."

The duration of your chosen adventure will determine the way you deal with taking time off. It may be a matter of taking your stuffy head and some Advil to the office in order to preserve those valuable sick days or scheduling your adventure on a holiday weekend so you only have to use two vacation days to get five full days away. If your adventure is longer than your job would allow, consider asking for a sabbatical. Explain to your boss how your adventure would enhance your work. Will your adventure give you a chance to brush up on a language, bring back new ideas, or make new contacts? If all else fails, don't be afraid to quit your job altogether. Yes, even though the economy's bad. This could be the perfect time to check out for a while and let the job market rebound. You'll come back armed with a more interesting résumé, refreshed and ready for the Adventure of Job Hunting.

"I can't leave my boyfriend."

Every new experience you have will only serve to make you a more interesting and energized girlfriend. He'll be there when you get back, and *if* he's not, he wasn't worth depriving yourself of adventure for. Your boyfriend's response to your proposed adventure will tell you a lot about him and the nature of your relationship. Is he supportive or does he try to talk you out of going? Is he worried that you'll change or is he excited for you to have new experiences? If he's trying to hold you back for fear of losing you, he's not your long-term guy. Don't sacrifice your opportunity for adventure today for a guy who won't be there tomorrow.

While these are the most common excuses, you may be able to come up with hundreds more. If you find that you're excuse-ridden, your issues with adventure may have more to do with your own deep-seated resistance to new experiences than you realize. Take this quiz to find out.

How Adventurous Are You?

When considering adventure, do you prefer the calm security of staying put in the Land of the Well-Known, do you carefully consider your adventure options before embarking, or do you throw caution to the wind and jump in with reckless abandon? Choose the answer that fits you best:

1. Your idea of adventure is
   a. Cave diving in Brazil.
   b. Hiking in your local mountains.
   c. Ordering extra foam in your latte.
2. Your boss mentions that he's going to need you to head up a six-month project in the London office. You
   a. Clean out your desk and go shopping for some new pub-crawling duds.
   b. Make a list of the pros and cons of taking the opportunity.
   c. Quit on the spot. You hate tea.
3. Your friends invite you to take a belly dancing class with them. You
   a. Grab your flowy skirt and meet them there!
   b. Tell them you'll think about it and order an *Art of Belly Dancing* DVD to check it out.
   c. Tell them you're sorry, but your hips just weren't made to swivel like that.
4. Your girlfriends are planning a weekend cruise to Mexico, but you've always worried about getting seasick. You
   a. Stock up on Dramamine and grab your bikini!
   b. Take a local boat ride and see how it goes.
   c. Bow out gracefully, blaming a prior commitment to feed your neighbor's cat.
5. Your coworker e-mails to tell you she has the perfect guy for you and invites you to meet him for drinks . . . tonight! Your reaction:
   a. Love to! How bad could it be? Worst case, you'll make a new friend.

   b. Tell her you'd love to have a chance to get to know him a bit better by e-mail or phone before agreeing to a date.
   c. No way! You don't know anything about this guy. He could be a serial killer.
6. You've always been content with your brunette locks, but your hairstylist is urging you to go blond. Your reaction:
   a. Great! You can't wait to find out if blondes really do have more fun.
   b. You pay a visit to the local wig store for a trial run before taking the plunge.
   c. What is she smoking? There's no way in the world you would ever even consider it!
7. A friend calls with an extra ticket for a weekend music festival a few hours away from home. You've got no plans. You
   a. Grab your sunscreen and you're out the door.
   b. Research the festival online to assess its safety before making your decision.
   c. Obsess over the lack of sanitary bathrooms, the crowds, and the sunburn potential.
8. You've got two weeks of vacation saved up along with a little bit of cash. You
   a. Go somewhere exotic you've never been, so you can fully experience the language, the food, and the culture.
   b. Book a trip that offers the comforts of home along with beautiful beaches, yummy food, and Wi-Fi.
   c. Enjoy being in your home with nothing to do but read and maybe venture out to catch a movie or two.
9. Your aunt and uncle come to town for a visit and want to take you to the new Latin-African-Asian fusion restaurant that just opened. You

a. Can't wait to try it! After all, it can't be any weirder than the sea urchin stew you had last week.
b. Tell them yes, but tuck a few granola bars in your purse just in case.
c. Tell them you're so sorry, but you have to work late and offer to meet them afterwards for a white wine spritzer.

10. Your city council is holding a hearing on an issue that you are very passionate about, and you're invited to share your perspective at the meeting. Problem is, you hate public speaking! You!
    a. Say yes and forgo the preparation. Your passion will carry you through!
    b. Accept the invitation and begin diligently preparing for your presentation.
    c. Tell them you'd love to, but unfortunately you feel a bad case of laryngitis coming on.

Give yourself 3 points for each *a*, 2 for each *b*, and 1 for each *c*.

0–12 points: You must chill! It is seriously time to bust out of your teeny-tiny comfort zone! Your fears are keeping you from experiencing your life to the fullest. Begin to overcome these fears by planning small, close-to-home adventures and then working your way up.

13–25 points: You are levelheaded and cautious, but have still managed to retain your sense of adventure. Try to expand your horizons a little. You may be missing out on some opportunities for adventure because your hesitancy hinders your spontaneity. You don't have to throw caution to the wind, but there's nothing wrong with putting it on the back burner for a while.

26–30 points: You're an Adventure Inspiration.

Life-Changing Adventures

Do not go where the path may lead, go instead where there is no path and leave a trail.

—Ralph Waldo Emerson

Whether you're an adventure newbie or a true-blue adventure junkie, we hope that by now your adventurous spirit is champing at the bit. If so, it's time to get serious and specific about the many, many exciting possibilities that are yours for the planning. These life-changing adventures range from travel adventures to adventure careers, from weekend trips to year-long excursions, but they all share one common requirement: the willingness to get off the couch and bust out of your comfort zone.

We've searched high and low for some of the best adventure travel ideas around and have compiled our very favorites. To make it easy for you to consider the options, we've broken them into five categories: International Adventures, Action Adventures, Wacky Adventures, Meaningful Adventures, and Adventure Careers. Of course, these are just a few, shared mostly to inspire you and get your adventure juices flowing. . . .

International Adventures

Explore the pyramids of Ancient Egypt
Island-hop through Greece
Ride horseback through the Costa Rican rain forest
Experience the bazaars of Marrakesh in Morocco
Learn to surf on Australia's Gold Coast
Run with the bulls in Pamplona, Spain
Luxuriate on the beaches of Khosa Mui in Thailand
Attend the Cherry Blossom Festival in Japan
Travel the Ring Road in Iceland

Any one of these adventures will change your life. Choose one, or better yet, experience them all. You may be thinking, *Oh sure, that sounds great, but how could I ever make a trip like that happen?* If so, it's time for you to meet the Lost Girls, three twentysomething women who decided that job security, boyfriends, and even apartments in Manhattan were not the end-all, be-all of life in their twenties. These women were just like you: They had jobs, they had fears, and no, they didn't have trust funds. Just like you, the Lost Girls were determined to make the most of their twenties. Here's how they did it:

> It was in New York City, dead-of-winter 2005, when we—Amanda, Jen and Holly—found ourselves in the midst of a collective quarter-life crisis. Sure, 20-something burnout may sound a tad to silly to anyone born before the advent of MTV, Atari or Guess! jeans, but long workweeks at stress-driven offices had taken their toll. Despite having creative gigs that fueled our passions, we were frustrated that we'd let our careers become our identities. We were starving for real connections with family, friends and significant others—who wants to date a woman already married to her job?
>
> It turns out, we weren't alone. Like millions of young women in our generation, we were plagued with doubts about the paths we were choosing. Though intense workdays left us little time for contemplation, we often found ourselves asking: What exactly were we doing with our lives? Could we ultimately commit to one career, city and lifestyle (and man), when so many opportunities lie before us? On our own, with no parents, advisers or a syllabus to guide us, you could say that we were a little, well, Lost. Okay, very Lost. So before making the ultimate choice of which

way to go as (gulp) adults, we decided to take a major detour, one we hoped might provide a little insight into these questions and just maybe, a road map to our futures. Kissing our jobs, boyfriends, apartments, families and our beloved Manhattan goodbye, we officially became "The Lost Girls," and started making plans for a yearlong, 35,000-mile journey around the globe. Loosely building an itinerary that began in South America and crawled eastward through Africa, the Middle East, India, Southeast Asia and Australia, we planned to explore the cultures, mindsets and lifestyles of our international counterparts, getting to know thousands of strangers so we could better know ourselves.

After being asked repeatedly why they went on their around-the-world adventure, and not being able to answer with just one reason, they instead offered these:

1. We'd rather wake up to the roar of the Amazon River than the screeching of an alarm clock.
2. Hiking the subway stairs: 14 calories burned. Trekking the Inca Trail: 14,000.
3. We'd rather get tan lines from lounging on the beach than worry lines from tackling endless to-do lists.
4. The real Wonders of the World can't be found on any map.
5. The world is filled with yummy desserts just screaming for a taste test.
6. Gazing longingly at your "exotic locales" screensaver hardly compares to watching the sunset over the Serengeti or diving with the wildlife along the Great Barrier Reef.
7. The phrases *burnout, multitasking*, and *quarter-life crisis* don't exist in most languages.

8. The cost of a Starbucks latte in the Big Apple will cover a week's lodging in Laos.
9. 'Cause we're suckers for guys with accents.
10. Sometimes you have to get lost in order to be found.

Inspired? Of course, you are! Want to learn more about their trip and how they made it happen? For all the details, check out their website, www.lostgirlsworld.com and look for their memoir, *Lost Girls and the Wander Year.*

Lest you think that an international adventure requires a year off and a trip around the world with stops in thirteen countries, read Mara's story:

MARA

"I always liked the idea of adventure and loved getting e-mails from college friends from exotic places around the globe, but the thought of actually doing something like that myself seemed pretty much out of reach. I never had any extra money or time to get to the gym, let alone plan some big trip. My moment of inspiration finally came when I received a 'farewell' e-mail from a coworker who was taking time off to go teach English in France. In Paris! I had always wanted to live in France and found myself just sitting there in front of my computer, seething with envy.

"In that moment, it finally hit me that there was really nothing stopping me from going anywhere I wanted to go. All I needed was enough money to live. I went home, canceled my cable, my bottled-water delivery, and my Netflix subscription. I drew a picture of a thermometer, which represented my savings, and put it on my refrigerator. By the end of the weekend, I had lined up a part-time job, which I kept for an entire year, until that thermometer was colored all the way to the top. It was a challenging year, but so worth it.

"I quit my job three weeks ago and I leave on Tuesday

morning for Europe. I'll be traveling for the first six months, some solo and some with friends, and then working as a farmhand in the Drome Valley for the rest of the time. Of course, I'm incredibly nervous, especially about the farm part, but beyond excited! The best part of this whole thing so far is that *I* made it happen."

Action Adventures

Women all over the world are taking hold of their inner adventurer and trying outdoor travel opportunities. As long as you are reasonably fit, you can have a thrilling vacation that really gets your adrenaline pumping. Here are some ideas of what you can do with a little time, money, and courage:

Climb Half-Dome at Yosemite National Park
Cycle through the Loire Valley in France
Parasail in Cancún, Mexico
Backpack to the top of Mt. Whitney in California
Sea kayak in Norway
Rock-climb in Wyoming
Go whitewater rafting in Virginia
Hot-air balloon over New England
Scuba dive among shipwrecks in the Caribbean

There are hundreds of tour companies that offer these and many more exciting action adventures, ranging from very affordable to pricey. The great thing about going with a guided tour is that you don't have to bother with the details. If you prefer, you can travel with a women-only or beginners-only tour group.

ERIN

"After college, I moved to Boston and began working for a large insurance company. Once I started living on my own in the 'real world,' I felt really small. Like everyone around me knew exactly where they were going and what they were doing, except for me. Life kind of closed in on me, and I fell into the rut of just working, coming home, eating dinner, watching TV, and doing it all over again the next day. Even though I had dreamed of hiking the Inca Trail ever since I was a little girl, adventure was now the farthest thing from my mind. I was just getting by, hoping that things would get a little more exciting as life went on.

"About eight months ago, I got a call from my best friend from high school, who was pretty much feeling the same way as me. She told me that her brother's girlfriend had just returned from Peru and had an amazing time. That conversation was the trigger that sparked our own adventure. Over the next six months, we planned and saved. I sold a bunch of stuff on eBay, stopped spending money on takeout, and even started riding my bike to work to save on gas money. Eliminating the takeout and adding the exercise also had the side benefit of getting me in shape for the hike!

"We landed in Quito exactly six months to the day from that first conversation. Standing at the top of Machu Picchu at dawn was definitely one of the most amazing experiences of my life. Since we returned home, life has been different. Our trip to Peru has given me more confidence in my daily life and in my own ability to take on challenges. We're already planning our next adventure!"

Wacky Adventures

Not up for an Action Adventure? How about designing your own crazy travel adventure? Your itinerary is limited only by your imagination. Be as creative as you want. Do you have a quirky interest or collection? There's probably a museum somewhere out there dedicated to showing it off. Do you love the circus? Visit the Circus World Museum in Baraboo, Wisconsin. Can't get enough jellybeans? Visit the Jelly Belly factory in Northern California. Love to tie things? Pay homage to the World's Largest Ball of Twine in Darwin, Minnesota. Want to celebrate your womanhood? Gather some girlfriends and visit the Museum of Menstruation in Maryland, which "educates visitors on the pleasant and unpleasant components of women's health from various cultures."

Here are some firsthand examples from our adventuresome friends:

- A couple of root beer–loving friends of ours took a few postgrad months off to travel to all the major root beer breweries in the United States, meeting with the owners, touring the production facilities, and of course, tasting the root beer.
- Three other girlfriends, all of whom were teachers and amateur photographers, decided to spend their summer driving around the country, photographing the tallest point in each state. They returned with amazing photos and unforgettable memories.
- Another group of women, who were all getting their Ph.D.s in English literature, spent their summer traveling to the graves of their ten favorite authors. They had a hilarious time on the road, and we're pretty sure they even earned some extra credit for their efforts.

If these wacky adventures are right up your alley, customize your own Weird U.S. Landmark Tour. For starters, your itinerary could include the Extraterrestrial Highway near Area 51 in Nevada, where you can search for UFOs, Gravity Hill in Pennsylvania, where your car will roll uphill, Bishop Castle in Colorado, a medieval castle à la *Lord of the Rings*, where you can stand in the fire-breathing dragon chimney, and the Wigwam

Village in Kentucky where you can—you guessed it—sleep in a tepee. But don't stop there. Log on to http://information.travel.aol.com/tourism-week/landmarks for more inspiration for your own weird wacky adventure.

Meaningful Adventures

If you just can't get over feeling like your vacation should have more purpose than collecting stamps in your passport or acquiring a savage tan, you might be interested in a meaningful adventure. Whether you have a week or a year, if you want to devote some time to helping others, a volunteer vacation is a great option for you. Do you like working with kids? Join AmeriCorps to work with a nonprofit organization that benefits children or volunteer at an orphanage in Zambia. Visit a new state while joining forces with Habitat for Humanity and help build houses for low-income families. Is saving the environment your thing? The Green Corps is a yearlong program that will prepare you for careers in environmental work and social change. It even offers stipends, health insurance, and student loan payment subsidies.

BRYNN

"Before I started graduate school, I spent three weeks of my summer in Ghana, working with women and children who were basically living on the street. We played with the kids, organized donated school supplies, conducted nutrition workshops, and helped the Shelter Director set up a computer network in her office. We didn't do anything extraordinary, really, but I think we made a big difference for the women and children there. A lot of my friends didn't understand why I would want to spend my last bit of free time doing volunteer work in Africa, but it was truly one of the best experiences of my life. I love lying on the beach in L.A. or shopping in New York as much as the next girl, but I am so glad that I decided to take the trip."

Volunteering: Read All about It

These are a few of the best books we've come across on the topic of meaningful adventures:

- *Delaying the Real World* by Colleen Kinder
- *Volunteer Vacations: Short-Term Adventures That Will Benefit You and Others* by Bill McMillon
- *How to Live Your Dream of Volunteering Overseas* by Stefano DeZerega and Zahara Heckscher

All these books are full of helpful information and will give you the tools you'll need to create a meaningful adventure within the United States and to the far reaches of the world.

Adventure Careers

Think you may be well suited for a job in a new place that actually pays you a salary? From teaching English in Thailand to working as an au pair in Sweden or a ski lift operator in Vail, opportunities abound. You may not live high on the hog while experiencing your working adventure, but you'll be having the time of your life.

LUCIA

Lucia is a twenty-seven-year-old medical student at Georgetown. After graduating from college, she worked in a hospital for a few years and then applied to be a tour guide in Nicaragua. Lucia wanted to spend some time overseas, but didn't want to end up with a lot of debt as she was entering med school. "I wanted to see the world and have some fun before going back to school, but didn't have any savings." Lucia made about thirty-one thousand dollars over the course of her year abroad, paid off some old credit card debt, and even managed to spend several weeks traveling through Central America after her tour gig ended. "I'm so glad I did what I did," Lucia told us. "I'm a little older than many of my fellow med school students who went straight through, but I think my experiences in Nicaragua will actually benefit my career. I'm certain that being bilingual will really give me an advantage in the medical field. Besides, now that I'm on this career track, when will I ever have the chance to have that kind of experience again?"

Read It and Work

Check out *The Back Door Guide to Short-Term Job Adventures* by Michael Landes. This book can help you find seasonal work all over the world, any time of the year. Another helpful resource is *Work Your Way Around the World* by Susan Griffith, which offers tons of suggestions for those who want to see the world, but need to keep earning.

Your Personal Adventures of a Lifetime

Where will your adventure take you? Quick! For this exercise, you'll need to grab your journal or a piece of paper; even a napkin will do. Start writing. Where do you want to go? Which parts of the country and the world have you always been curious about or drawn to? What cultures excite and interest you? How about social issues? Which ones are you willing to devote some time to? What obstacles do you need to overcome in order to pursue your desired adventure? What practical steps will be necessary? How long will it take you to save for your intended adventure? Are there people in your life with whom you could imagine pursuing these adventures? Who will be the naysayers in your life, and how will you respond to them when they challenge your plans?

Right here, right now could be the first step to one of the most amazing experiences of your single life and perhaps of your lifetime. Whether it's a crazy and memorable road trip with good friends or a two-year stint in the Peace Corps, seeking out adventures is undeniably one of the most valuable and fulfilling things you can do.

Every Day an Adventure

An adventure-prone person is not simply someone assaulted by a set of adventurous circumstances. Rather, he or she is one who perceives the possibility for adventure where others do not.

—John Griffin

When we hear the word *adventure,* most of us think of trudging through the Amazon with machete in hand, whitewater rafting down the Zambezi, or any of the other exciting travel adventures we've talked about. And to all these adventures, we say, "Yes!" But did you know that you can have adventures each and every day of your life without having to leave town or even the comfort of your own home? It's true. Adventure is lurking everywhere. Discovering it has everything to do with your perspective on your everyday life and the world around you. Whether you are at the top of Mount Rainier or eating a tuna sandwich at the new deli around the corner from your office, adventure is yours for the taking. A perfect example of this perspective is David Silberkleit, author of *A New Adventure Every Day.* Before David wrote his book, he had tried just about every adventure around. He had been a ski instructor, commercial glider airplane pilot, scuba diver, sailboat racer, rock climber, and motorcyclist. No doubt his passport was overflowing with stamps from exotic locales.

When it was all said and done, this is what he concluded: "To my surprise, all my adventures led me to a lesson I hadn't expected. I discovered that I didn't need to go anywhere or plan any trips to be adventurous. Adventure was all around me. I discovered that I could find adventure anytime right where I was."

Everyday adventures are essential because they give us a renewed interest in our lives and help us find joy in the midst of the inevitable hassles of life. They offer a fresh perspective and infuse our lives with fun and creativity. Here are some suggestions of how to create adventure at every turn:

Adventures at Home

Have a picnic on the floor in your living room.
Keep a bottle of champagne in your refrigerator and find a reason to celebrate.
Cook a meal featuring cuisine from an exotic country.
Sleep in a tent in your backyard.
Host Art Saturday. Invite friends to spend the day creating at your house—painting, making jewelry, bookbinding, or anything else creative.
Bury a time capsule.
Rearrange your furniture.

Adventures about Town

Go apple picking in the fall.
Visit a nearby museum and linger for a while in front of your favorite painting. Bring a sketch pad and try your hand at creating a reproduction.
Go to a drive-in movie. In your pajamas.
Attend a local high school play. Bring flowers for the lead performers.

Wander through the children's section at your local library and check out all your favorite childhood books. Spend an entire weekend reading them.

Send a message in a bottle.

Write a letter to the editor.

Adventures in Relationships

Show up at your friend's office and convince her to let you treat her to lunch. Don't take "I'm too busy" for an answer.

Send a letter of appreciation to your favorite junior high school teacher.

Spend a whole day with a friend's kids. Take them to the zoo, the beach, or the park.

Send a card to your parents, thanking them for all they've done for you. Be specific.

Send your mom flowers on *your* birthday.

Record your grandparents telling the story of their courtship.

Learn to say "I love you" in five different languages.

Solo Adventures

Go to an outdoor concert by yourself.

Join your local chapter of Toastmasters and conquer your fear of public speaking.

Take yourself to dinner. (Drive-through doesn't count.)

Take a martial arts class.

Try out for local community theater.

Sit in an empty chapel for an hour.

Take a trapeze lesson.

Watch *Breakfast at Tiffany's*. Holly Golightly will inspire you to see possibilities for adventure in the everyday.

No matter where you are—at home, in your office, with friends, walking through the grocery store, or by yourself, it's up to you to create your own adventurous life. When you develop a sense of wonder about yourself and the world outside your door, you will soon find your whole life becoming more adventuresome.

> *People travel to wonder at the height of the mountains, at the huge waves of the seas, at the long course of the rivers, at the vast compass of the ocean, at the circular motion of the stars, and yet they pass by themselves without wondering.*
>
> —*Saint Augustine*

30 Before 30 Adventures

If you're going to live your single life to the fullest, you've got to have a plan. And if there's one thing we know for sure, it's that all good plans begin with a list. Your assignment: Make a list of thirty adventures you'd like to have before you turn thirty. If you happen to be over thirty, no problem, just make it a "thirty-five before thirty-five" list. These can be small, everyday adventures or big, Life-Changing Adventures. Ideally, you'll end up with some of both. Don't edit your list of adventures based on what you think is possible or plausible; just write.

For inspiration, and to help get your adventure juices flowing, here are some fun ideas from our focus group members:

- Drive a motorcycle. I want to drive a real motorcycle, like a Harley. (Meg, 24)
- Learn sign language. How powerful to be able to communicate in that way. (Kate, 27)

- Swim with dolphins. This is something I have dreamed about since I was eight years old. It may sound silly, but to me it would just be the most thrilling experience. (Ashley, 21)
- Go on a police ride-along in a big city. My cousin did this in Dallas and had a blast. I'm sure I'd be scared of what we could encounter, but that's part of the thrill! (Jana, 22)
- Learn to windsurf. I'm sure it's actually harder than it looks, but how exhilarating to be out there in the waves with the wind pushing you along! (Rachel, 25)

Forget about old age; *these* should be your golden years—full of exhilarating, challenging, and fun adventures. This decade is your chance to fully experience life, expand your perspective, learn more about who you are, and become a person who finds adventure everywhere she goes. So no more sitting around, making excuses. Whether you're swimming the Bosphorus, sleeping under the stars in Death Valley, or running a 5K, you will look back on your adventurous single life with a heart filled with gratitude, incredible memories, and not an ounce of regret.

> *Twenty years from now you will be more disappointed by the things you didn't do than by the ones you did. So throw off the bowlines. Sail away from the safe harbor. Catch the trade winds in your sails. Explore. Dream. Discover.*
>
> *—Mark Twain*

Chapter 13

You Can Get a Great Married Life!

Getting a fabulous single life in your twenties paves the way to a successful marriage. When you make the most of your twenties and refuse to become another casualty of young marriage, you have a clear shot at a happy and fulfilling marriage and family. As a confident, self-aware woman in your late twenties or early thirties, you will be able not only to choose a great husband, but to be a great wife as well. Instead of looking back on your life filled with regret, you will be grateful that you made the decision to embrace your twenties as a time of personal growth and self-awareness.

Don't let this amazing opportunity of your twenties pass you by. Grab hold of it and live it to its fullest. Promise yourself right here and now that you will use the Ten Keys to get your own fabulous life *now*. Since you won't be making lifetime vows to a man while you're making the most of your single life, it's time to make life-changing vows to yourself.

My Vows to Myself

I promise to be a true friend, in good times and in bad.
I will work faithfully to make peace with my family, till death do us part.
I promise to pursue a career path that fulfills my sense of purpose, through triumphs and defeats.
I vow to get control of my finances and maintain financial stability, in plenty and in want.
I will place a premium on my emotional health, through happiness and sadness.
I vow to honor my body and accept it, without reservation and forsaking all harsh judgment.
I pledge to become independent from my parents, for richer or for poorer.
As God is my witness, I commit to clarify my spiritual beliefs.
I vow always to respect, honor, and cherish my sexuality for the sacred gift that it is.
I promise to bust out of my comfort zone and pursue a life of adventure, wherever the path may lead me.
I thus commit to myself this day. ***These are my solemn vows.***

Now take a moment to write some of your own vows. You might find it helpful to go back through each chapter to remind yourself of the specific areas that were especially helpful to you.

Vow #1~Friendships

I vow to ______________________________.

I pledge to begin ______________________________.

I commit to stop ______________________________.

Vow #2~Family

I vow to ____.

I pledge to begin __________________________________.

I commit to stop ___________________________________.

Vow #3~Career

I vow to ____.

I pledge to begin __________________________________.

I commit to stop ___________________________________.

Vow #4~Finances

I vow to ____.

I pledge to begin __________________________________.

I commit to stop ___________________________________.

Vow #5~Emotions

I vow to ____.

I pledge to begin __________________________________.

I commit to stop ___________________________________.

Vow #6~Body Image

I vow to ____.

I pledge to begin __________________________________.

I commit to stop ___________________________________.

Vow #7~Independence

I vow to ______________________________.

I pledge to begin ______________________________.

I commit to stop ______________________________.

Vow #8~Spirituality

I vow to ______________________________.

I pledge to begin ______________________________.

I commit to stop ______________________________.

Vow #9~Sexuality

I vow to ______________________________.

I pledge to begin ______________________________.

I commit to stop ______________________________.

Vow #10~Adventure

I vow to ______________________________.

I pledge to begin ______________________________.

I commit to stop ______________________________.

And this is our solemn promise to you: If you honor your vows to get a life before you become a wife, you will love the life you get. The ring can wait, but your life cannot.